The Value-Added Tax:
Orthodoxy and New Thinking

The Value-Added Tax: Orthodoxy and New Thinking

edited by

Murray L. Weidenbaum
Center for the Study of
American Business

David G. Raboy
Patton, Boggs & Blow

Ernest S. Christian, Jr.
Patton, Boggs & Blow

Kluwer Academic Publishers
Boston/Dordrecht/London

Distributors:

for North America: Kluwer Academic Publishers, 101 Philip Drive,
Assinippi Park, Norwell, MA 02061

for the UK and Ireland: Kluwer Academic Publishers, Falcon
House, Queen Square, Lancaster LA1 1RN, UK

for all other countries: Kluwer Academic Publishers Group,
Distribution Centre, Post Office Box 322, 3300 AH Dordrecht, The
Netherlands

Library of Congress Cataloging-in-Publication Data

The Value-added tax : orthodoxy and new thinking / edited by Murray L.
  Weidenbaum, David G. Raboy, Ernest S. Christian, Jr.
     p.   cm.
  Includes index.
  ISBN 0-7923-9002-4
  1. Value-added tax--United States. 2. Spending tax--United
States. 3. Value-added tax--Law and legislation--United States.
I. Weidenbaum, Murray L. II. Raboy, David G. III. Christian,
Ernest S.
  HJ5715.U6V343   1989
336.2'714'0973--dc19   88-34036
                                                      CIP

Printed in the United States of America

CONTENTS

ACKNOWLEDGEMENTS

This volume was written to be a resource for the next serious public debate on the subject of value-added and other consumption-based taxes. It seeks to combine a discussion of theoretical issues with an analysis of practical problems such as tax incidence, trade implications and administrative difficulties.

The Center for the Study of American Business at Washington University has made analysis of major tax proposals a high priority research emphasis since its inception in 1975. As a result of a long association with Dr. David Raboy and Ernest Christian, the CSAB's director, Dr. Murray Weidenbaum, was approached with the idea for this volume. Messrs. Raboy, Christian, and Cliff Massa III had begun to research the pragmatic concerns associated with a consumption or value-added tax independently of the Center's own research on the theoretical economic issues. Joining forces to produce this volume seemed to be a logical way of making the results available to individuals interested in the various policy aspects of consumption taxes and especially value-added taxes.

The editors and authors bear the responsibility for the viewpoints presented in the material to follow, but they would like to acknowledge the debt of gratitude owed to a host of individuals. We have benefitted greatly from their comments and criticisms.

Each chapter was edited and helpful comments were offered by Kenneth Chilton, associate director, and Melinda Warren, writer/analyst, at the Center for the Study of American Business. In addition, valuable comments and criticism were received by Messrs. Raboy, Christian and Massa from senior executives of major corporations who reviewed the chapters examining the various aspects of a value-added tax. Despite their disparate views and experiences, these individuals have been unwaveringly dedicated to probing analysis and have, over an extended period, shared their insights. We express appreciation for the advice and counsel provided by: Michael Axt, Claude Burleson, Stephen Conafay, Kenneth Johnson, Ted Killhefer, John Loffredo, John Mendenhall, William Modahl, Sandy Navin, Patrick Nugent, C. P. Powell, James Pratt, Charles Rau, Robert Scott, Ira Siegel, Burton Smoliar, and

Ellan Wharton. Any inaccuracies or shortcomings that remain in the book are solely our responsibility.

We wish to thank Marjorie Shane, Jennie Glasgow and Alice Konicki for original manuscript preparation. A debt of gratitude is owed Christine Moseley and Melinda Warren for final editing and for converting these manuscripts into form suitable for publication.

Researching and compiling sources of data can be difficult and time-consuming. Sincere appreciation is expressed to Donna Steele for her very capable research assistance.

Ernest Christian, Jr.

David Raboy

Murray Weidenbaum

INTRODUCTION

IF, WHEN YOU SAY "CONSUMPTION TAX," YOU MEAN ...

by Ernest S. Christian, Jr. and
Cliff Massa III

Much has been said and written about consumption taxes in the United States, but mostly in a theoretical context. Dozens of scholarly treatises have been published, along with innumerable papers and speeches most of which were more argumentative than illuminating in nature. Audiences have sat through uncounted conferences on the merits or evils of consumption taxes, depending on the speakers' perspectives. There have been only three comprehensive legislative proposals to which these theories and arguments could be applied, no one of which was acted upon in the Congress.[1]

Purveyors of conventional wisdom have suggested that this theoretical context might be replaced within a year or two by actual consideration of a federal-level consumption tax. Some see enactment of such a tax as a desirable -- or at least a necessary -- means for reducing the federal deficit. The National Economic Commission, which was created by legislation in 1987 to recommend deficit reduction measures, was perceived by many skeptics and proponents alike to be the Trojan Horse which would carry a consumption tax

---

[1]The proposals were H.R. 7015, "The Tax Restructuring Act of 1980," introduced by Rep. Al Ullman; S. 1102, "The Business Transfer Tax Act of 1985," introduced by Senator William Roth; and H.R. 4598, introduced by Rep. Richard Schulze in 1986 to enact a "Business Alternative Minimum Tax."

proposal into the federal government's fiscal policy debate in 1989. Others see international developments which could pressure the U.S. into enacting a consumption tax with border adjustments for imports and exports as a trade policy initiative. These observers anticipate enactment of such tax systems by Canada and Japan, which would leave the U.S. alone among major industrialized democracies in our reluctance to make use of such a system. Both Canada and Japan, which account for about 40 percent of U.S. imports and about 35 percent of U.S. exports annually, could enact such border adjustable value-added taxes within a year.

But conventional wisdom is often wrong or contradicted by *other* conventional wisdom. As this book went to press in the fall of 1988, the two major parties' presidential nominees were vying for dominance as the *anti*-tax-increase champion; neither one was promoting a new system in order to increase taxes and reduce the deficit. Members of Congress also have been noticeably cool in their responses over the years to consumption tax proposals. Their skittishness is routinely explained in part by reference to the defeat in November 1980 of the late Rep. Al Ullman (D-OR), then Chairman of the House Ways and Means Committee, who had advocated a tax restructuring package which was based on a value-added tax. Now, their litany of political reasons for opposing such taxes includes the adverse reaction to former Arizona Governor Bruce Babbitt's call for a national consumption tax during his 1988 campaign for the Democratic presidential nomination. These latter bits of conventional wisdom suggest that debating federal consumption taxes may remain an academic exercise for the near term. Only time will tell who are the better prophets.

But the *possibility* that the new President and the 101st Congress will at least look into the subject has created a sense of urgency during the last year or two. More is being written on the subject, and more people are talking about it. The current flurry of activity may be only another false start, but if it is for real, the debate will shift from theories to hard realities in very short order.

This collection of 11 chapters seeks to contribute to the quality of the next serious public debate by linking the abundance of theoretical commentaries with practical questions and problems. These chapters represent a multi-disciplined effort to connect both the large body of economics literature on the subject and the prevailing popular view about "consumption taxes" with the numerous real-world questions which must be answered. All of these aspects should be considered if any such tax is ever to be intelligently debated in this country, much less properly structured and implemented. Just as the issues themselves are diverse, there is considerable diversity of opinion on nearly each one, as will be evident in the 11 separately authored chapters which follow.

For example, is it possible that the term "consumption tax" itself may be a misnomer which is no more properly applied to a sales tax or a tax on value added than to the present corporate tax on net income or to payroll taxes on wages and salaries? This conclusion would be so distinctively and substantively different from the popular view that, if correct, it could radically alter the decisions of policymakers. Even the *consideration* of this alternative view will affect the terms of the debate, no matter the level of support which it ultimately attains.

On what may be the eve of a watershed debate, the rhetoric on consumption taxes is still bouncing back and forth between genuine confusion and downright pettifoggery. The passionately expressed views are reminiscent of the contradictions so artfully presented in the following.[2]

> If, when you say whiskey, you mean that devil's brew, the poison spirit, the bloody monster that defiles innocence, dethrones reason, destroys the home and creates misery . . . then I am certainly against it with all my heart. But, if when you say whiskey, you mean the oil of conversation, the philosophic wine, the ale consumed when good fellows get together, . . . then certainly I am in favor of it.

The spectrum of perceptions and opinions about consumption taxes is just about as wide as that for John Barleycorn. It is as if people are talking about different subjects. To some extent, they are. Like the six blind men of Indostan describing an elephant, one's opinions about a consumption tax are likely to be shaped by what part of the beast one gets hold of first.

Much of the problem arises from the nomenclature itself. This is especially unfortunate, not because the "consumption tax" label is necessarily inaccurate when applied to certain tax systems, but because it tends to prejudice one's assessment of specific tax systems and to stifle an open-minded debate. The mere use of the label by proponents and opponents alike has substituted loose terminology and political biases for rigorous and thoughtful analysis.

The confused and emotional state of the current consumption tax

---

[2]The original version of this exquisitely equivocating statement of opinion is generally thought to have been presented during congressional debates about temperance in the 1800s. A specific version is presented in *Alcohol Education in Oregon Schools: A Topic Outline and Resource Unit for Teachers* (State of Oregon: Alcohol and Drug Section, Mental Health Division, Board of Control, 1968), p. 77.

debate can soberly be portrayed by paraphrasing the Whiskey
Speech.

> If, when you say consumption tax, you mean a tax on the bread for my
> table and the clothes on my back, a tax which raises all merchants' prices,
> a tax which bears most heavily on the poor, a tax which fuels the federal
> spending machine, then I am most certainly against it. But if, when you
> say consumption tax, you mean a small and equitable tax on all producers
> of goods and services, a tax which is measured by the "value added" by
> each, a tax which extracts a fair measure of revenues from foreign com-
> petitors in our markets, a tax which enables American-made goods to
> compete abroad, a tax which can lower the federal deficit and even reduce
> income and payroll taxes, then certainly I am in favor of it.

So, the problem which lies ahead is this. When we say
"consumption tax," what are we talking about and do we really
understand all that we think we know about the subject?

PRACTICAL DEFINITION OF A CONSUMPTION TAX

The currently popular, almost journalistic view is that a
"consumption tax" is just what the label implies -- a tax paid by consumers on the prices of goods and services they purchase, thereby
making consumption more costly than it otherwise would be. What
most people have in mind is a retail sales tax and the accompanying
line of reasoning which is as follows. Under such a tax, the total cost
consumers pay is the price of the item plus the amount of the sales
tax which is collected by the store at the cash register and printed on
the receipt. This tax-induced increase in the total cost of consumer
goods and services then creates a regressive economic effect on
lower-income individuals who must spend a greater portion of their
incomes, in general, and a substantially greater portion in purchasing necessities alone. In order to avoid regressivity, this line of
argument goes, purchases of necessities must be exempted from tax,
or arcane devices such as refundable income tax credits must be
provided to lower-income families.

As in the case of any tax, economists question whether the consumer who "pays" the sales tax is the one who actually bears the real
economic incidence or burden of that tax and whether the goods
purchased are actually more costly than otherwise would be the
case. The rest of us, politicians and plebians alike, usually adhere to
the notion that the person who pays a tax is the one who bears the
burden of that tax. After all, it is *our* bank accounts which are
reduced when we pay a tax.

In the case of a sales tax, very few consumers would agree with any economic theory that the tax paid at the cash register is actually borne to some degree by the companies (or, more accurately, by their employees and/or shareholders) which produce and sell us the goods. It would be difficult to explain how companies have been forced to reduce the price of their goods by the amount of the tax in order to get us to buy the same quantities of those goods. Instead, most people consider that the price of the goods would be the same whether taxed or not and, if taxed, the cost would be the price *plus* tax.

Given this deeply-rooted and widely-accepted perception, points of view about the benefits and evils of consumption taxes are well defined and strongly held. If nothing else changes, a noisy dispute is certain to erupt among various businesses and other economic groups if or when a consumption tax debate is initiated in earnest in Washington. Assuming the previous flirtations with federal consumption taxes are reliable forecasters of the future, you will not need a program to identify the players; the rosters of opponents and supporters are predictable and the arguments can be recited by rote. The resulting "debate" will produce massive amounts of the proverbial heat and smoke, but there is not likely to be much light breaking through the haze.

But circumstances are changing. Business executives have taken a much stronger interest recently in understanding consumption taxes in general and value-added taxes in particular, primarily as a result of federal budget deficits, trade deficits and proposals for a generic or subtraction method value-added computation. The possibility that a federal value-added tax might actually be considered has disrupted the comfortable practice of pontificating on the subject without fear of having to convert theories into actual practice. Where speeches and commentaries previously could trot out the traditional virtues and vices of consumption taxes -- and the same attribute is a virtue to one speaker and a vice to another -- theories are being put to a more rigorous intellectual test by some who may have accepted the traditional views in earlier years, but largely without assessing what was being said.

WHAT THIS BOOK IS ABOUT

In this changing environment, the purpose of this book is to raise and consider questions about the features and effects of tax proposals which are commonly called "consumption taxes" and to do so in the context in which many policymakers and taxpayers probably would analyze tax proposals, given sufficient quiet time to do so.

Issues are presented from the perspective of the practical problems which would affect, or would arise from, the imposition of such taxes. No attempt has been made to produce one more scholarly treatise on the subject, although several such works are noted in the following chapters as sources of information and analysis. The intention instead is to discuss in some detail a range of economic, political, practical and technical questions which should be of interest to taxpayers and tax policymakers alike.

Chapter 1 sets the stage for Chapters 2 through 11 by explaining why the subject matter is current and relevant and by presenting some of the real political problems and opportunities associated with consumption taxes. It also establishes the context of the U.S. consumption tax debate and provides an overview of economic and political issues.

A recurring theme in many of the following chapters is the presentation of alternative ways of looking at the fundamental nature and results of particular forms of consumption taxes. For example, Chapter 2 discusses the potential elements of a definition of "consumption tax." A sales tax and two value-added tax systems are assessed under such a definition, with the practical effects of differing formats being considered.

Chapters 3 and 4 present two views of the economic incidence of a multi-stage value-added tax and a single-stage sales tax. The first view is the traditional analysis, which concludes that the ultimate economic burden of the tax is borne by consumers (hence the "consumption tax" label). An alternative "shared incidence" analysis is also offered, which concludes that such a burden is shared among consumers, workers and owners of capital in proportions that are dictated by market forces. The varying implications of the two analyses are also reviewed.

This book is not intended to establish the correctness of any particular viewpoint. Rather, it is largely a means for organizing a discussion of issues which obviously are not yet fully developed in the literature or otherwise, and of focusing attention on certain critical choices upon which a whole series of other decisions depend.

For example, Chapter 5 reviews the basis for providing exemptions for certain goods or services and the consequences of doing so. The discussions note the relationship between exemptions and the fundamental analysis of whether the tax is considered to be primarily a tax on consumers or a tax which is dispersed among consumers, workers and owners of capital.

This same process of presenting alternative views in order to provide a more informed basis for decisions is to some degree carried forward through the remaining chapters. Chapter 6 considers potential problems of transition to a value-added tax and provides macroeconomic data about which sectors are most likely to encounter such problems. Again, one's perception about incidence affects one's conclusions about transition issues.

Chapter 7 discusses in some detail the international trade effects of a value-added tax and the relevance of substituting such a tax for existing U.S. taxes. Once again, the incidence analysis plays a critical role by influencing the terms of the debate over trade effects. The Appendix to Chapter 7 is a substantive presentation on the effects of monetary exchange rates in a border-adjustable value-added tax environment.

Chapter 8 describes the issues which affect how a value-added tax can readily be applied to financial services. This material is particularly provocative, given the European experience which suggests that such services generally should be ignored by value-added tax systems.

Chapters 9 and 10 provide some numerical analysis of sectoral impacts and macroeconomic effects of consumption taxes. Chapter 9, in particular, explores the potential, relative impact of a value-added tax on different business sectors of the economy in relation to existing federal taxes. Chapter 10 discusses macroeconomic effects of a consumption-based tax. Chapter 11 discusses issues of compliance and administration.

THE VALUE-ADDED TAX AS THE SUBJECT FOR DISCUSSION

While the roster of broadbased consumption taxes includes three general categories -- a national sales tax (imposed at the point of sale to ultimate consumers), a consumed income tax or expenditures tax (imposed on income which is available for consumption expenditures after removing savings), and value-added taxes (imposed at each stage of the production and distribution process for goods and services) -- the national sales tax and the consumed income tax do not appear to be high on any list of viable options.[3] Neither category has been the subject of a major legislative effort at the federal

---

[3]Other types of consumption taxes are much more limited in their application and do not fall within the realm of "broadbased" taxes. These include excise taxes on specific items, such as the federal taxes on gasoline, diesel fuel, tires, telephone services, alcoholic beverages, tobacco products, etc.

level in the United States or apparently in any other major trading nation. However, value-added taxes are already imposed in the European Common Market and other countries, and the governments of Canada and Japan have prepared major tax reform packages which are based on the implementation of a value-added tax.

Within the value-added category, the "invoice and credit" mechanism is the most widely known, since it is this format which is used in Europe. However, increased attention is being given to what is usually called the "subtraction method" of value-added taxation.[4] As Chapter 2 will more fully develop, the subtraction method is a generic method of value-added computation. The introduction of a Business Transfer Tax (the BTT) by Senator William Roth (R-DE) in 1985, the initial discussion drafts of the Canadian government's proposal and Rep. Richard Schulze's Business Alternative Minimum Tax (the BAMT) have generated a new look at the range of issues associated with consumption taxes.[5]

In addition to being a topic of current interest, the basic subtraction method also presents a format in which the alternative analysis of consumption taxes is more readily explained. For both reasons, the value-added tax is the principal subject for discussion in the succeeding chapters, with some emphasis on the generic or subtraction method as a current and topical example for analysis. However, the analyses and commentaries presented here can also be applied to other forms of consumption taxes. There does exist a widely-held view that the *form* of a consumption tax and even of a value-added tax can affect economic incidence and, thus, affect the conclusions which follow from that overriding analysis. Two approaches to this form versus substance debate are presented in Chapter 2 and Chapter 4.

Several important topics are discussed in this book, but no attempt has been made to present all of the issues and problems which a value-added tax proposal would raise in this country. For example, the treatment of governments, governmental agencies and traditionally tax exempt organizations is one major substantive area which is not addressed. Certain politically volatile matters such as the "money machine" argument are mentioned only briefly. The

---

[4]The "subtraction method" label is one of three popular labels for specific mechanical rules under which a value-added tax is calculated. The "invoice and credit method" and "addition method" are the other two. Succeeding references to a generic value-added tax and a subtraction method value-added tax are interchangeable.

[5]A revised Canadian proposal which is likely to be submitted for consideration is a hybrid version of the invoice and credit and the subtraction method VAT systems.

quasi-legal/quasi-economic arguments about the General Agreement on Tariffs and Trade (GATT) legality of a subtraction method value-added tax which includes border tax adjustments is not analyzed here.

Each of these subjects is important, and thoughtful analysis of each will be essential to any serious public debate about a potential U.S. value-added tax system. The authors hope to address these and other matters at a later time. But as with any work on so large a subject, there comes a point at which one concludes that enough is enough. For now, "enough" is represented by the following 11 chapters.

A conscientious effort has been made to present information objectively and to describe alternative points of view, with restrained expressions of opinion and conclusions by the authors of individual chapters. The reader is urged to weigh the presentations, sift out any biases and come to the conclusions which seem appropriate.

Whatever the final conclusion, the reader should come away from this material with the following message. *Approach this subject with caution!* There is a great deal more involved than the simplistic picture brought to mind by the term "consumption tax."

The Value-Added Tax:
Orthodoxy and New Thinking

1

SHIFTING TO CONSUMPTION AS A FEDERAL TAX BASE: AN OVERVIEW

by Murray L. Weidenbaum and
Ernest S. Christian, Jr.

For years, economists have debated the respective merits of income and consumption bases for taxation. The United States uses consumption-based taxes far less than most other developed Western nations. In 1985, the 23 members of the Organization for Economic Cooperation and Development obtained an average 30 percent of their revenue from taxes on consumption (see Table 1-1). For the United States, the ratio was 18 percent.

Many people believe that it is fairer to tax people on what they take from society, rather than on what they contribute by working and investing. In the nineteenth century, classical economist John Stuart Mill made this point in advocating the exemption of saving as part of a "just" income tax system. In the 1940s, American economist Irving Fisher argued that the income tax involved double taxation of saving and distorted the choice of individuals in favor of consumption. According to this view, not only is the income tax unjust, it encourages consumption and leisure at the expense of thrift and enterprise.

The U.S. Treasury actually proposed a "spendings tax" in 1942 as a temporary wartime measure to curb inflation. The proposal was quickly rejected by Congress. A major political argument against the expenditures tax -- then and now -- is that the exemption of saving would favor the rich who are better able to save large

Table 1-1

PERCENTAGE DISTRIBUTION OF TAX REVENUES IN SELECTED COUNTRIES BY MAJOR SOURCE, FISCAL YEAR 1985

Country	Income Taxes	Social Security Taxes	Taxes on Consumption	All Other
Austria	54%	0%	33%	13%
Australia	26	32	33	9
Belgium	41	33	24	2
Canada	44	13	32	11
Denmark	55	4	34	7
Finland	50	9	37	4
France	17	44	29	10
Germany	35	36	26	3
Greece	17	35	43	5
Ireland	34	15	45	6
Italy	36	35	25	4
Japan	46	30	14	10
Luxembourg	45	25	24	6
Netherlands	26	44	26	4
New Zealand	69	0	23	8
Norway	40	21	37	2
Portugal	29	26	43	2
Spain	28	42	26	4
Sweden	42	25	26	7
Switzerland	41	32	19	8
Turkey	45	5	44	6
United Kingdom	39	18	31	12
United States	43	29	18	10
AVERAGE	40%	26%	30%	4%

Source: American Council for Capital Formation.

portions of their incomes. Proponents of an expenditures tax respond that it can be made as steeply progressive as desired. Moreover, the recent trend in income taxation in the United States has been away from progressivity and toward a flatter, more proportional revenue structure. The 1981 and 1986 tax acts are striking cases in point. Another objection to the consumption base is that it would favor the miser over the spendthrift, even when both have similar spending power or ability to pay. The response offered to this argument is that consumption uses up the resources available to the nation, while work and saving add to these resources.

In practice, much of the impact of shifting to a consumption base would depend on how the tax is structured. The two major alternatives are an expenditures tax levied on total purchases within an accounting period and a value-added tax collected on each purchase. In theory, the base of the two taxes is the same -- the value of goods and services purchased. The yields could be similar.

AN EXPENDITURES TAX

An expenditures tax would be collected in much the same manner as the income tax. The annual taxpayer return would continue to be the heart of the collection system. Only one major change would be made; the portion of income that is saved would, in effect, be exempt from taxation.

For a while, the United States was moving toward an expenditures tax, albeit indirectly and in modest steps. The establishment of Individual Retirement Accounts (IRAs) enabled many federal taxpayers to defer paying taxes on amounts saved and invested in an IRA (up to $2,000 a year). Also, the first $100 of dividends received by a taxpayer was excluded from gross income. The Tax Reform Act of 1986, however, greatly reduced the incentives for investing in IRAs and eliminated the dividend exclusion. Having so recently curtailed deductions for saving, it is unlikely that Congress will in the near future reverse course and effectively exempt all saving by shifting to an expenditures tax.

A VALUE-ADDED TAX

Attention has shifted to forms of national sales taxes, notably a value-added tax. Such a consumption-based tax could be levied in addition to the currently collected taxes (although substitutions are possible). After having lain dormant for nearly a decade, interest in a value-added tax in the U.S. has reemerged primarily because of the conjunction of two economic factors -- budget and trade deficits.

Sources of Revenue For Deficit Reduction

There are political and economic proponents of additional federal tax revenues who want to use such revenues for two *inconsistent* policy objectives -- reducing the federal budget deficit and satisfying pent-up demand for new or increased domestic spending programs. Both pressures are well understood, although the latter is not spoken of in public very often.

Although less clearly understood, it is also likely the case that we are near the end of the era in which the income tax can provide major new revenues to the federal government. As the result of recent tax reforms, primarily in 1986, the base of the income tax has been broadened just about as much as is politically possible.

Income tax rates were drastically reduced in 1986 primarily as the direct result of a strong political force which is still at work. High marginal rates of tax, which were born in a war-time era and designed to apply to the rich, were being applied to a broad range of people in the newly affluent middle class who certainly do not consider themselves to be "rich." Having substantially reduced tax rates twice in the 1980s, it will be exceedingly painful for the Congress to reverse course and reimpose high rates of tax on income. The appetite for low tax rates was whetted, not satisfied, when the old idea of steeply "progressive" rates was effectively discarded almost without comment.

As a potential revenue raiser, the sheer *size* of a value-added tax base is unequaled by the current income tax base or payroll tax base, each of which has been severely limited by political judgments over several decades. The value-added tax base roughly corresponds to the total output of goods and services in the economy plus imports and minus exports. For example, a comprehensive value-added tax base in 1987 might have amounted to approximately $2.5 trillion.[1] That year a value-added tax of 3.5 percent on the comprehensive base could have raised approximately the same revenue as the present corporate income tax with its generally applicable rate of 34 percent. A value-added tax of about 16 percent could have raised

---

[1]For this general purpose, the comprehensive base is computed as the total amount of personal expenditures ($2,966 billion) less the values of all housing services ($469 billion), which totals $2,497 billion. Sources: *Economic Report of the President* (February 1988), Tables B14 and B104.

about the same revenue as the present individual income tax which applies 15 percent and 28 percent rates.

Computing a Value-Added Tax

An expenditures tax can be calculated via a "top down" approach, building on the records that are already available to provide the data needed for enforcement of corporate and personal income taxes. In contrast, a value-added tax (a VAT) represents a very different way of collecting a general tax on consumption. It is, in effect, a sophisticated and comprehensive sales tax which avoids the double counting otherwise inevitable when the same item moves from manufacturer to wholesaler to retailer. In total, a VAT should be equivalent in yield to a single-stage sales tax levied at the retail level.[2]

A firm's value-added is the difference between its sales and its purchases from other firms. As shown in Table 1-2, value-added can also be estimated by adding labor and capital inputs supplied by the firm itself -- represented by wages and salaries, rent and interest payments and profit.

A variety of approaches has been suggested for collecting the new tax. The most familiar is the invoice and credit method (see Table 1-3). Under this approach, the tax is computed initially on a company's total sales and the firm is given credit for the VAT paid by its suppliers. To a substantial degree, the VAT would be self-enforcing.

In practice, the collection of the VAT may not be as simple as it is in concept. That would be the case if certain transactions were exempted (such as food) and if non-profit institutions and government enterprises were treated differently. Exemptions are no minor matter in terms of the administrative complexity that they generate. In France, a long and extensive debate occurred over whether or not Head and Shoulders anti-dandruff shampoo was a medicine (tax-exempt) or a cosmetic subject to the full VAT. Food eaten away from the business at which it was purchased may be tax-exempt. What happens if a McDonald's sets up tables outside of the restaurant?[3]

---

[2]Charles E. McLure, Jr., "The Tax on Value Added: Pros and Cons," *Value Added Tax: Two Views* (Washington, D.C.: American Enterprise Institute, 1972), pp. 1-68; Charles E. McLure, Jr., "Value Added Tax" in Charls E. Walker and Mark Bloomfield, editors, *New Directions in Federal Tax Policy for the 1980s* (Cambridge, Mass.: Ballinger Publishing Co., 1983), pp. 185-213.

[3]J. Gregory Ballentine, "The Administrability of a Value-Added Tax," in Walker

Table 1-2

TWO METHODS OF COMPUTING
VALUE ADDED IN PRODUCTION AND DISTRIBUTION

Item	Raw Materials Producer	Manu- facturer	Whole- saler	Retailer	Cumulative Total
Purchases of inputs	--	$100	$500	$800	$1,400
Value Added:					
Wages	$60	$275	$200	$100	$635
Rent	10	25	40	50	125
Interest	10	50	25	25	110
Profit	20	50	35	25	130
Total Value Added	$100	$400	$300	$200	$1,000
Sales of output	$100	$500	$800	$1,000	$2,400

Note: Value added can be estimated in two ways:
(1) Deducting purchases from sales of output ($2,400-$1,400 = $1,000) or,
(2) Adding inputs by the firm itself (excluding inputs supplied by others) ($635 + $125 + $110 + $130 = $1,000).

The "Business Transfer Tax" Proposal

While budget deficits and trade policy may increase the political and economic interest in a value-added tax, the introduction in 1985 of the Business Transfer Tax (BTT) proposal by Senator William Roth, a senior member of the Senate Finance Committee, generated concerns that such taxes might *not* have the financial effects on businesses and consumers which have long been assumed. The substance and *structure* of the proposed BTT attracted attention and in some cases generated considerable alarm.

and Bloomfield, p. 297.

Table 1-3

COMPUTING THE VAT USING THE CREDIT METHOD

Item	Raw Materials Producer	Manu- facturer	Whole- saler	Retailer
Sales of output	$100	$500	$800	$1,000
Less purchases	-0	-100	-500	-800
Value added	$100	$400	$300	$200
Tax on total sales	$10	$50	$80	$100
Credit on purchases	--	-10	-50	-80
Tax liability	$10	$40	$30	$20

Note: Assumes 10 percent VAT on a consumption basis.

As a generic value-added tax computed by the basic subtraction method (without the more familiar invoice and credit mechanisms), the BTT raised some doubts about the traditional analysis of value-added taxes. Could it be that consumption taxes in general -- or at least this particular consumption tax -- might *not* be passed along in full to consumers? Could ardent business proponents of consumption taxes find that they had actually been promoting a tax which becomes just one more *business* cost rather than a tax that is borne solely by consumers? Coupling the BTT proposal with the fact that the Canadian government was also discussing a subtraction method value-added tax at that time resulted in a period of substantive study by business executives, as well as professional analysts, of the real-world effects of such taxes.

PROS AND CONS OF A VAT

Reasons for Favoring a Value-Added Tax

Proponents of a VAT contend that it is economically neutral, because ideally it would be levied at a uniform rate on the entire consumption base. It does not distort choices among products or methods of production. Thus, shifting to more capital-intensive and perhaps more profitable methods of production does not influence the tax burden. Nor is the allocation of resources across product markets, and industry lines affected. In these regards, the VAT is far superior to the existing array of selective excise taxes. In addition, advocates of a VAT point out that, in contrast to an income tax, there is no penalty for efficiency and no subsidy for waste.

One argument in favor of the U.S. adopting a VAT is that so many other nations have adopted this form of taxation. It fits in better than other taxes with the growing international character of production. The VAT has become one of the revenue workhorses of the world. Virtually every important country in Europe imposes the tax, and it has spread throughout the Third World.[4] France has used value-added taxation since 1955, and other members of the European Common Market have done so since the late 1960s or early 1970s.

To some degree, international developments have also helped to increase interest in a value-added tax. Proposals have been made by the Canadian and Japanese governments to implement income and sales tax reforms while enacting border-adjustable value-added taxes. If successful, the efforts would leave the United States as the only major industrialized democracy which does not utilize a tax system that allows imports to be taxed at the border and exports to leave the country free of such tax. Interest in the United States in enacting a comparable proposal for income and/or payroll tax reductions with an offsetting value-added tax could be heightened by Canadian and Japanese action.

At first blush, a VAT would seem to help reduce this nation's presently large trade deficit. However, many economists believe that fluctuations in exchange rates would largely offset these initial effects and result in little change in the balance of trade. This controversy is discussed in detail in Chapter 7 and its Appendix.

Basis of Opposition

Opponents of a VAT offer an extensive list of shortcomings. They contend that a VAT, like any consumption-based revenue source, is inherently regressive. Those least able to pay face the highest overall burdens. Such regressivity can be softened by removing food and medicine from the VAT base or by making refunds

---

[4]McLure, "Value-Added Tax," p. 186.

to low-income taxpayers, but these variations make the collection of the tax more complicated. It would also provide some opportunity for people in the underground economy to avoid paying taxes.[5]

Assuming a VAT is included in the price of purchases, it registers in all of the price indices and, hence, exerts an inflationary force on the economy. The counter-argument is that this is only a one-time effect (occurring when the tax is enacted or increased). Also, the inflationary impact could be offset by appropriate changes in monetary policy, albeit at times with an adverse effect on the levels of production and employment. Opponents also charge that a VAT would invade the area of sales taxation, traditionally reserved for state and local governments.

Imposition of a VAT in the United States is said to require establishing a new tax collection system by the federal government and new recordkeeping on the part of taxpayers. The Treasury Department, based on European experience, believes it would need 18 months after enactment to begin administering a VAT.[6]

OTHER FUNDAMENTAL ISSUES

Any debate about value-added taxes quickly sparks renewed discussions of many long-standing, fundamental issues of tax policy such as the saving rate in the United States by both individuals and corporations, the relative burden of tax borne by capital and labor, taxes on individuals versus taxes on corporations, the relative burden of tax on one type of business compared to another, and the effects of the tax system on international trade. Affecting all of these issues are two recurring questions. Who pays the tax? Who bears the economic incidence?

For example, the anticipated boost to personal saving resulting from a value-added tax rests on the assumption that such a tax is borne by consumers and thus will make consumption relatively more expensive than saving. But if the tax is *not* borne primarily by consumers and is, instead, a proportional tax on the output of labor and the output of capital, will there be a boost to personal saving? Would corporate saving be enhanced if this proportional tax on la-

---

[5]See Joseph A. Pechman, "A Consumption Tax Is Not Desirable for the United States," in Walker and Bloomfield, pp. 271-74; and George N. Carlson, "A Federal Consumption Tax," in ibid., pp. 275-95.

[6]For a negative evaluation of the British experience, see John Blundell, "Britain's Nightmare Value Added Tax," *Heritage Foundation International Briefing* (Washington, D.C.: Heritage Foundation, June 13, 1988), pp. 1-11.

bor and capital were substituted for the corporate income tax, which presumably is borne primarily by capital? Conversely, would the increase in the relative cost of labor prove to be a source of regressivity, even if a value-added tax is not assumed to be passed on to consumers?

The issue of taxing corporations versus taxing individuals takes on a unique characteristic when considering a value-added tax. In the income and payroll tax contexts, the corporation is the entity which writes the check to the government, and no effort is made to allocate such taxes to individuals as shareholders or employees of the corporate payors. But in a value-added context, the corporation writes the check while individuals as consumers are assumed to be bearing the burden. Why does this distinction exist?

Collecting certain taxes from corporations and then pretending that such tax burdens are *not* actually borne by individuals (either as shareholders, employees or consumers) is a lamentable political process which should have been abandoned long ago. In an era in which hundreds of billions of dollars of *individuals'* pension funds, IRAs, insurance policy assets and personal investments are in the form of corporate stocks and bonds, it is difficult to understand the argument that *people* are not bearing the cost of the tax on corporate profits. Perhaps a free-wheeling debate about the nature of the relationship between incidence and payment of value-added taxes could at least lead to similar considerations with respect to income and payroll taxes.

There is a burgeoning concern within the business community that a value-added tax may weigh more heavily on some lines of business than others. Do these concerns arise because managers see their businesses (i.e., their shareholders) as paying the tax or because they think that their customers would pay it?

The possibility of exempting certain goods from a value-added tax presents the most stunning example of how important it is to consider very carefully the question of who pays the tax and who bears the economic incidence. Assume, for example, that the value-added tax is a tax on producers of goods or services, comparable in that respect to the present corporate income tax and payroll taxes. If a value-added tax were substituted for present taxes and if certain commodities such as food and medicine were exempted from tax, the result would be essentially the same as exempting the producers of those commodities from the corporate income tax and payroll tax. How would that affect the flows of investments to, and the values of stock in, taxable and nontaxable companies?

To the extent that international trade advantages can be obtained by substituting a border-adjustable value-added tax for some existing tax, any favorable change in the trade price of goods will depend heavily on whether the value-added tax has the same or similar incidence as the tax it replaces. The presumption that a value-added tax would have a favorable effect on trade does not mesh easily with the presumption that such tax is paid in full by consumers.

MACROECONOMIC EFFECTS

On the basis of expected 1990 levels of economic activity, a one percent VAT would yield approximately $20-40 billion in federal revenue (depending on the coverage of the tax). Thus, at a five percent rate, the VAT might virtually eliminate the $150 billion annual deficit in the federal budget. Even with exemptions for food, housing, and medical care, the estimated annual receipts from a five percent VAT would be approximately $60 billion.

However, fiscal flows of such magnitude likely would generate a variety of other impacts on the economy. For example, these estimates of the yield of the VAT assume that the Federal Reserve will follow an accommodating monetary policy, with a somewhat inflationary effect.

Because the withdrawal of such a substantial amount of purchasing power would act as a depressant on the economy, a tax of that magnitude likely would be phased in over a period of time. One econometric analysis concludes that the economy would grow about one percent more slowly for each percent of VAT and that inflation would be one and a half to two percent higher during an initial adjustment period.[7]

In policy terms, the institution of a VAT in the United States in the 1990s should properly be viewed in contrast to likely alternatives:

- Increases in income tax rates;
- Reductions in general outlays for defense and entitlements; or
- Continued high levels of deficit financing.

Each of these three alternatives would be accompanied by substantial burdens or costs, although they would differ from those generated by the imposition of a consumption-based tax such as a VAT. Reversal of the 1980s trend toward lower marginal income

---

[7]Joel L. Prakken, "The Macroeconomics of Tax Reform," in Walker and Bloomfield, pp. 117-66.

tax rates would reduce the incentives to work, save, and invest. Substantial further reductions in military and civilian spending might, depending on individual value judgments, impair the achievement of vital national objectives -- such as protecting the national security or maintaining the living standards of the elderly. Continued high levels of deficit spending would bring their own set of drawbacks, ranging from high real interest rates to upward pressure on the dollar and thus on the foreign trade deficit.

OUTLOOK

Taxpayers may prefer a low-rate VAT to the income tax if their apparent attitude toward sales taxes is any indication. Yet, politicians fear VAT because they fear it is regressive. Companies marketing consumer products fear that the higher prices will reduce their sales and profits. Conversely, companies selling capital equipment and business services tend to take a more sympathetic attitude toward this form of government revenue, which would lighten the tax burden on their customers and, hence, tend to expand their markets. The validity of such long-held views is questioned, in Chapters 2, 3 and 4, however.

Some observers of national policymaking are reluctant to support any new tax on the assumption that the added revenues would make it harder for members of the Congress to turn down proposals for ambitious new government spending programs. In their view, the budget deficit likely would change little.

Selective Excise Taxes

Considerable support exists for a partial move toward federal consumption or sales taxes, which would be accomplished by linking the tax to an important policy objective. For example, some propose an energy tax to help slow down the rising imports of oil. A $5 a barrel oil import fee would raise about $17 billion in 1990. A more ambitious measure to dampen energy demand -- a $5 a barrel tax on domestic and imported oil -- would yield approximately $21 billion in the same year. One argument against such selective taxes is that they discriminate against a single form of energy, petroleum. A comprehensive five percent tax on all domestic energy consumption, in contrast, is anticipated to bring $16 billion a year into the U.S. Treasury.

More modest tax proposals include raising the federal excise rate on beer and wine to equal the rate on distilled spirits -- a $6 billion revenue-raiser in 1990. Doubling the tax on cigarettes from 16 cents to 32 cents a pack would yield $3 billion. Finally, linking the tobacco and alcohol excises to the rate of inflation would increase Treasury revenues $1 billion a year by 1990. Clearly, the federal government does use selective sales taxes to raise revenue, although not to the extent that state and local governments do. Nevertheless, the annual yield of federal excises is substantial. As shown in Table 1-4, this form of taxation produced over $32 billion in revenue for the Treasury in the fiscal year 1987.

Also, in the case of a comprehensive VAT, linkage to a popular expenditure program would make passage more likely. Suggestions include initiatives on education, health care, and investment.[8]

Value-Added Tax As a Substitute

Although the current political interest in a value-added tax has arisen primarily from its potential to raise revenues to reduce the federal deficit, the *substitution* of a value-added tax for all or portions of existing income and payroll taxes is also a possibility. In fact, the most recent proposals in the United States have explicitly included such proposals.

In 1980, H.R. 7015 was introduced by Rep. Al Ullman. It provided for individual and corporate income tax rate reductions, liberalized depreciation rules, expanded retirement savings provisions and reduced Social Security taxes, all of which were offset by a 10 percent tax applied to a moderately-narrow value-added base (which excluded food, housing, medical care, farmers, fisherman, mass transit, interest and exports).

In 1985, Senator William Roth introduced S. 1102, which called for a credit against Social Security tax liabilities based on Business Transfer Tax (BTT) liabilities under a five percent rate applied to a base similar to the earlier Ullman proposal. The bill also included a sense of the Senate provision which called for using the net BTT revenues (after the Social Security credit) to reduce individual tax rates and to provide increased individual saving incentives. In February 1986, Senator Roth outlined explicit income tax rate reductions and investment-related provisions which would be funded by revenues from an eight percent BTT (after the Social Security credit) applied to a much broader base than his earlier proposal in S. 1102.

---

[8]"Tax Policy Options," *Capital Formation* (May 1988), p. 3.

Table 1-4

REVENUE FROM FEDERAL EXCISE TAXES
Fiscal Year 1987

Source	Amount (in billions)	Percent of total
Alcohol	$6.0	18%
Tobacco	4.8	15
Highway:		
Gasoline	8.7	
Diesel fuel	2.8	
Tires, etc.	1.8	
Subtotal	13.3	41
Airports and airways	3.0	9
Telephone	2.5	8
All other	2.9	9
	$32.5	100%

Source: *Budget of the United States Government, Fiscal Year 1989.*

In 1986, Rep. Richard Schulze introduced H.R. 4598, which called for repealing the corporate minimum tax and enhancing the capital recovery provisions with revenues from a seven percent Business Alternative Minimum Tax. Credits would be allowed against the corporate income tax and Social Security liabilities.

Substitution of a value-added tax for some portion of existing taxes seems a likely feature of any legislation for several reasons.

Politically, the process of enacting a new tax is all but certain to require the building of a coalition from diverse interests. The "cost" of blending such diversity could well include reductions in existing income or payroll rates and/or re-enactment of prior income tax provisions which were repealed or restricted in 1986. Economically, the incidence debate could produce pressures to compensate in some way for the burdens of the new tax. It is interesting to speculate about the diversity of proposals which could arise -- payroll tax cuts, low income credits, corporate rate cuts, capital formation provisions -- depending on one's perspective.

TOO MUCH REVENUE: IS THERE ANY RESTRAINT?

The value-added tax is widely perceived as an almost unlimited source of federal tax revenue. That is true only in the sense that a relatively low rate of value-added tax -- compared to the present high rates of corporate and individual income taxes -- would raise substantial amounts, if applied to a comprehensive base. Despite this theoretical revenue potential, there are obvious practical restraints, not the least of which is the percentage of GNP that may be extracted in taxes without stifling the economy.

Consider the possibility that Congress merely enacts a generic value-added tax which is paid by the producers of goods or services in proportion to the value that is added by each and that is understood to be the substantial equivalent of the present corporate income tax and payroll tax. Having in mind that corporate income taxes are already approximately one-third of corporate profits (as computed for income tax purposes), is it realistic to suppose that such a value-added tax would be imposed to extract another one-third or that the value-added tax rate might be increased another percentage point or two so that the combination of corporate income tax and value-added tax payments would equal or exceed corporate profits?

Alternatively, assume that the popular view prevails and the value-added tax is considered to be a tax on consumption. Two commonly-voiced concerns would immediately come to the fore. One is that the value-added tax is a "money machine" which can readily be increased a percentage point or two almost unnoticed in the general mix of price fluctuations, state sales taxes, etc. The other concern is that any consumption tax is a major burden on consumers which may cause political revolt and could be enacted only at great political danger to all incumbents. Both concerns are expressed by opponents, but it is difficult to see how both can be correct.

SUMMARY

In any event, the short-term outlook is for a substantial increase in the tax burden levied by the federal government on private corporations. Specifically, as a result of the Tax Reform Act of 1986, corporate income tax payments in 1990 are expected to reach approximately $130 billion -- double the 1986 total and more than triple the amount collected by the Treasury in 1983.

The corporate tax increases in the 1986 law -- coupled with the more modest revenue bills passed in 1982 and 1984 -- more than offset the substantial corporate income cuts enacted in 1981 as part of the supply-side Economic Recovery Tax Act. Total corporate income tax payments to the federal government in 1991 are estimated to reach about $140 billion, or 40 percent more than they would have been had the pre-1981 tax law remained in effect.

The impact of taxation on business is most uneven. Increasing reliance on consumption taxes would likely hit consumer-oriented companies particularly hard. However, a VAT would likely be a lower burden on a highly profitable industry than a simple rate increase on corporate profits. In contrast, increasing excise taxes selectively could wind up pitting one industry group against another, with substantial incentive for businesses to use the political process to achieve advantages or avoid disadvantages.

In short, the yawning federal deficit is reviving interest in another round of tax "reform." Recent tax changes designed to be "revenue neutral" have shifted the tax burden from the low-saving sector (families and individuals) to high-saving sector (businesses). Some form of VAT is thus likely to be debated and perhaps inaugurated in the near future. The economic impacts of such a shift in the basis of taxation must be carefully examined beforehand. Winners and losers are unavoidable in any major tax change, but Congress should obtain a clear understanding of its benefits and costs before embracing a major new revenue source.

2

IF, WHEN YOU SAY "VALUE-ADDED TAX," YOU MEAN . . .

by Ernest S. Christian, Jr.

SETTING THE STAGE: PAYMENT VS. INCIDENCE

The value-added tax (VAT) is the form of "consumption tax" that is most likely to be considered for enactment at the federal level. It is also a source of confusion that has habitually caused reasonable people to take opposing views as if they were talking about two different taxes. Fact is, they probably are.

A tax on value added, as such, may not be a consumption tax at all. Such a tax is imposed on and paid by the producers of goods or services in proportion to the value added by each. From the standpoint of who pays, such a tax more resembles the present corporate tax on net income than a retail sales tax, which is what most people have in mind when they say consumption tax.

On the other hand, it is possible to convert a tax on value added into a tax that more resembles a sales tax paid by consumers. Chapter 3 also discusses two opposing views expressed in the substantial body of economics literature that add to the confusion on the subject. Both views tend to ignore who pays the tax and to focus, instead, on who bears the ultimate economic burden of the tax.

A traditional view described in Chapter 3 suggests that consumers bear the economic incidence of a value-added tax even if the tax, as such, is *paid* by corporations and other producers of goods and services. By skipping over payment and assuming that the amount of tax paid by producers is automatically passed on to purchasers in the form of a higher price, adherents of this point of view readily conclude that any form of value-added tax is a consumption tax.

This supposedly traditional view of a value-added tax would appear to be inconsistent with the traditional view of the present corporate income tax. While there has long been some general acknowledgement that a tax paid by corporations measured by net income must at some point be borne by "people," no one has characterized the present corporate income tax as a "consumption tax."

An alternative view described in Chapter 3 suggests that the economic incidence of a value-added tax is indeterminately shared by consumers, workers, and the owners of capital without regard to whether the nominal *payor* of the tax is a corporation that produces goods and services or is a consumer who purchases goods and services. This shared-incidence analysis consistently ignores payment of the tax with all forms of taxes; not just with the value-added tax. Adherents would, for example, suggest that the present corporate tax on net income, any form of value-added tax, and even an outright sales tax, may all have qualitatively similar effects on the price and quantity of consumer goods and services.

Even though taxes in general are normally evaluated primarily in terms of the amount thereof and who pays it, there has long been a strong tendency to apply the different standard of economic incidence to a value-added tax. Within limits, it is useful to focus on the ultimate economic burden of a value-added tax. For example, as discussed in Chapter 7, absent an understanding of economic incidence, it is not possible to evaluate properly the potential international trade effects of a value-added tax. Chapter 5 points out that numerous critical choices in structuring a value-added tax, such as whether to provide exemptions for the value of food or medicine, also depend on an understanding of economic incidence. Certain widely presumed secondary consequences, such as altering the relative preference between saving and consumption, may in the final analysis also depend on the economic incidence of a value-added tax.

On the other hand, when extended too far, emphasis on the economic incidence of the tax -- instead of on who pays the tax as such -- tends to lose its practical utility; especially if used to define a consumption tax and to determine if a value-added tax fits that definition. For instance, pushed to its extreme, the shared-incidence analysis might suggest that there is no such thing as a consumption tax that is greatly different from any other tax in terms of its effect on the price or quantity of goods and services sold. At the other extreme, the traditional view discussed in Chapter 3 leads to the

improbable conclusion that a tax imposed on and paid by corporations in proportion to the value added by each is a consumption tax,
even though the present corporate tax measured by net income is
not.

Moreover, in order to be consistent in making certain comparisons between a value-added tax and other existing or potential
taxes, it is necessary to look first at who pays the tax. For example,
Chapter 9 undertakes to compare the sectoral allocation of a value-
added tax to that of the present corporate tax on net income. This
critical comparison is measured by potential changes in the relative
amounts of taxes paid by corporations in different lines of business.
There is no practical way to quantify and compare potential changes
in economic incidence.

FOCUSING ON PAYMENT: INITIAL INCIDENCE

By focusing primarily on who pays a tax in the sense of the payor
whose bank account and cash flow are reduced, as occurs when we
all pay our income tax on April 15th, this chapter establishes a definition of a hypothetical "consumption tax" based on four criteria that
may make such a tax discretely different from other taxes. These
criteria are first applied to a retail sales tax and then to two potentially different forms of a value-added tax. The question is whether,
when judged by consistent application of the same criteria, any form
of value-added tax is the equivalent of a sales tax.

The emphasis here on payment of the tax may be viewed as a
way of determining initial incidence as distinguished from economic
incidence, which is discussed in Chapter 3. The difference is largely
one of timing.

Congress and other tax policymakers only address the question at
the time a new tax is enacted or when some existing tax is changed
in a major way. On that occasion and for some period of time
thereafter, the incidence of the tax (in all senses of the word) is on
the nominal payor -- the taxpayer. Thereafter, the ultimate economic burden of the tax may be dispersed throughout the economy
in various indeterminate amounts. In the past, at least, Congress
and other tax policymakers have felt that they have had no way of
quantifying these shifts in incidence. Even if they did, they normally
would have no occasion to later revisit the question.

The reaction on the part of most payors (or burden-bearers) of a
value-added tax is similar. Given the fact that the ultimate economic burden of a value-added tax or any other tax probably is as

diffuse and uncertain in amount as suggested by the shared-incidence analysis described in Chapter 3, their first and last question is likely to be the same: "Who pays the tax?"

PRACTICAL DEFINITION OF A CONSUMPTION TAX

The total taxable base of both a comprehensive single-stage retail sales tax and of a comprehensive multi-stage value-added tax can be said to equal the total value of all goods and services purchased by consumers, just as the total taxable base of an income tax can be said to equal the total amount of net income. Accordingly, both a sales tax and a value-added tax can be said to be consumption-based taxes, similar to the way in which the present income tax can be said to be an income-based tax. Given the difference between an income base and a consumption base, and the potential significance of that difference, that fact alone might be sufficient to define both a sales tax and a value-added tax as consumption taxes.[1]

Important as it is, the nature of the value-added tax base is not, however, what most people primarily have in mind. The currently-prevailing definition of a consumption tax that most people have in mind is as follows.[2]

> A consumption tax is a tax paid by consumers levied at the time they make a retail purchase in proportion to what they spend, which makes consuming more expensive than it otherwise would be.

Clearly, the primary emphasis is on payment of the tax by the consumer and the increase in the cost to the consumer of a taxed item of goods or services.

POTENTIAL DEFINITIONAL ELEMENTS OF A CONSUMPTION TAX

Proceeding forward toward the objective of trying to apply this general definition in a more precise way to some particular form of tax, four questions come to mind that ought to be asked about any

---

[1]In the case of a comprehensive single-stage sales tax, the maximum taxable base is generally considered to be equal to total personal consumption expenditures. As discussed later, the maximum value-added tax base is at least that large. Potentially, the value-added tax base may be larger; much closer to GNP.

[2]No consideration is given in this chapter to a consumed income tax or any other form of expenditures tax which allows a deduction for savings and makes consuming more expensive than savings.

tax: (i) what is the taxable base; (ii) who is the payor of the tax; (iii) what is the event which causes payment of the tax to be due; and (iv) what is the immediate, discrete result of the tax other than to collect revenue? Consideration of these questions suggests four definitional elements. A tax might be called a "consumption tax" because the taxable base is the value or price of goods and services purchased by consumers; because the taxpayer is the consumer; because the event which causes the tax to be paid is the act of making a consumer purchase; or because the tax makes consumption more expensive than it otherwise would be.[3]

Application of These Criteria to a Sales Tax

In the case of the familiar retail sales tax, the first three definitional elements clearly are present. The sales tax is a stated percentage of the value or price of the goods or services purchased that is paid directly by consumers on the occasion of making a retail purchase. Insofar as the fourth element -- whether the tax makes consumption more expensive -- very few consumers likely agree with any economic theory that the seller *may* in some unstated degree have taken the tax into account in setting the underlying price of the goods in order to sell the desired volume of goods. Instead, they consider that the price of the goods is the price of the goods and, if taxed, the cost to them is the price *plus* tax. In the absence of any ability to *quantify* the price adjustment that may have been made for each item of goods and services in the same precise way as the tax is associated with each item, consumers are not likely to be convinced otherwise.

Most people recognize that there is some price elasticity in their demand for goods. In theory, if goods cost sufficiently more, they will buy less. Indeed, that is exactly what most people foresee from a sales tax; perhaps not in their own case because sales tax rates generally are low, but certainly in the case of others who are less able to afford the additional cost.

Thus, in a practical sense, the fourth definitional element is present also -- consumption is more expensive than it otherwise would be. A retail sales tax fits the baseline definition and is precisely

---

[3]For the purposes of this chapter, which is concerned primarily with initial incidence as reflected by payment, consumption is considered to be more expensive if the cost to consumers of a taxed item is greater by the amount of the tax. Consumers may or may not continue to purchase the same total volume of taxed items. As discussed in Chapter 3, consumers would bear the *total* economic incidence of the tax only if they continued to purchase the same volume.

what most people have in mind when they say "consumption tax."

Application of These Criteria to a Value-Added Tax

Having established a baseline definition of a consumption tax, and the definitional elements upon which that conclusion is based, the next logical step is to apply the same criteria to a value-added tax to see if it is the equivalent of a sales tax.

The following Consumption Tax Scorecard reflects a preliminary comparison of the familiar retail sales tax and the general idea of a value-added tax without specificity as to any particular form of VAT.

CONSUMPTION TAX SCORECARD

Consumption Tax	Sales Tax	Value-Added Tax
(1) Taxable base = total consumption	Yes	Yes
(2) Paid by consumer	Yes	?
(3) Paid when consumption occurs	Yes	?
(4) Makes consumption more expensive	Yes	?

Because the taxable base of any comprehensive value-added tax can be said to be at least equal to total value or price of all goods and services purchased by consumers, the first element in our Consumption Tax Scorecard can be filled in with a "Yes." At this point, we cannot fill in the rest of the scorecard. We must first discuss two forms of value-added tax that may have similar taxable bases, but which may be radically different insofar as how they fit the remaining three definitional elements.

Fork in the Road: Two Different Value-Added Taxes

This brings us to the fork in the road where two forms of the VAT diverge -- even though both may be called value-added taxes and even though both may have the same or similar bases. After a brief definition of each, it is necessary to apply to each of them separately the three remaining definitional elements of a consumption tax.

Generic Value-Added Tax. Although it appears nowhere in the literature on the subject, and may be a little off the mark in a dictionary sense, the term "generic value-added tax" is here used to describe the fundamental concept and basic structure of a tax on value added in its simplest form. In essence, a generic value-added tax is a tax imposed on and paid by corporations (and other businesses) in proportion to the value they "add" to the goods and services they produce and sell. The value added by any company is the amount it receives from the sale of goods and services minus the amount it pays to other companies for goods and services.

This calculation of value *sold* minus value *purchased* to arrive at value *added* is made periodically, usually quarterly with an annual reconciliation. The amount of tax paid is the tax rate multiplied by the value added during the accounting period.

In theory, over some period of time all these separate "increments" of value added by countless numbers of companies that produce and sell goods and services will equal the total value of goods and services produced and sold; just the same as if all goods and services were produced and sold by one company.[4] Such a single-company comparison presents a useful illustration. If all goods and services were produced and sold by General Everything, Inc., all value would have been added by that company and the tax would be the tax rate times gross receipts.[5]

Invoice and Credit VAT. The invoice and credit VAT is more well-known than the generic product. This is the form of value-added tax widely utilized in Europe and elsewhere abroad, which has been the object of most of the writing on the subject, and is what most people have in mind when they say "value-added tax."

---

[4]In the interest of simplicity, this discussion gives no attention either to imports which are produced abroad and subject to tax at the border or to exports of goods and services the value of which does not enter into the tax base.

[5]Although misleading in the case of the value added by financial institutions, in the case of a company which produces and sells goods, a value-added tax may readily be analogized to a gross receipts tax with an adjustment mechanism. The adjustment mechanism avoids the pyramiding effect that would occur when Company A sells raw materials to Company B for $100X and Company B manufactures a product which it sells to Company C for $200X. Under a regular gross receipts tax, total taxable receipts would be $300X; whereas if Company B produced both the raw materials and product, taxable receipts would be only $200X. It is widely noted in the literature, too often to cite, that one reason for adopting value-added taxes in some European countries was to avoid this pyramiding effect under pre-existing "turnover" taxes in those countries.

The invoice and credit VAT starts with exactly the same concept and framework as the generic value-added tax. There is then appended to that framework various versions of a system of invoices and credits that undertakes to identify, accumulate and roll forward to the final sale of consumer products the amount of tax paid by each producer or seller on all the "increments" of value that are said to be reflected in the final sales price to the consumer. That amount of tax may or may not be separately stated to the consumer. Whether or not separately stated, the retailer owes a tax equal to the tax rate multiplied by the final sales price; minus, however, a credit for all the "previously paid" taxes as shown on the invoices furnished to him by his suppliers.

Is a Generic Value-Added Tax a Consumption Tax?

Let us return to our Consumption Tax Scorecard and try to answer the three open questions about a generic value-added tax, the first of which is: Do consumers pay the tax?

The answer is, "No, not unless when you say 'pay,' you mean something different from the way we have heretofore applied that term; and not unless you consider that consumers pay the present corporate tax on net income." The initial incidence of a generic value-added tax and the present corporate tax on net income should be the same. Both are *paid* by corporations in the sense that it is the corporation's cash flow or bank account that is reduced when quarterly or annually it writes checks to the Treasury in payment of its tax.

That concept of initial incidence is exactly what most of us have in mind when we pay our income tax on April 15 or when we pay a sales tax at the cash register. That is also what the Congress has in mind when it periodically amends the tax laws to rearrange the relative aggregate amount of taxes paid by corporations and paid by individuals. In the Tax Reform Act of 1986, the $120 billion reduction in income taxes paid by individuals was funded by a $120 billion increase in taxes paid by corporations.

When people say that a value-added tax is paid by consumers, they mean that the amount of tax nominally paid by the corporation or other business that produced and sold goods and services is actually passed on to consumers in the form of a higher price for those goods and services.[6] But why would it be assumed that a tax paid by

---

[6]In that case, the bank account and cash flow of the corporation would be only temporarily reduced. The only real cost to the corporation would be an implicit

corporations measured by value added is automatically passed on to consumers in the form of a higher price, when a tax paid by corporations measured by net income is not assumed to be passed on to consumers?

This "pass-on" assumption appears to arise from indiscriminately characterizing any value-added tax as an *ad valorem* tax, merely because the aggregate base of that tax may be equal to the total value of goods and services produced and sold. As discussed in Chapter 3, a traditional view among many economists has been that *ad valorem* taxes -- the various duties and imposts of an earlier time and the excise and sales taxes of today -- are paid by the purchasers in the form of a higher price whether or not separately stated as a tax. Apparently, that is because typically an *ad valorem* tax is measured by the value of each item of goods and is, therefore, directly *associated* with that item. One colorful quotation from an early 19th century commentator illustrates the attitude about *ad valorem* taxes that is still popular today.[7]

> Taxes upon every article which enters into the mouth, or covers the back, or is placed under the foot . . . taxes on everything on earth, and the waters under the earth . . . . The schoolboy whips his taxed top -- the beardless youth manages his taxed horse, with a taxed bridle, on a taxed road; -- and the dying Englishman, pouring his medicine, which has paid seven per cent, into a spoon that has paid fifteen per cent -- flings himself back upon his chintz bed, which has paid twenty-two per cent. . . .

A generic value-added tax paid by corporations is *not* associated with any particular item of goods or services produced and sold in the economy or finally sold to consumers, any more or less than is the corporate tax on net income. When the countless numbers of corporations -- many of which sell only to other corporations -- periodically calculate and pay a tax on the amount of value they added during that period (or on the amount of net income they derived), could one really imagine that any identifiable amount of that aggregate amount of tax is somehow associated with particular items of goods and services purchased by consumers in the way of an excise tax, a sales tax or some other form of actual *ad valorem* tax?

---

interest payment for the period between the time it paid the tax and the time it was reimbursed by the customer. The first real payor of the tax would be the consumer who would bear the initial incidence of the tax.

[7]Reverend Sidney Smith, *Review of Seybert's Statistical Annals of the United States*, p. 291.

Unless one wishes to change the definition of "paid," and to engage in certain assumptions that are highly debatable and that are not applied to the corporate income tax, we should fill out our Consumption Tax Scorecard as follows:

CONSUMPTION TAX SCORECARD

Consumption Tax	Sales Tax	Generic Value-Added Tax
(1) Taxable base = total consumption	Yes	Yes
(2) Paid by consumer	Yes	No
(3) Paid when consumption occurs	Yes	No
(4) Makes consumption more expensive	Yes	No

While one might have some hesitancy in marking number (4) with a flat "No," knowing that some indeterminate amount of any corporate tax -- whether measured by value added or net income -- may ultimately find its way into the price of what the corporation sells, the scorecard is correct for the purpose of consistently applying to all forms of taxes a uniform standard based on initial incidence as reflected by payment. Viewed from that perspective, even though the aggregate tax base can be said to be the same as the tax base of a comprehensive sales tax, a generic value-added tax more resembles the present corporate tax on net income than a sales tax.

Is an Invoice and Credit VAT a Consumption Tax?

Let us return, again, to our Consumption Tax Scorecard and try to answer the three open questions about an invoice and credit VAT, the first of which is: Do consumers pay the tax?

Under the invoice and credit VAT, although calculated differently, the amount of each company's tax liability and the amount of tax that each company "remits" to the Treasury during each accounting period, is the same as under the generic value-added tax.[8] The two distinguishing features of the invoice and credit VAT are as follows. First, each company which sells goods or services to another company provides the purchaser an invoice which *associates* with those goods and services the amount of VAT paid up to that point.[9] Second, this invoice also entitles the purchaser to a credit for the stated amount of tax when he, in turn, must pay a tax on the further value that he adds as reflected in the sales price to his own customer later on.

This process continues on through the chain from one manufacturer to another, to retailers and finally to the consumer where the credit mechanism stops. Because of the close association of an amount of tax with particular goods and services and because each company acquires, for an agreed price, goods or services plus a tax credit, the basic idea is that each company that sells to another can more readily collect the separately stated tax from its customer.[10] When the succession of invoices finally gets to the retailer, he has a credit equal to the tax rate times the wholesale price. The assumption is that the retailer will charge the consumer a separately stated VAT equal to the tax rate multiplied by the retail price, take his credit and remit the balance to the Treasury. If all companies, including the retailer, have been successful in passing on the tax, it is clear that an invoice and credit VAT is the equivalent of a sales tax and is, therefore, a consumption tax.[11]

Based largely on the European experience and experience in the United States with various separately stated state taxes imposed prior to the retail level, many believe that the invoice and credit sys-

---

[8]Typically, in the case of an invoice and credit VAT, companies are said to "remit" the tax instead of having paid it. That is because of the assumption, derived from and reinforced by the structure of the tax, that each company will be reimbursed by its customer for the separately stated tax.

[9]The amount of tax associated with each item of goods and services is arrived at by multiplying the sales price times the tax rate. This is supposed to represent the tax on the increment of value that was added by the seller as well as the tax on all increments of value previously added by others.

[10]Chapter 4 discusses the difference between a tax levied on the tax-inclusive price of goods and services (where the price includes the tax) and a tax levied on the tax-exclusive price of goods and services. In both instances, the tax is separately identified; in the one case as a component of the price and in the other case as an addition to the price.

[11]It will be recalled that in the case of the generic value-added tax which does not involve invoicing a separately stated tax, we rejected the notion that corporations (and other businesses) are mere collectors or remitters of the tax who are automatically fully reimbursed by customers and, finally, the consumer. We reached that conclusion largely on the basis that the generic value-added tax is not associated with any particular item of goods or services and could be recovered, if at all, only through the corporation's overall pricing structure.

tem will cause the tax to be passed on as a matter of course. If it does not actually cause a pass-on of the tax, certainly the invoice and credit mechanism makes it more likely that a larger portion will roll forward arbitrarily attached by invoice to particular goods and services. This viewpoint is consistent with the traditional view among many economists that an *ad valorem* tax is paid by consumers.

The following practical circumstances suggest that all or a large part of the tax will, in fact, be passed on from one business to another and finally on to consumers. Many people in business are convinced that they can more readily pass through to their customers -- whether commercial or retail -- an invoice and credit VAT that is a separately stated tax. Because they believe that such a tax can be passed on, they will vigorously attempt to do so. Separate identification of the tax and the forced association of the tax with each sale of a product should cause marketing executives to become more involved in recovering the corporation's tax "cost" than at present. One gets the impression that the present corporate income tax is an after-the-fact occurrence that is of far more importance to the chief financial officer than to the head of marketing.

Producers and sellers, as well as consumers, of certain products such as gasoline and telephone services are by long tradition and familiarity conditioned to separately stated federal excise taxes associated with the goods and services. More broadly, nearly all consumers are conditioned to paying sales taxes. It may be that many people have a different and more receptive attitude toward paying slightly more for a product if that additional amount is separately stated as a tax than they do toward paying an equivalently greater, unexplained higher price for the product itself.

We have classified a separately stated, single-stage retail sales tax as a consumption tax paid by consumers. Most people would agree. If consumers are willing to pay a separately stated sales tax, it is reasonable to conclude that they will have no different attitude about paying a separately stated VAT. Therefore, each of the corporations (or other businesses) involved in the multiple stages of an invoice and credit VAT prior to the final retail sale should be reasonably confident that the tax can be passed on and should be willing to reimburse one another and keep the tax rolling forward to the consumer.[12] Compared to a sales tax, the major difference

---

[12]Anecdotal information, plus their continued use of the invoice and credit VAT, indicates that companies in Europe are reasonably confident that most of the tax is passed on. The invoice and credit VAT has been in use in Europe for years without any suggestion, insofar as the author knows, that the tax is paid *twice* in those countries where the VAT is first remitted by each producer and seller and then separately

should be that the Treasury collects revenue sooner, as each corporation -- early in the process far ahead of any final retail sale --
remits an incremental amount of tax and seeks reimbursement from
its customers.

On that basis, we should fill out our Consumption Tax Scorecard
as follows:

CONSUMPTION TAX SCORECARD

Consumption Tax	Sales Tax	Invoice and Credit Value-Added Tax
(1) Taxable base = total consumption	Yes	Yes
(2) Paid by consumer	Yes	Yes or probably
(3) Paid when consumption occurs	Yes	Yes or probably
(4) Makes consumption more expensive	Yes	Yes or probably

At the very least, the invoice and credit VAT far more closely
resembles a sales tax than does the generic value-added tax. If any
form of tax measured by value added is a consumption tax as
heretofore defined, this is it.

We have given great weight to the pass-on mechanics of the
separately stated tax in concluding that the consumer is probably the
payor of the tax in the sense of being the first one who experiences
any real reduction in his or her bank account or cash flow as a result
of the tax as such. Once having arrived at the consumer level
(where it is indistinguishable from a sales tax), whether the invoice
and credit VAT will have any determinable effect on the prices and
quantities of goods and services sold, or on the returns to capital or
labor, is a question of economic incidence dealt with in Chapter 3.
The initial incidence, as reflected by payment, is primarily on the
consumer.

---

stated and collected at the retail level from the consumer.

WHAT CONCLUSIONS CAN BE REACHED FROM THE VALUE-ADDED TAX BASE ALONE?

It should be clear that merely because the base of a tax is value added (instead of net income, gross receipts or some other plausible amount) does not mean that the tax is a "consumption tax." Both a generic value-added tax and an invoice and credit VAT have similar or mathematically equal bases. The former is a tax on corporations and other producers of goods and services. The latter is the substantial equivalent of a sales tax.

Consumption-Based vs. Output-Based

A value-added tax can be characterized as a "consumption-based" tax because, generally speaking, the total amount of tax collected by the Treasury should at least equal the tax rate times the total value or price of all goods and services purchased by consumers. On the other hand, leaving aside for the moment that not all goods and services are purchased by consumers, a value-added tax can also be characterized as an "output-based" tax. Because the total value or price of all goods and services purchased must be equal to the total value or price of all goods and services produced and sold, a VAT may be considered output-based.

Thus, in broad concept, one may look at the value-added tax base primarily in terms of gross national product (GNP) which is supposed to represent the total value produced in the economy as measured by the final sales price of domestically produced goods and services. (See Table 2-1.) One may also look at it primarily in terms of personal consumption expenditures which is the largest component of GNP. The choice between these two points of emphasis may depend on whether we are talking about a generic value-added tax imposed on and paid by corporations and other producers of goods and services or are talking about an invoice and credit VAT that closely resembles a sales tax paid by consumers.

In the case of a sales tax or any form of value-added tax considered to be the equivalent of a sales tax paid by consumers, the normal shorthand method is to ignore all other components of GNP and to state the taxable base as being equal to personal consumption expenditures; in this case $2,430.5 billion.[13] The long way around to

---

[13]A revenue estimator or anyone else seeking to be precise would probably exclude from personal consumption expenditures imputed consumption such as the rental value of owner-occupied housing and foreign travel expenses. After these and other minor adjustments, the consumption base for 1984 would probably be about

Table 2-1

GROSS NATIONAL PRODUCT 1984
(billions of dollars)

GNP	$3,772.2
Components of GNP:	
Personal Consumption Expenditures	$2,430.5
Gross Private Domestic Investment	$ 664.8
Net Exports	$ (58.9)
Government Purchases	$ 735.9

Source: U.S. Department of Commerce, *Survey of Current Business*, July
          1987. Although comparable GNP data are available for subse-
          quent years, 1984 data are used here in order later to make
          consistent comparisons with certain income tax data taken from
          the *Statistics of Income* for 1984 which is the most recent year
          available.

reach the same result would be to start with GNP and subtract gross
private domestic investment ($664.8 billion) and government pur-
chases ($735.9 billion), and then add net exports ($+58.9 billion).
This also equals a taxable base of $2,430.5 billion.

In the case of a generic value-added tax on corporations and
other producers of goods and services, there would, however, be no
particular reason to subtract from GNP that portion of output purchased by the government ($735.9 billion). Income derived from
sales to the government is not excluded from the tax base of the present corporate tax on net income.[14] Accordingly, from this "output"
perspective, the value-added tax base might be $735.9 billion larger
than personal consumption expenditures. The total could be around

$2,050.6 billion.

[14]Normally, where the value-added tax is considered to be the equivalent of a
sales tax paid by the purchaser, sales to government are "zero rated" or otherwise
exempted on the theory that if the government collected a tax on its own purchases, it
would merely be swapping dollars from one pocket to another. The obvious
assumption is that the government (as a purchaser-consumer) both pays the tax and
bears the ultimate economic burden of that tax. No such assumption is made with the
corporate income tax. It is not apparent why any such assumption should be made
with a generic value-added tax imposed on and paid by corporations and other producers.

$3,166.4 billion which is less than GNP for 1984 only by the amount of gross private domestic investment (producers' durables, etc.), which can appropriately be considered intermediate inputs that ultimately show up in personal consumption expenditures or government purchases.[15]

Both of these potential value-added tax bases -- $2,430.5 billion in the case of the invoice and credit VAT and $3,166.4 billion in the case of the generic value-added tax -- assume no exemptions. Various forms of exemptions are likely in the case of an invoice and credit VAT. Exemptions are basically inconsistent with a generic value-added tax. Therefore, the disparity between the two potential tax bases may be even greater.[16]

Significance of the Value-Added Base

Whether viewed from the perspective of output or the perspective of consumption, the significance of the value-added tax base should not be obscured by attempts here or elsewhere to put a label on the tax or to fit it within some definitional framework. The fact is that value added is a plausible tax base that exists as an alternative to the present net income base. In recent years in the United States, in Canada, in Japan and, perhaps, elsewhere, increasing attention has been given to imposing a tax on value added (with the tax structured either to be paid by the producers of goods and services or to be paid by the purchasers of goods and services).[17]

There are obvious reasons why there might be great interest in

---

[15]In accounting for GNP, $181.1 billion for investment in residential housing is included along with producers' durables, etc., in gross private domestic investment. At least a portion thereof is housing produced and sold to owner-occupiers as a final product and probably should be included in the base of a generic value-added tax.

[16]While, at a minimum, it would normally be expected that various "products" such as food, medicine and housing (as distinguished from imputed rent which is already excluded from the base) would be exempted in the case of an invoice and credit VAT paid by consumers, such exemptions are inconsistent with a generic value-added tax imposed on and paid by corporations. Assume, for example, that a generic value-added tax were substituted for the present corporate tax on net income. Would it make sense to exempt corporations that produce and sell food, medicine or housing from the "corporate tax"?

[17]As pointed out in Chapter 1 and elsewhere, versions of a Business Transfer Tax have been introduced in the U.S. Congress. Those taxes are versions of a generic value-added tax. Canada came close to imposing a generic value-added tax modeled after the Business Transfer Tax, although Canada now appears to be headed toward taxing value added by means of a border-adjustable sales tax. Based on press reports in the summer and fall of 1988, Japan may undertake to tax value added by either a "simplified" method that resembles the Business Transfer Tax or by some other means that more resembles a sales tax.

the value-added tax base both in the United States and elsewhere. Although in years past, the emphasis was primarily on the potential trade effects of a value-added tax, today the focus is more on the revenue potential either to pay for deficit reduction as in the United States in 1989-90 or to pay for tax reform achieved by lower individual and/or corporate income tax rates.[18]

Typically, reform of the income tax has been aimed at achieving a broad-based/low-rate tax. Given its broad base and consequent revenue potential at a lower rate of tax, a tax on value added may be the ultimate broad-base/low-rate tax. Many foresee substantial advantages of equity and efficiency, wholly apart from the revenue potential of a value-added tax. Nevertheless, the revenue potential -- which frightens some and intrigues others -- is the dominant factor.

Comparisons Between Value-Added and Income Tax Bases

Why is the revenue potential of a value-added tax considered to be so great? It is sometimes said that the value-added tax base is much larger than the net income base. In some ways that is true. In other ways, not. This can be illustrated by the following comparisons for the year 1984 which is the latest year for which official income tax data from the *Statistics of Income* are available.[19] (See Table 2-2.)

As might be expected, personal consumption expenditures (PCE) are not as large as an expansive definition of personal income as derived from the National Income and Product Accounts (NIPA).[20]

---

[18]In both Canada, and apparently in Japan, consideration of the value-added tax has arisen primarily in the context of income tax reform centered around lower income tax rates. In Canada, for example, income tax reform has been almost parallel to the Tax Reform Act of 1986 in the United States. Although it played no direct role in the process, the Business Transfer Tax was introduced in the U.S. Congress during the early stages of the Tax Reform Act of 1986. There was some speculation at the time that a tax on value added might have been used to pay for lower income tax rates.

[19]Use of 1984 figures in making these comparisons also emphasizes that the only purpose here is to illustrate approximate proportions between various key elements of a value-added base and an income base; not to in any way make revenue estimates or otherwise to be precise about the numerical results of what might or might not be done in the context of 1989-90. In 1986, and subsequently, changes were made in both the individual and corporate income tax bases. Those changes do not, however, greatly alter the proportions shown here.

[20]PCE does not include that portion of personal income that is saved; nor does it include purchases by government.

Table 2-2

COMPARISON OF TAX BASES:
INCOME VS. VALUE ADDED IN 1984
(billions of dollars)

Income Tax Base	
Individual	
· Taxable Income	$ 1,671.2
Adjusted Gross Income (AGI)	$ 2,214.8
NIPA Personal Income	$ 2,784.7
Corporate	$ 257.1
Value-Added Tax Base	
Total Personal Consumption Expenditures (PCE)	$ 2,430.5
Less Imputed Amounts	316.0
Less Other Excluded Amounts	63.9
Adjusted PCE Tax Base	$ 2,050.6
Add Government Purchases	735.9
Expanded Value-Added Base	$ 2,786.5

Sources: Internal Revenue Service, *Statistics of Income 1984*; U.S. Department of Commerce, *Survey of Current Business*, July 1988.
Adjusted gross income is calculated without state tax refunds and
above-the-line adjustments to income. The amount of personal
income shown here, as derived from the National Income and
Product Accounts (NIPA), includes only those elements that are
comparable to AGI and taxable income. Thus, for example,
transfer payments are not for this purpose included in personal
income. PCE has been reduced by imputed rent as well as by
other miscellaneous imputed amounts, by religious and welfare
activities and by the expenses of foreign travel.

That is, however, not the relevant comparison. From the perspective of realistic policymaking choices, the comparison should be
between a value-added tax base and the maximum taxable income
base that is likely to exist. The primary consideration should be the
possibility of incremental change. Comparisons must be made

under alternative assumptions that the value-added tax may be an additional tax or may be substituted for all or some portion of the existing income tax. Comparisons must also take into account whether the value-added tax is primarily a tax on individuals (invoice and credit VAT) or a tax on corporations (generic value-added tax).

If the value-added tax is considered to be a tax on individuals in their capacity as consumers, the following comparisons are relevant:

1984 Taxable Income	1984 Adjusted PCE
$1,671.2 billion..	$2,050.6 billion

1984 Excess of AGI Over Taxable Income	1984 Adjusted PCE
$543.6..	$2,050.6 billion

Because adjusted PCE is about 20 percent larger than taxable income, an invoice and credit VAT could readily be *substituted* for the individual income tax. A value-added tax rate of 14.5 percent would raise as much revenue and any higher rate would increase revenue collections.[21] Because adjusted PCE is about four times greater than the excess of AGI over taxable income, a very low rate of value-added tax could be *added* on top of the individual income tax; probably much more readily than trying to surmount the major political hurdle that would be involved in increasing the taxable income base to more nearly correspond to AGI.

At then-prevailing tax rates, the 1984 taxable income base would have to have been increased by $113.31 billion to raise as much revenue as a 1 percent comprehensive invoice and credit VAT. Even if taxable income were increased by $543.6 billion to equal AGI, the revenue would be the same as a 5 percent tax on value added in 1984.

At the other extreme, if the value-added tax is considered to be a tax on corporations and other producers, the following comparisons are relevant.

---

[21]In 1984, individual income tax collections were $301.9 billion. Although marginal income tax rates ranged from 11 to 50 percent, the effective tax rate relative to taxable income of $1,671.2 billion was 18.1 percent.

1984 Corporate Income Tax Base	1984 Expanded Value-Added Base[22]
$257.1 billion	$2,786.5 billion

1984 Corporate Payroll and Income Tax Base[23]		Corporate Portion of 1984 Expanded Value-Added Base[22]
Income	$ 257.1	
Compensation	1,502.1	
Total	1,759.2 billion	$2,229.2 billion

Because the value-added base is, generally speaking, the gross output value of goods and services, it includes the output value of *labor* as well as the output value of *capital*. The value-added base includes *compensation* paid to employees, just as it includes amounts paid to capital in the form of dividends and interest.

One way to look at it -- and many will -- is that under a value-added tax, companies cannot "deduct" wages paid employees; whereas under the corporate net income tax, they can. Another way of looking at it -- which seems more meaningful -- is that a generic value-added tax is roughly the equivalent of a corporate tax on net income *plus* an employer-paid payroll tax.[24]

Obviously, the corporate portion of the 1984 expanded value-added base would exceed by many times the corporate income tax base for 1984 as well as the total amount of corporate profits (which, by any measure, are net of compensation paid employees and interest payments for the services of borrowed capital). If imposed at a 3

---

[22]Obviously, not all value is added by corporations. For present purposes of rough approximation, 80 percent of the value-added base is attributed to corporations and 20 percent is attributed to unincorporated businesses. The National Income and Products Accounts for 1984 show that corporate compensation to employees was about 90 percent of total private sector compensation and that corporations accounted for about 75 percent of the private business sector portion of national income.

[23]According to the *Statistics of Income* for 1984, total wages and salaries from *all* sources were $1,807.1 billion. The National Income and Product Accounts for 1984 show corporate compensation paid to employees as $1,502.1 billion.

[24]The inclusion of the value added by labor (measured by the price or wages paid for it) is the largest single difference between the corporate income tax base and the value-added base. Chapter 3 outlines a set of amendments that could be made to the corporate income tax and the FICA payroll tax to conform the bases of those taxes to the value-added base.

percent rate in 1984, the corporate portion of a generic value-added tax would have been essentially equal to corporate income tax collections in 1984.[25]   A 6.5 percent generic value-added tax is about equal in revenue to the corporate income tax *plus* the corporate portion of the employer's share of the payroll tax in 1984.[26]   A generic value-added tax imposed at any substantially higher rate could quickly produce tax liabilities that exceed the ability of most corporations to pay; having in mind that while the value-added base includes wages to employees, corporations have paid those wages and the amount thereof is not available for payment of taxes.[27]   The same is true for interest and dividends paid for the services of capital.

CONSIDERATIONS RELATED TO TAX ADMINISTRATION AND COMPLIANCE

Nearly all conventional works on the subject, as well as most idle commentaries, devote an overwhelming amount of attention to the fascinating, detailed mechanics of the invoice and credit VAT. Starting with the assumption that any value-added tax is some exotic import, most people talk about the great complexity of the invoice and credit VAT, the long period of time it would take to put in place such an unfamiliar system, and the great burden on businesses -- small and large -- in dealing with all the invoices and other paper work.[28]   There have been suggestions that as many as 20,000 new

---

[25]According to the *Statistics of Income* for 1984, corporate income tax collections were $64.0 billion. A 3 percent rate applied to the expanded value-added base of $2,229.20 billion yields $66.88 billion.

[26]The National Income and Products Accounts for 1984 show that employers paid $106.3 billion in FICA payroll taxes. If one assumes that 80 percent (or $84.80 billion) was paid by corporations and added $64.0 billion for income taxes paid by corporations, the total is $148.0 billion. A 6.5 percent rate applied to the 1984 Expanded Value-Added Base of $2,229.20 billion yields $144.89 billion.

[27]Under the present two-tier income tax system, wages paid by corporations to employees are deducted and not taxed to the corporation, but they are taxed to the recipient-employees. If a generic value-added tax were substituted for the corporate income tax, wages paid employees would not be deducted in arriving at the value-added base, although they would be included in the taxable income of the recipient-employees.

[28]It would be easy to overstate the complexity of invoicing. Most businesses, small and large, are accustomed to dealing with invoices that reflect the price of goods or services plus separately stated taxes. In the case of many smaller, local businesses, these taxes probably are primarily sales taxes or sometimes various business-transaction taxes. In the case of larger, multi-state enterprises, there are likely to be a whole range of local, state and federal (excise) taxes that are accounted for separately

revenue agents would be required if an invoice and credit VAT were enacted.[29] This has led some to suggest the generic value-added tax (or subtraction method VAT as popularly referred to) as a simple solution that does not involve invoicing.[30] A generic value-added tax may be simple, but it simply is not a "consumption tax" within the baseline definition that most people have in mind.

It is not the purpose here to rehash all the arguments about why an invoice and credit VAT may or may not be complex and difficult to implement. Suffice it to say, however, that while that tax may seem new and different from a federal tax perspective, it may not be from the perspective of state tax and local taxes many of which are separately invoiced both in commercial transactions between companies and to consumers.

THE CHALLENGE AND THE OPPORTUNITY

Even within the rigid confines of this chapter, it would appear that the issues presented by a value-added tax are many, varied and perplexing. That impression probably increases the more chapters one reads. Those issues are, however, present with the current tax system in one way or the other, and reflect uncertainty about it in much the same way. A value-added tax may not be enacted, but if debated, that process may tell us as much about the present system as about any alternative.

It would be a challenge to construct a value-added tax that would fit within all the conflicting considerations that are likely to be brought to bear in 1989-90. That challenge also presents an opportunity. Instead of remaining mired in preconceived notions or becoming embroiled in details, we ought to step back and take the opportunity to decide what tax base we have now and what tax base we would prefer to have in the future.

---

from the price of goods and services.

[29]Whether they were dealing with a generic value-added tax or an invoice and credit VAT, it would seem that the principal task of revenue agents would be the same -- to be certain that every company had within the applicable accounting period remitted or paid the correct amount of tax to the Treasury; whether arrived at by subtracting from value received the amount of value purchased or by crediting against the tax owed on sales the amount of tax deemed paid on purchases.

[30]Presentationally -- to the Congress and others -- this approach is simple and can be done in connection with the income tax return for most companies. Whether, in fact, it is simpler to do yet another iteration in addition to the regular income tax and the alternative minimum tax, remains to be seen.

3

WHO BEARS THE BURDEN OF CONSUMPTION TAXES?

by David G. Raboy and
Cliff Massa III

For decades, discussions of consumption taxes routinely have begun with either an explicit or implicit presumption that the ultimate burden or "incidence" of the tax rests solely upon consumers in the form of higher prices for the goods and services which are subject to that tax. Proponents and opponents alike have generally accepted the proposition that the "consumption tax" label is an accurate and descriptive term for the tax systems to which it is routinely applied.

Given this fundamental agreement, controversies in consumption tax debates have tended to arise only with respect to a range of second-level subjects on which there are widely differing views. The second-level subjects include such concerns as: the effects of such taxes on consumption and saving and the merits of those effects; the need to reduce the regressivity of such taxes; the desirability of reducing or eliminating the tax with respect to necessities (food, housing, medical care, etc.); the effects on a country's exports and imports; and so on.

In recent years, an alternative analysis of incidence which was a part of earlier consumption tax debates has resurfaced. This analysis concludes that consumption taxes are not borne *solely* by consumers but instead are borne by individuals in *three* different capacities -- as consumers, as wage earners, and as providers of capital services (i.e., as owners of and lenders to business entities).

Increased attention is being given to this new approach to incidence analysis as a result of two legislative proposals -- the introduction of the subtraction method Business Transfer Tax (BTT) by Senator William Roth (R-DE) in 1985 and the consideration of another subtraction method value-added tax (VAT) by the Canadian government. Apparently, it is the subtraction method system itself -- in contrast to the familiar invoice and credit system used in Europe -- which presents a perspective on consumption taxes that had not been widely considered in this country. (A subtraction method value-added tax is a VAT in its most generic form. An invoice and credit method of collection may be considered as an "option" to a generic VAT.) If the alternative analysis attracts substantial support, then debates over saving versus consumption choices, the regressivity issue, exemptions for necessities, trade effects and other subjects will occur in a substantially different context.

Conclusions concerning the incidence of consumption taxes have had and will continue to have a very substantial impact on domestic economic policy decisions. The traditional analysis of consumption tax proposals has given rise to strongly-held opposing views, depending upon the advocate's opinions about the secondary effects mentioned previously. Predictable schisms are created within the business and political communities, in particular, as well as within the academic and economic communities. If the consumption tax is borne by individuals in roles other than as consumers, the terms of debate almost certainly would be substantially changed.

Substantive federal tax policy decisions for the 1990s are likely to be affected by policymakers' conclusions about the political and economic effects of consumption tax proposals. Reviewing the traditional analysis and studying the alternative analysis are increasingly important prerequisites to a well-informed policy debate. For this reason, the following discussion of the two incidence analyses is of some importance.

WHAT IS MEANT BY "INCIDENCE" OF A TAX?

A series of questions is posed by the "incidence" issue. What is meant by the incidence or burden of a tax? Does the burden exist only for the company or the individual who writes the check to the government? How many levels of economic effects should be incorporated into an incidence analysis? Can a monetary value be computed for the effects that consumption taxes may have on economic decisionmaking?

The definition of incidence which is applied here follows the general economic literature on "differential incidence." The original definition was developed by Richard Musgrave, who defined differential incidence as ". . . the difference in the distributional results of two tax policies that provide equal yield in real terms; or to put it differently, that provide for money yields adequate to finance a given set of real expenditures of government."[1] Stated somewhat more simply, the incidence of a tax falls upon the individuals whose real incomes are adversely affected by that tax in comparison to the effects of a different tax. This definition by Musgrave is generally accepted in the economics literature.[2]

Therefore, to analyze incidence, the real income situations of individuals are compared under two tax systems which yield the same amount of real tax revenue. Because government spending (both in absolute amount and composition) is held constant, the differential effects of the two taxes can be isolated without concern for the distributional effects of transfer payments and other forms of government spending. The concept of differential incidence will be applied in the subsequent discussion of the alternative analysis in order to compare a multi-stage consumption tax remitted by businesses to the existing income and payroll taxes paid by firms.

The proper time to measure distributional effects is the point at which the economy has fully adjusted to the new tax -- that is, after a new "equilibrium" has been reached following the innumerable adjustments which individuals and companies make to tax system changes.

Unfortunately, this "general equilibrium" approach can be unwieldy and impractical because one wave of adjustments produces another wave (usually smaller) which produces yet another and so on for a period of time until the new equilibrium occurs. To minimize the difficulties, shortcuts generally are taken in the analysis. This is often the case when incidence analysis is developed by the Treasury Department or by the staff of the Congressional Joint Committee on Taxation in conjunction with tax legislation. The results of such analysis usually fall somewhere between the limits of purely static analysis (which assumes no adjustments within the economy) and truly dynamic analysis (which assumes that behavior

---

[1] Richard A. Musgrave, *The Theory of Public Finance* (New York: McGraw Hill, 1959), p. 212.

[2] A related approach, which is applied in the three simple examples on pages 52-57, compares the effects of imposing a new tax on a previously non-taxed economy. Implicit in this type of analysis is a comparison of one type of tax, imposed on a previously non-taxed economy, with another type of tax.

will be affected over time by the change in tax law).

THE TRADITIONAL ANALYSIS -- CONSUMPTION TAX BURDENS ARE BORNE BY CONSUMERS

The traditional analysis concludes that the incidence of consumption taxes falls solely on consumers because such taxes are fully shifted forward in prices and consumers continue to purchase the same quantities of goods and services at higher prices. Businesses, or their owners, which remit such a tax to the government, are found to be collectors of the tax, but they do not bear any of the economic burden of the tax.

The usual point of departure for this analysis is a discussion of a final-stage sales tax levied on an *ad valorem* basis, such as a retail sales tax of 5 percent. The tax is levied only at the point of sale to an ultimate consumer, and the tax clearly is added to the total purchase price of goods on the sales receipt. The retailer then pays to the taxing jurisdiction the total amount of tax collected from consumers. On its face, the single-stage sales tax appears to be borne solely by the consumer since, but for the tax, the prices paid by consumers would be lower by the amount of the tax.

An extensive history of the debate on the incidence of consumption taxes is provided in the Appendix to this chapter. The arguments for both the "traditional" and "alternative" views have been continuously developed from the 1600s up to the present. However, for purposes of this chapter, only a brief review of contemporary commentaries is required to illustrate the differing views.

Two contemporary microeconomics textbooks which are widely used in undergraduate and graduate economics courses present the traditional analysis as applied to an *ad valorem* tax on the value of output (like a VAT) and an *ad rem* tax on a unit of output, both under conditions of perfect competition.

In the long run the entire amount of the tax has been shifted into prices. *Even though the firm ostensibly "pays" the tax, in fact the burden is borne by consumers* (emphasis added).[3]

In this post-tax long run equilibrium, each firm produces . . . the output before the tax . . . but there are fewer firms so industry output . . . is less than both initial output and short run output. *Price has risen so that the new equilibrium price exceeds the old by the amount of the tax* (emphasis

---

[3]Walter Nicholson, *Microeconomic Theory* (Illinois: Dryden Press, 1978), p. 334.

added).[4]

Once the assumption of full forward shifting was accepted for the single-stage sales tax, analysts and authors found it plausible that a multi-stage consumption tax such as a VAT is shifted forward in a similar fashion. The imposition of a 5 percent VAT at each stage along the production and distribution chain (offset by a credit for VAT imposed through the previous stage) achieves the same tax at the consumers' level as the single-stage sales tax. Thus, the multi-stage VAT is considered to be identical to a single-stage sales tax, regardless of the differences in mechanisms of remittance to the government. The fact that the VAT is multi-stage is considered to be simply a difference in the method and timing of collection.

Numerous academic articles and public policy papers in recent years have reinforced the traditional analysis (although there has been little presentation of the original analytical support). An article measuring the incidence effects of tax reform changes in Korea in 1976 states:

> Indirect taxes are assumed to be shifted forward in the price of goods on which they are levied. A household's tax burden will be in direct proportion to its consumption of the taxed goods.[5]

Similarly, when the Treasury Department produced distribution tables for an invoice and credit VAT, it was assumed that the tax would be fully shifted forward in prices.[6] Stating that "a consumption type value-added tax is similar to a retail sales [tax] in terms of its economic effects,"[7] the Treasury report asserts that a 10-percent VAT covering about 77 percent of total consumption expenditures would produce a total consumer price increase of 8 percent. Thus, full forward shifting is assumed.[8]

A study undertaken by the Australian government reaches a somewhat less certain conclusion but generally presumes the shift forward in price:

> To the extent that the tax is passed on in the price of domestic goods and

---

[4]C. E. Ferguson and J. D. Gould, *Microeconomic Theory* (Illinois: Richard D. Irwin, Inc., 1975), p. 298.

[5]Peter S. Heller, "Testing the Impact of Value-Added and Global Income Tax Reforms on Korean Tax Incidence in 1976: An Input-Output and Sensitivity Analysis," International Monetary Fund Staff Paper (June 1981), 28(2), p. 384.

[6]U.S. Department of the Treasury, *Tax Reform for Fairness, Simplicity, and Economic Growth, Volume 3: Value-Added Tax* (Washington, D.C.: U.S. Department of the Treasury, November 1984), pp. 20, 21.

[7]Ibid., p. 17.

[8]Ibid., p. 21.

services, its incidence falls on final consumers and does not enter into industrial costs.[9]

Publications by U.S. accounting firms generally assume that a VAT would be fully shifted forward in price and borne by consumers. A Coopers & Lybrand publication concludes:

> A value-added tax is a multi-stage tax on consumer goods and services. To the consumer, the value-added tax is similar to a retail sales tax in that the ultimate purchaser of the goods or service bears the burden of the tax. . . .[10]

The same conclusion is presented in a study published by the American Institute of Certified Public Accountants (AICPA):

> Theoretically, VAT is a tax on the value added to goods and services by each separate processor in the production and distribution chain. In actuality, it is a tax on the increase in the sales price of goods and services as they pass through that chain. Ultimately, however, it is a tax on consumption -- on the amount spent for the product by the final consumer. The consumer ultimately bears the burden of the tax, even though the actual payer of the bulk of the tax is the manufacturer or processor.[11]

A study prepared for the Financial Executives Research Foundation argues that a VAT constitutes a ". . . proportionate increase in costs. As such, it presumably is passed forward and reflected proportionally in the prices of all consumer goods and services."[12] The report points out, however, that "[i]ndividual companies at all levels will be tempted to take advantage of competitive strengths, or be forced to suffer from competitive weaknesses, as the effects of price increases move forward and consumer reactions move backwards through the system."[13]

Charles McLure argues that the incidence of a VAT depends on whether it is "destination-" or "origin-based." Virtually all of the existing VAT systems are destination-based -- that is, goods are taxed in the country of consumption as a result of a rebate of taxes from the country of export and of an import tax imposed in the

---

[9]Mark Buyer, *An Analysis of the Case of a Broadly-Based Consumption Tax in Australia* (Sidney, Australia: Department of the Parliamentary Library, Legislative Research Service, March 1985), p. 2.

[10]Coopers & Lybrand, *Focus on the Value-Added Tax* (March 1986), p. 5.

[11]American Institute of Certified Public Accountants, *Alternatives to the Present Tax System for Increasing Saving and Investment*, (Washington, D.C.: AICPA, October 1985), p. 29.

[12]Dan Throop Smith and Bertrand Fox, *An Analysis of Value Added Taxation in The Context of The Tax Restructuring Act of 1980* (Washington, D.C.: The Financial Executives Research Foundation, 1981), p. 12.

[13]Ibid., p. 13.

country of consumption. However, McLure states that under an origin principle where there are no border tax adjustments, a VAT is in fact a production tax, whereas ". . . the base of a destination-principle tax is consumption rather than production. . . . International competitive pressures ensure that the likely incidence of consumption-based taxes is on consumers; by comparison, producers are likely to bear the burden of production taxes."[14]

Traditional analysis also generally concludes that the *method* for computing and remitting the multi-stage VAT does not affect the incidence. In the traditional analysis, a subtraction method VAT and an addition method VAT are found to be fully reflected in the price of goods and services, as is the case with the invoice and credit method VAT which is used in Europe.[15] The similarities with respect to computation and/or remittance between such multi-stage VATs and other business taxes, such as corporate income taxes and payroll taxes, are not generally considered to be relevant in the traditional analysis.

In summary, the traditional view of consumption taxes begins with a single-stage *ad valorem* tax and observes that prices to consumers would be lower but for the tax. The analysis extends this conclusion to a tax which is imposed at each stage of production and distribution, with an offset for taxes imposed at each prior stage, and concludes that the incidence of such taxes also rests on consumers. Similarities between the computation and remittance of some multi-stage consumption taxes and existing business income and payroll taxes are acknowledged but are not considered relevant.

THE ALTERNATIVE ANALYSIS -- "CONSUMPTION TAXES" ARE BORNE BY LABOR, CAPITAL AND CONSUMERS

Whereas the traditional analysis begins with the highly visible, single-stage retail sales tax to demonstrate that the burden falls on

---

[14]Charles E. McLure, Jr., *The Value-Added Tax* (Washington, D.C.: American Enterprise Institute, 1987), p. 31.

[15]The invoice and credit VAT uses the sales invoice to specify an amount of VAT with respect to each taxable transaction. A business is liable for the aggregate VAT shown on its sales receipts, less a credit for the VAT shown on its purchase receipts. A subtraction method VAT requires the aggregation of all taxable sales and the subtraction of all previously taxable purchases. The tax rate is applied to the balance. The addition method VAT requires the compilation of a specified set of payments to employees, owners and lenders, and the tax rate is applied to the sum of such payments.

consumers, the alternative analysis begins with the much less visible, multi-stage application of a VAT under the subtraction method (this has been described as a generic VAT). Using the latter approach, this analysis contends that a VAT is a proportionate tax on the factors of production. In this view, the value-added tax is a tax on labor and capital services, rather than a tax on goods and services themselves.

First, a brief discussion and definition of economic "value added" is presented, and then a comparison of a VAT to existing corporate income and payroll taxes is undertaken.

A Definition of "Value Added"

Manufacturers acquire raw materials, component parts, energy, services, and other inputs and then combine/transform them into a product with a value which is greater than the sum of the purchased resources and parts that went into it. This excess of the product's value over the sum of the values of its inputs arises from the services of capital and labor which have been applied by the manufacturer to convert the various inputs into a more valuable, single product.[16]

This value added is readily computed for the company by subtracting the value of the inputs which it purchases from the value of the products which it sells. The difference is the value which it has added through application of capital and labor services. Value added can also be measured by adding the payments made to the providers of labor and capital. Under the addition method approach, value added is equal to the sum of the firm's total labor costs (both cash and non-cash compensation) and the costs of its capital services (interest paid to lenders, dividends paid to shareholders and profits retained and invested by the company). Under either a subtraction or addition method, value added clearly is computed as the amounts distributed to two general categories of individuals -- those who provide their personal labor and those who provide their capital (whether as debt holders or equity holders).

Therefore, the most basic definition of a VAT is a proportionate tax on the incomes of the factors of production -- that is, the

---

[16]Value added discussions generally use the manufacturing process as the example to explain the multi-stage development of value added in the economy, and this practice is continued here. However, service businesses also generate economic value added. No inference should be drawn from this text that professional services (e.g., attorneys, accountants, doctors, etc.), distribution services, construction services, financial services, transportation services, etc., should be excluded from a value-added tax base.

incomes to capital and labor. Because a pure VAT ultimately applies to the value added by every business from the first producer of raw materials through the retail seller (i.e., the company which sells to a non-business user) of all goods and services in the economy, the multi-stage VAT is applied to the same tax base as a single-stage consumption tax at the retail level.

Comparing Existing Business Taxes to a VAT

Given this basic definition of value added, the alternative analysis proceeds to compare a VAT to the principal taxes on businesses under present law -- the corporate income tax[17] and the employer's portion of Social Security payroll taxes. After reviewing the general presumptions about the incidence of such taxes and then assessing the similarities between such taxes and a VAT, the analysis concludes that there must be a qualitative similarity in the incidence of a VAT and of a combined income and payroll tax structure.

The incidence of the corporate income tax is not generally agreed upon. Some argue that it is borne by shareholders, while others assert a mixed incidence on both shareholders and consumers. There is little apparent support for the proposition that the burden of the corporate income tax falls solely on consumers.

There is disagreement about who bears the brunt of the payroll tax as well, but few consider its incidence to be similar to a single-stage consumption tax. While some would argue that it is borne partially by labor and partially by consumers, many would argue that the ultimate bearer of the payroll tax is labor which, but for the tax, would realize higher wages and/or more work opportunities.

Given these substantial differences in the presumptions about the incidence of existing business taxes and the traditional analysis of consumption taxes, the alternative analysis considers a series of amendments which would convert the existing corporate income and payroll taxes into a VAT. This process purports to illustrate qualitative similarities between these two existing business taxes and a VAT.

The first amendment would repeal the deductibility of interest at the corporate level. As a result, all types of payments to capital -- i.e., interest, dividends and undistributed profits -- would be taxed at the corporate level.

---

[17]The individual income tax is also relevant to the extent that it applies to shareholders of S Corporations and to partners and sole proprietors of businesses. For simplicity, this discussion will refer only to the corporate tax.

The second amendment would replace the existing depreciation system with immediate expensing and a full loss offset. The value added in a physical capital asset would be taxed only as such value added arises in the multiple stages of production and construction, *not* when the final product is being used as a capital asset by a manufacturer.

The third amendment would deny a corporate-level deduction for the wide range of preferred, non-wage compensation and fringe benefits. Thus, all non-wage compensation would be taxed at the corporate rate.

A fourth amendment would shift the employee's portion of the Social Security payroll tax to the employer and repeal the income cap for the payroll tax, thereby doubling the business payroll tax rate and applying it to all wages.

A final amendment would lower the corporate income tax rate and increase the payroll tax rate so that the two are equal.

These amendments clearly would change the magnitude and scope of each tax. But assessed individually, no one amendment seems likely to transform these existing business taxes from systems borne by shareholders and labor (and perhaps partially by consumers) to systems borne exclusively by consumers.

The alternative analysis asserts that when the two tax systems are revised by *all* of the amendments, the resulting tax structures essentially would duplicate the elements of a value-added base. The revised corporate income tax would apply to interest, dividends, and retained profits (which are payments for capital services), and to non-cash compensation (which is partial payment for labor services). The payroll tax would apply to all wages (which is the remaining payment for labor services).

The alternative analysis also approaches this subject from the opposite perspective which begins with a theoretically pure VAT and then amends the VAT to reflect potential political realities of the type which have shaped the existing corporate income and payroll tax systems. Consider two major amendments to a pure subtraction method VAT.

First, because a VAT may be viewed by some observers as a tax on labor (especially in the context of a subtraction VAT which clearly applies to *all* labor costs), a partial deduction for payroll might be allowed.

Second, U.S. taxpayers and policymakers are comfortable thinking in an income tax context and may have trouble with the expensing feature for capital assets under a VAT. Therefore, a depreciation variant could be enacted in lieu of expensing (although no existing VAT system uses the depreciation variant).

These two amendments to a pure VAT base would produce a variant with striking similarities to the corporate income tax and presumably would suggest a similar incidence as well. Clearly, such tinkering could transform a VAT into something which resembles existing business taxes, but would such actions change the incidence of a VAT?

The alternative analysis asserts that there is no logical basis for concluding that the traditional incidence analysis is correct in the context of either the revised VAT or the revised income and payroll tax systems. Instead, the alternative analysis finds fundamental similarities between existing taxes remitted by business and a multi-stage VAT remitted by businesses -- similarities which suggest to proponents of the alternative analysis that the incidences of these tax regimes are qualitatively similar.

In general, this approach stops short of concluding *precisely* what that incidence is, in large measure because it is uncertain who bears the burden of existing taxes. The existing systems are probably borne in part by labor, in part by the owners of capital, and in part by consumers of goods and services. Therefore, the alternative analysis of consumption taxes concludes that there is a shared burden associated with a VAT which is qualitatively similar to existing taxes, although not necessarily having quantitatively identical proportions.

This chapter has used, for illustrative purposes, a subtraction method VAT. Considerable debate exists on whether the VAT method is relevant to the incidence outcome. This subject was discussed in Chapter 2 and will be revisited from a different perspective in Chapter 4.

Support in the Literature

The alternative analysis is beginning to attract support, both in the academic and business communities. Two popular economics textbooks were quoted above in support of the traditional analysis. Two other popular economics textbooks support the alternative view:

> The price rises and the quantity sold diminishes as a result of the tax. The price rise is less than the amount of the unit tax. *The 50 cent increase in the price represents that portion of the unit tax that is passed on to the consumer, the remainder of 40 cents is the burden on the entrepreneur* (emphasis added).[18]

---

[18]James M. Henderson and Richard E. Quaundt, *Microeconomic Theory: A*

So long as the market supply has a positive slope, the specific tax will be paid partly by the buyer and partly by the firm.[19]

The dichotomy in views about consumption taxes expressed in these four economics textbooks is also working its way into public finance textbooks on the undergraduate and graduate levels.[20]

Several business and economic writers have presumed the soundness of the traditional analysis as noted above, but others are considering or are adopting the alternative. For example, the public accounting firm of Arthur Andersen & Co. is not certain about the effect on consumers of the subtraction method VAT represented by Senator Roth's Business Transfer Tax. A 1986 publication by the firm argues that the incidence is uncertain. It may be shifted to consumers, or it may result in lower profits, depending on general business and specific industry conditions.[21]

Other publications by tax professionals profess an uncertainty as to the nature of the shifting of incidence. Consider the 1977 report from the Special Subcommittee of the Committee on General Income Tax Problems of the American Bar Association's Section on Taxation:

> Many of the theoretical arguments and discussions of a VA tax are centered on the concept of "forward shifting." The question here is whether a VA tax is in fact shifted forward to the consumer in higher prices or is absorbed by business in lower profits.
>
> The answer seems to be that it is and it isn't, depending on such factors as the stage of the business cycle in which it operates, the nature of the business, the elasticity of the supply and demand for the product, and the efficiency of the particular business organization selling the product.[22]

A study prepared more recently by the Canadian Federation of Independent Business also considers the possibility of shared incidence, at least in some circumstances:

> Since traders do not bear the tax on their inputs and charge the output tax

---

Mathematical Approach (New York: McGraw-Hill, 1971), p. 126.

[19] A. Koutsoyiannis, *Modem Microeconomics* (New York: St. Martin's, 1979), p. 169.

[20] See, for example, Musgrave, *Theory of Public Finance*, p. 289. Musgrave concludes that, depending on the cost structure of the firm, a unit or *ad valorem* tax will be partially shifted, fully shifted or more than fully shifted.

[21] Arthur Andersen & Co., "The Business Transfer Tax -- A VAT by Any Other Name," *Tax Legislative Update* (February 3, 1986), p. 4.

[22] "Report of the Special Subcommittee of the Committee on General Income Tax Problems on the Value-Added Tax," *Report of the Special Committee on the Value Added Tax of the Tax Section of the American Bar Association* (1977), p. 428.

on their sales to their consumers, the formal incidence of the tax largely falls on the consumer. The effective incidence may be shared, however, by other stages in the chain of production and distribution. For example, the imposition of VAT may stimulate shifts in the pattern of consumption away from taxed goods and towards untaxed goods. Producers and retailers may attempt to arrest these shifts by reducing margins which may force some out of business. The incidence of taxation is a complex subject, and whilst most economists would agree that VAT is fully shifted forward to the consumer in the long term, it is possible that business bears some of it in the short term.[23]

Finally, there are authors who have affirmatively argued that consumption taxes should be viewed as proportionate taxes on incomes associated with the factors of production. For instance, Edgar Browning states:

> Using a simple differential incidence model, it is shown that allocating such taxes to consumption is inconsistent with widely held methodological tenets of tax incidence analysis, and also in practice has produced errors and logical inconsistencies. In contrast, the analysis suggests that allocation of individual output taxes to factor earnings avoids these problems.[24]

The assumption that a VAT is a tax on factor incomes is also employed by Chiou-nan Yeh in a paper which assesses the long run incidence of a VAT in a growth model of the economy. Yeh argues that if the rates of tax on wages and profits are the same under an income tax and if the rate of a VAT that replaces such taxes is the same, then the VAT and the income tax are identical.[25] The concept of a VAT as a proportionate tax on factor incomes is also strongly supported by Norman Ture.[26] And McLure asserts a similar result, but only with respect to the "origin-principle" VAT.[27]

---

[23]Graham Bannock, *VAT and Small Business: European Experience and Implications for North America* (Canada: Canadian Federation of Independent Business and National Federation of Independent Business Research and Education Foundation, 1986), p. 16.

[24]Edgar K. Browning, "Tax Incidence, Indirect Taxes, and Transfers," *National Tax Journal* (December 1985), p. 525.

[25]Chiou-nan Yeh, "The Incidence of the Value-Added Tax in a Neoclassical Growth Model," *Public Finance* (No. 2/1979), p. 281.

[26]Norman B. Ture, *The Value-Added Tax -- Facts and Fancies* (Washington, D.C.: IRET, 1979).

[27]McLure, p. 31.

THREE EXAMPLES IN SUPPORT OF THE ALTERNATIVE ANALYSIS

The earlier discussion of the alternative analysis focused on a multi-stage tax. To illustrate the application of that analysis to a single-stage tax which compares with that used in the traditional analysis, three simple models are presented below: (1) a simple economy which faces specified financial constraints (with five companies producing identical goods for identical costs); (2) the same simple economy modified by an increase in the money supply; and (3) a simple economy with four companies producing different products which face different demand elasticities. These examples assume a profit-maximizing strategy by all companies, which is a generally accepted economic concept. All three examples illustrate the fundamental flaw in the traditional analysis. In order for consumers to bear the full burden of a consumption tax, the price of goods and services must rise by the full amount of the tax *and* consumers must continue to purchase the same quantities as if in a non-tax world. Traditional analysis has considered only the price effects.

Incidence Under Financial Constraints

The first example provides for the imposition of an *ad valorem* tax on a simple economy. The key factor in this example is that, as with the real world, a financial constraint exists on the economy; total purchasing power or total output in the economy is fixed in real terms. Therefore, when a new tax is imposed on this constrained economy, something has to give. For purposes of the example, it is assumed that the tax revenues are removed from the economy and not reinserted in a domestic income support program or other program which would offset the tax.[28]

> An economy has a total purchasing power of $10,000,000 in real terms. There are five identical firms producing an identical product, and all the money in the economy is spent on this product; there is no saving. The firms sell directly to the public; there is no separate distribution sector. Each firm has annual fixed costs (representing previous capital expenditures) of $200,000, and each unit of output involves variable labor costs of $10.

---

[28]Implicitly, the move from a non-tax world to a consumption tax world is being compared to a move to, say, a world with a corporate income tax. In the latter case, business clearly would be affected. Of interest are the effects of a consumption tax on business income.

Before the implementation of the tax, the unit price of the good is $20, which covers costs and produces a normal profit. Given those constant labor costs, each company will produce as much as the constant purchasing power in the economy will absorb at the given price.

In a non-tax world, each firm sells 100,000 units at $20 a piece. Labor employed by each firm earns $1,000,000 and, with $200,000 of fixed costs, each firm earns $800,000 in profit. Total industry profits are $4,000,000, and total labor earnings are $5,000,000. Consumer welfare is measured by total consumption, which is 500,000 units.

A 10-percent *ad valorem* tax is imposed to fund a non-domestic government program. Each firm fully shifts the tax forward in price by increasing its price until the after-tax price equals the price before the implementation of the tax. Since the tax is levied *ad valorem*, the price must rise to $22.22. Because the economy is constrained to purchase $10,000,000 worth of goods, each firm sells 90,009 units. Each firm's total revenue is $1,999,999, of which $199,999 is remitted to the government, $200,000 is fixed costs and $900,090 is paid to labor. Each firm makes profits of $699,910.

The effect of a 10-percent *ad valorem* tax which is fully shifted forward in price is to force consumers to bear part of the burden. Total consumption has dropped from 500,000 units to 450,045 units.[29] But consumers are not the only ones affected. Total industry profit has dropped from $4,000,000 to $3,499,550 -- a drop of about 15 percent. In addition, total payments to labor have dropped from $5,000,000 to $4,500,450 -- a drop of about 10 percent.

Because there is a real financial constraint on the economy, a tax which is fully shifted forward in price carries an incidence that will fall on capital and labor, as well as consumers. In addition to reducing the quantity which consumers can purchase, the tax results in reduced profits and wages.

This model presents a very simple example to illustrate the central theme of the alternative analysis. Within this example, other options are also available. One of the five firms may shift less than all of the tax in order to improve its market share. This could trigger a bidding war in which competition results in a less than full shifting by all companies. It may also be that, as production declines, the demand for labor drops, and as a result, wages are negotiated downward. In any event, in this example the imposition

---

[29] In economic terms, actual loss to consumers is measured by consumer "deadweight loss." As an approximation, this deadweight loss has two components. The first is the additional amount paid on units which consumers are still able to purchase. The second is the general discontent associated with constrained consumer choice, i.e., the inability to purchase the pre-tax quantities.

of a new tax on an economy with a full forward shift approach requires that *something* must give. The economy cannot purchase the same levels of all goods and services as it did before the implementation of the tax.

Incidence Under an Increasing Money Supply

Clearly, no industrial economy is so simple or so easy to model. As noted at the beginning of this chapter, general equilibrium analysis is too complex to use in such examples, and shortcuts must be taken to exclude some effects.

One factor which is not easily dismissed -- and is often very controversial -- is the potential change in monetary policy. Much has been written about the ramifications of the actions of a country's central bank during the implementation of a consumption tax. Some claim that accommodation of a new tax by the Federal Reserve Board (Fed) in the U.S. in the form of an equivalent increase in the money supply would allow companies to successfully shift the tax forward. The presumption is that this additional money in the economy would allow consumers to pay higher prices while continuing to purchase the same quantities of goods and services. However, it does not appear to matter whether the Fed "accommodates" the tax by increasing the money supply or not, because, in most cases, simply increasing the money supply does not change the underlying real economy and reactions to the tax. To illustrate, consider the following two cases.

Instead of treating the $10,000,000 of purchasing power in the preceding example as real purchasing power, treat it as the total money supply. If, under case #1, the Fed holds the money supply constant at $10,000,000, the outcome is as described above. When five companies fully shift the tax in price, the quantities purchased will drop, and profits and wages will drop as well.[30]

If, under case #2, there is an *increase* in the money supply, the effects will differ, depending on whether or not the expansion is expected or a surprise. Most economists would agree that anticipated changes in the money supply have no effects on the real economy. All prices and incomes simply increase in proportion to the monetary expansion. It is only when changes are unexpected that

---

[30]This assumes no change in money velocity, which is the speed with which the money supply turns over in the economy. If velocity were to increase because of a tax, the results would be more similar to the case where money supply expands. If the consumption tax is neutral between saving and consumption, there is no reason to believe that money demand or money velocity change because of the tax.

monetary shocks can have real effects.

If a consumption tax were added to existing taxes, most economic actors would expect a Fed response. For this reason, the safest assumption is that the Fed would increase the money supply to the extent that prices are raised -- 11 percent in the example -- and that this change would be expected. But what happens when an 11 percent increase in the money supply is fully anticipated? First, consider such an expansion without a new tax. *Absent* a new tax and after some lag and adjustment, all prices and factor payments could be expected to increase by 11 percent and, in real terms, nothing would have changed. In the example, all of the costs and the product price would have increased by 11 percent, but each firm would be in the same real position as before.

If the money increase occurs simultaneously with the implementation of the tax, firms would not be content to charge $22.22 for goods because there would be no forward shifting in *real terms*. In order to fully shift the tax in real terms, they must charge $24.69, which produces the after-tax nominal price of $22.22 equivalent to an inflation-adjusted after-tax price of $20. This is where the firm began and where it must remain if the tax is to be fully shifted. The other numbers -- nominal revenues, profits, labor costs, fixed costs -- would also increase, but each firm still could only sell approximately 90,000 units. *Real* revenues, profits and labor costs would be the same as if there were no monetary expansion.

Therefore, unless the increase in the money supply is unexpected, a money supply expansion does not appear to be capable of mitigating the effects of a fully shifted tax. Firm profits, labor payments, and consumption would still decrease. The money supply accommodation would not change the shared incidence of the new tax.

Incidence with Differing Demand Elasticities

A slightly more sophisticated example takes into account the different consumer demands facing different sectors of the economy. The financial constraint is ignored; instead different firms face different demand elasticities.[31]

---

[31]Consumer responsiveness to price changes is measured by the price elasticity of demand. This is defined as the percentage change in quantity demanded, due to a one percent increase in price. Thus, an elasticity of 2 means that for every one percent increase in price, there will be a two percent reduction in quantities purchased. An elasticity of 1 is called a unitary elasticity and indicates a proportionate response to price changes. Demand is elastic if the elasticity exceeds 1. Demand is considered

The example is structured to begin at a point of equilibrium. There are four firms representing sectors which produce different products. It is assumed that each product market is highly competitive with many firms in each industry. To simplify comparisons among firms, the example must assume that they have identical capital investments/fixed costs. If these costs are identical, then equilibrium requires that all firms be maximizing profits and have the same level of profit, thereby earning the same maximum return in a stable situation. The fixed costs for each firm are assumed to be $2,000. Each firm has a different output level and price, but each faces a common wage rate of $10 per unit. (The output levels and prices were chosen arbitrarily to fulfill the equilibrium requirements and are not the only possible combinations.)

From this equilibrium position, each firm can respond to the new tax in a way which maximizes profit. The result is a short-run phenomenon only and implies no long-run equilibrium. The item of interest in the example is the initial tax-shifting strategies of profit-maximizing firms which face different demands for their products when a 10-percent *ad valorem* tax is imposed.

What differentiates each industry is the consumer response to price increases. Firm A faces inelastic demand of -0.5 (a 1 percent increase in price results in a .5 percent decrease in sales), Firm B faces unitary demand of -1, Firm C faces elastic demand of -2, and Firm D faces highly elastic demand of -2.5.

Firm A, facing inelastic demand of -0.5 in the non-tax world, produces and sells 100,297 units of a good priced at $17. The firm enjoys profits of $700,079 after paying wages of $1,002,970. If a 10-percent tax is imposed and the firm does not attempt to shift the tax forward in price, it would still sell 100,297 units, but its profit would drop to $529,573. If it shifts one-half of the tax forward in price (requiring a grossed-up 5.3 percent price increase), units sold drop by only 2.6 percent to 97,657. Profits also fall, but only to $594,225. If the firm fully shifts the tax forward, requiring an 11.11 percent increase in price, profits fall only slightly to $661,074. Thus, a firm facing inelastic demand will find it to its benefit to shift the tax forward in price.

Firm B, with unitary elasticity of -1, sells 78,004 units at a pre-tax price of $19 per unit for a profit of $700,042. If the firm does not attempt to shift the tax forward in price, the firm's profit will drop to $551,830. If one-half of the tax is shifted forward, unit sales will drop by 5.3 percent to 73,898, but profits of $589,190 should be realized. If the firm fully shifts the tax, profits will drop only to $622,034. For a firm facing unitary demand and the cost structure in this example, profits are maximized by shifting the

---

inelastic if the elasticity is less than 1.

tax forward.

Firm C, facing an elasticity of -2, prices its good at $20 per unit and sells 70,200 units for a profit of $700,000. When the tax is imposed, if it does not shift the tax forward, the firm's profit will drop to $559,600. If the firm shifts one-half of the tax, it can achieve a profit of $559,989. But if it attempts to fully shift the tax, necessitating an 11 percent price increase, unit sales will drop by 22 percent, and profits will fall to $544,000. Therefore, a firm with a cost structure similar to Firm C's and facing an elastic demand of 2 will maximize profits by only partially shifting the tax, because price increases result in greater than proportionate drops in unit sales.

Firm D, facing the very elastic demand -2.5, sells 58,501 units at a unit price of $22 for profits of $700,017. If the firm does not attempt to shift the new tax, unit sales remain the same, but profit drops to $571,314. If the firm attempts to shift one-half of the tax, unit sales drop to 50,804 and profit drops to $548,821. Fully shifting the tax results in even lower profits; unit sales would drop to the point where profits were only $505,013. A firm facing very elastic demand will maximize profits only if it does not attempt to shift the tax at all.

This highly stylized example is not sufficiently sophisticated to indicate how high the elasticity must be before tax shifting becomes a less than optimal pricing strategy. Whether profits can be increased because of tax shifting depends not only on the price elasticity facing the firm, but the firm's cost structure as well.

Still, some general conclusions can be drawn. Unless the demand for all goods in the economy is inelastic, it is unrealistic to assume that firms acting in self interest can always successfully shift consumption taxes (or any new tax or other cost) forward in price. Even a simple, single-stage *ad valorem* tax will not be fully shifted forward if demand is elastic. Thus, even on the most primitive level, the conventional wisdom concerning the incidence of consumption taxes is worthy of challenge. If profit-maximizing companies, acting in their own self interest, determine that the best strategy is to not shift part or all of a tax forward in price, then the part that is not shifted must be borne by the owners of capital or by labor.

APPENDIX: A BRIEF HISTORY OF THE DEBATE ON THE INCIDENCE OF CONSUMPTION TAXES

The issue of the incidence of consumption taxes has been debated for hundreds of years with the same result: the traditional wisdom holds that consumption taxes are borne solely by consumers with an articulate minority arguing that the incidence is shared among the factors of production and consumers. This was true during the earliest debates, and it is true today.

The debate can be traced back to at least the 1600s where excise taxes were proposed in England and Holland. The first English excise tax was introduced in 1643 and was assumed by most writers to be a tax on consumers:

> The earliest writers to propose a system of excise taxes did not look much further than the surface fact that the excise was a tax on a consumable commodity, and therefore presumably a tax on consumption.[32]

This belief that consumers carried the tax was considered an argument in favor of excise taxes. In 1659, Francis Cradock wrote:

> [T]he General Excise (so much decryed and Petitioned against) in its proper Constitution, is the most equitable of Impositions: no man being charged with it, but he that sels it for profit, to the consumption of the Commodity, who in truth pays it insensibly without complaint.[33]

The first economist to write on incidence was Thomas Munn in 1664. It was his belief that excise taxes, contrary to the conventional wisdom, could not rest with the poor. If taxes caused the prices of necessities to rise, then wages must rise and, therefore, the excise would be shifted to employers. This was a good thing because the rich would be ". . . forced to abate their sinful excess and idle retainers."[34]

Another view, given by William Waterhouse in 1662, held that the poor did not bear the burden of excise taxes because ". . . money raised upon the poorer sort, returns to them again."[35] Thus, the tax was viewed as a loan that would produce more employment and higher wages.

Despite the writings of Munn and others, the belief that an excise was borne by poor consumers became the prevalent doctrine of the time. In the next century, however, the debate was rejoined as classical theories of economics began to develop. F. Faquier, in 1756, wrote that ". . . [t]he Poor do not, never have, nor even possibly can pay any tax whatever."[36] In Faquier's view, wages were always set at a subsistence level. Thus, if a tax increased prices, wages must rise

---

[32]Edwin R. A. Seligman, *The Shifting and Incidence of Taxation* (New York: Columbia University Press, 1927), p. 23.

[33]Ibid., pp. 24, 25.

[34]Ibid., pp. 25, 26.

[35]Ibid., p. 26.

[36]Ibid., pp. 28, 29.

and the tax would be shifted to producers in the form of lower profits.

The possibility of shared incidence had been expressed by a contemporary of Faquier, known only as a Friend of Truth and the Christian Religion, who wrote the following in 1743:

> Everyone admits that Quantity and Vent give a Price to any Commodity; it is therefore to be considered in what Cases the Quantity can be commanded or ascertained, in proportion to the Vent, and in what Cases it cannot; for where it can, the Duties will lie on the Consumer; but where it cannot, it will evidently lie on the Producer or Maker as often as the Quantity exceeds the Vent.[37]

Thus, supply and demand conditions were expected to affect the incidence of the consumption tax.

Adam Smith, writing in 1776, argued that taxes on necessities would raise the wage rate and would be shifted to producers while taxes on luxuries would fall on the consumers of luxuries. Thus, it is in the interest of the rich to oppose taxes on necessities because they will always be borne by producers (presumably including the rich as owners of capital) whereas the rich will pay tax on luxuries only proportionate to their consumption of luxuries.[38]

The classical economist David Ricardo, writing in the early 1800s, disagreed with Adam Smith's belief. In his view, taxes on production would always be borne by consumers because there is a normal rate of profit which must be maintained for businesses to survive. The only way for business to maintain the requisite profit level is to shift consumption taxes forward in price.[39] However, many neoclassical writers, such as Alfred Marshall, developed modern theories of the competitive firm which suggested a shared incidence depending on supply and demand conditions.

The first American writer to consider a VAT was Thomas S. Adams. In proposing a VAT, Adams had little to say on incidence. He did argue, however, that more broad-based taxes are easier to shift then taxes with more narrow bases:

> [B]ecause moderate taxes on net income are shifted less and less readily than taxes on gross business; and in particular because taxes on net income are imposed only when the taxpayer has earnings from which to pay them . . ., net income has come to be accepted as the more equitable, certainly the more merciful, basis.[40]

---

[37]Ibid., p. 71.

[38]Ibid., p. 146.

[39]Ibid., p. 147.

[40]Thomas S. Adams, "Fundamental Problems of Federal Income Taxation,"

Adams' argument for a VAT rests more on simplicity arguments than equity considerations. A contemporary of Adams, K. M. Williamson, acknowledges that there is some basis for a shared incidence under certain situations and sums up the existing debate in the 1920s:

> There is no complete agreement as to the incidence of the tax even under normal competitive conditions. One advocate, tho proceeding in most of his argument on the assumption that the sales tax is shifted, maintains that "where the profits of an industry are large, the one percent tax is not a substantial item, and may under strong competitive conditions be wholly or partially absorbed by the dealers. Where profits are small, however, every bit of the smallest tax must and will be shifted to the buyer. Opponents assert that, if the tax is not shifted, being borne by the seller, it would be a tax on gross income, discriminating against businesses whose profits form only a small part of their sales. . . . Some are concerned over the fear that in a falling market it would be difficult if not impossible to shift the tax. . . . But some sales tax advocates deny that such taxes could not be shifted even in a buyer's market, stating that "a merchant may be unable to shift a relatively high overhead, but a sales cost that 'runs with the goods' operating at the time upon all competitive sellers will be shifted in the price."[41]

Williamson concludes that ". . . the tax, whatever its incidence in the immediate future, would normally be a burden on consumers."[42]

Once again, through the 1920s, the conventional wisdom was that consumption taxes would lead to higher prices and be borne by consumers. Seligman, however, notes that higher prices may result in part of the tax burden being shifted to producers because, "[t]he producer may shift the tax entirely and yet his restricted sales may lead to lower profits."[43]

Probably the period of the most intense debate on the incidence of consumption taxes was the 1940s and 1950s. Eminent scholars lined up on two polar extremes with one side arguing that consumption taxes were fully borne by consumers while the other side argued that consumers were not affected at all, the entire burden being shifted onto the factors of production. Between these two extremes, some scholars found room for a shared incidence view with the tax burden divided among consumers, capitalists and workers.

The first salvo was fired in 1939 by Harry Gunnison Brown.

Quarterly Journal of Economics (August 1921), p. 552.

[41] K. M. Williamson, "The Literature on the Sales Tax," *Quarterly Journal of Economics* (October 1921), p. 624.

[42] Ibid., p. 633.

[43] Seligman, p. 12.

Brown argued that the conventional wisdom was wrong and that any general consumer tax must be shifted onto the factors of production:

> A good many persons too readily conclude that such a general tax must raise all prices. But there are important considerations which such persons overlook. Such a general tax cannot reduce the output of goods unless workers are willing to remain idle -- for there is no untaxed line to go into -- or unless owners of capital or land are willing to let their capital or land lie idle and to receive no income at all from it. Surely, most men would, in time, accept wages very considerably lower rather than be chronically idle, and most owners of capital would rather have greatly reduced returns on their capital rather than let their capital depreciate unused and get no returns at all. . . . We cannot expect, therefore, that a general tax on output would cause permanent cessation of production or that it would, as a long-run phenomenon, bring any appreciable decrease. Why suppose, then, that it could, in the long run, make prices higher?[44]

One of the issues hotly debated during this period was what assumptions should be made concerning monetary policy. It was generally agreed that monetary expansion was a necessary condition for general price increases. The debate centered around whether any cause and effect relationship existed between the implementation of a consumption tax and monetary action. Brown argued against any causal relationship:

> An increase in the volume of circulating medium, whether it be through the issue of additional money or an expansion of bank credit, tends definitely toward a higher range of prices. But there is certainly no obvious connection between a general tax on the output of goods and an increase of the volume of circulating medium. There is, therefore, no basis in monetary theory for supposing that a general tax on all goods will make average prices permanently higher.[45]

Brown concludes that a general expenditure tax can only fall on the factors of production, regardless of whether prices rise or stay the same:

> The incidence of a general output tax is . . ., in practical effect, the same as if it raised all prices (as most of the public seems to suppose it does) without either decreasing or increasing money incomes. For in either case there is a subtraction, proportioned to the tax, from the real incomes of wage receivers, interest receivers, and recipients of land rent.[46]

Another article, written by two contemporaries of Brown, used microeconomic price theory to investigate two types of output taxes

---

[44]Harry Gunnison Brown, "The Incidence of a General Output or a General Sales Tax," *Journal of Political Economy* (April 1939), p. 254.

[45]Ibid., p. 255.

[46]Ibid., p. 257.

-- a specific tax and an *ad valorem* tax. The authors investigated these taxes under conditions of pure competition and under conditions of "monopolistic competition."[47] Under pure competition, the authors concluded that a specific (per unit) tax would raise prices, but not by the full amount of the tax, implying a shared incidence. Under an equal rate *ad valorem* tax, prices would be higher, but as later critics pointed out, this is not a fair comparison because an equal rate *ad valorem* tax will yield more revenue. Under monopolistic competition, according to the authors' results, shared incidence will still be evident.[48]

An elegant delineation of the shared incidence theory was offered by Paul Studenski in 1940:

> The incidence of a tax on value added cannot be easily determined, for it is subject to a great many varying influences. Inasmuch as the tax would become a part of the entrepreneur's costs of production, it would affect his profits and his pricing and production policies. He would try to shift the incidence of the tax forward to consumers by raising prices or, if this cannot be done, shift it backward to his employees, land owner, lenders of money, or suppliers of raw materials by offering them lower wages, rents, rates of interest, and prices. Finally, if neither can be done, the entrepreneur would try to introduce improvements in the methods of production which would lower the costs thereof sufficiently to absorb at least a part of the tax. If he fails in the accomplishment of either objective, he must content himself with lower profits; and, if he cannot earn any profits, he must go out of business.[49]

Studenski rejected both the view that only consumers would bear a VAT and the view that only the factors of production would bear the tax:

> [I]t can scarcely be asserted that the incidence of the value-added tax would always be on the consumers and that the tax is merely a new type of a consumption tax. Nor is it possible to accept the opposite theory, advanced by some writers, that the incidence of the tax could never be on

---

[47]"Monopolistic competition" was a microeconomic theory of the firm that was popular in the 1940s and 1950s. This theory considered a situation where, even though there was competition among firms, each firm might have sufficient market power to affect price. In the perfect competition model, no firm has enough market power to affect price and can only determine the profit maximizing quantity given the market determined price. The monopolistic competition model was thought to bridge the gap between pure competition and pure monopoly (or even oligopoly). The theory was an attempt to realistically model industry conditions for many American industries.

[48]Elmer D. Fagan and Roy W. Jastram, "Tax Shifting in the Short-Run," *Quarterly Journal of Economics* (August 1939), pp. 563, 589.

[49]Paul Studenski, "Toward a Theory of Business Taxation," *Journal of Political Economy* (October 1940), p. 653.

the consumers, inasmuch as the tax applies to all business enterprises and does not change their competitive positions, and that the tax is likely to be distributed among the various factors of production in the exact proportion of the amounts of income obtained by them. The tax on the value added must be considered as being primarily a production tax. The fact that its incidence may be shifted, in part at least, to consumers does not establish it as a consumption tax, for the tax is adjusted to the peculiar features of production rather than to the peculiar features of consumption.[50]

The staunchest defender of the view that any general sales or production tax would be borne solely by consumers was John F. Due. Due placed heavy emphasis on the proposition that the economy was characterized, not by pure competition, but by "monopolistic competition" where individual firms could set their own prices because some market power was enjoyed. In such a world, "a producer ascertains as well as he can the direct cost attributable to each unit, allocates overhead on some more or less arbitrary basis, and adds a certain percentage for profits."[51]

A theory in which firms shift taxes forward in price is not sufficient to prove that consumers bear the burden of such taxes. This is because reduced profits and wages from decreased output due to higher prices can result in part of the burden being shifted onto capital and labor. In order for the tax to be fully borne by consumers, it is necessary to explain how aggregate demand remains the same after the tax. Due, employing the macroeconomic theories of his day, attempted to establish a general theory in support of the traditional view of incidence.

His explanation of how a general consumption levy would be borne solely by consumers is as follows: It is assumed that after the implementation of the new tax, firms, employing cost-plus pricing mechanisms, will raise prices by the amount of the tax. Consumers will end up spending the same amount of money on goods, but because prices are higher, will purchase fewer units. This drop in demand will result in unemployment and less use of capital. At this point, the government will step in and restore full employment through increased government spending and will adopt an accommodative monetary policy which raises prices while restoring aggregate demand. Thus, consumers will end up paying the tax.[52] Note

---

[50]Ibid., p. 654.

[51]John F. Due, *The Theory of Incidence of Sales Taxation* (New York: King Crown Press, 1942), p. 16.

[52]John F. Due, "A General Sales Tax and the Level of Employment: A Reconsideration," *National Tax Journal* (June 1949), p. 123.

that in order to sustain the traditional theory, a causality running from the tax to other fiscal and monetary policies is necessary on top of a theory that states that firms will always increase price by the amount of the tax.[53]

In 1952, Earl R. Rolph published an article which attacked the traditional wisdom that was defended by Due. His opening paragraph gives a flavor of the debate:

> The doctrine that consumers can and do pay excise taxes has lived a long life; it is among the most ancient opinions held by both professional and lay groups about economic affairs. The theory has successfully survived revolutions which have torn other segments of economic thinking to tatters. So strongly is it entrenched that the few assaults made on it directly have been scarcely noticed. Yet the theory has highly vulnerable aspects of a rather obvious character. If excise taxes raise prices to consumers, what shall be done about monetary theories which hold that an increase in aggregate demand is a necessary condition for a rise in the general level of prices?[54]

Rolph reiterated Brown's earlier arguments and stressed that with a general excise tax, firms could not move out of taxed products into untaxed lines. Thus, "[a] system of completely general and uniform taxes leaves the composition of output unchanged, does not raise product prices, and reduces the money incomes of resource owners and does so proportionately."[55]

A response came from Due in 1953. He put added emphasis on the reality of competitive conditions facing U.S. industry:

> The nature of competitive conditions is important, particularly as it determines the extent to which immediate price adjustments can be made in response to the tax. With the traditional case of perfect competition, sellers cannot directly raise prices; price adjustments must come about from adjustments to market supply, or from the consequences of the sales tax revenue upon demand. With the more common non-perfectly competitive case, direct immediate price increases by sellers are possible and without question frequently occur.[56]

Due also reiterated the argument that the uses of the tax revenue

---

[53]In Chapter 3, it has been argued that simply changing the money supply does not change the underlying real elements of the economy and that expected monetary changes, which only affect the unit of exchange, cannot change the real burden of a tax. Modern monetary theories generally agree that real aggregate demand cannot be affected by an expected change in the nominal money supply.

[54]Earl R. Rolph, "A Proposed Revision of Excise-Tax Theory," *Journal of Political Economy* (April 1952), p. 102.

[55]Ibid., p. 105.

[56]John F. Due, "Towards a General Theory of Sales Tax Incidence," *Quarterly Journal of Economics* (May 1953), pp. 256, 257.

had to be considered, and that the decreased quantities purchased due to price increases would be made up by government purchases. Since factor demand would remain the same, the tax would be successfully shifted to consumers. This would require, in addition, accommodative monetary policy.[57]

Due concludes that competitive conditions will result in immediate price increases following the introduction of a general spending tax. If aggregate demand is not reduced (requiring in his view, increased government expenditures and an expanding monetary policy), the tax will rest on consumers. Rigidities in factor prices will make it difficult to shift the tax onto labor. He argued that the Brown-Rolph conclusions were based on narrow and unrealistic assumptions and that their ". . . conclusions are of limited usefulness as a basis for policy considerations."[58]

Richard Musgrave, writing in 1953, added to the debate on incidence. He agreed that the effects of a tax were, in part a function of monetary scenarios and general government fiscal policy. Under different scenarios, there would be different outcomes for commodity and factor price reactions as a result of a new consumption tax. With a constant money supply, product prices would remain the same and the tax would be absorbed by reduced factor payments. In order for factor payments to remain the same and product prices to rise, the money supply must be increased.[59] Musgrave also considers scenarios where the government can purchase goods tax free.[60]

Musgrave argues that it is not an absolute price change (an increase in consumer prices or a decrease in factor prices) that matters for incidence, but rather changes in relative prices. Concerning a substitution of a consumption tax for an income tax, he states:

> The conventional conclusion is that this substitution relieves those who save and places the entire burden on the consumer. . . . While the conclusion is substantially correct, the reasoning involves two fallacies. First, we cannot be sure that the prices of consumer goods will rise. It may also be that consumer-goods prices are unchanged, while cost payments to factors are reduced. . . . Second, and assuming that prices did rise, no conclusions as to incidence can be drawn therefrom. . . . [I]ncidence depends on

---

[57]Ibid., pp. 260, 261.

[58]Ibid., p. 265.

[59]Note, however, that if factor prices remain the same in nominal terms after a monetary expansion, in real terms factor prices have dropped due to the new inflation and, as a result, factor prices continue to absorb part of the burden of the tax. This point seems to be missed by both Musgrave and Due.

[60]Richard A. Musgrave, "On Incidence," *Journal of Political Economy* (August 1953), p. 312.

changes in relative price, and these are independent of changes in absolute prices or price levels.[61]

The relative price of concern to Musgrave is the price of consumer goods relative to the price of capital goods. If the two move
in tandem, then the tax is not a tax on consumers; if the price of
consumer goods increases relative to capital goods, then the tax falls
on consumers, according to Musgrave. He finds that the issue is
hazy but concludes that most likely the tax falls on consumers.[62]

Due restated his position a decade after Musgrave's article. That
the incidence issue was still unresolved was evident in Due's writing:

> A major unresolved controversy in the field of public finance is that of
> whether or not consumers "bear" sales taxes. The traditional argument
> that they do . . . has been questioned by some of the top scholars in the
> field including Rolph, Break, Stockfish, Buchanan, and to some extent
> Musgrave.   Yet the traditional doctrine remains generally accepted,
> within the profession and outside.[63]

In this article, Due argues that, for incidence purposes,
researchers should not compare taxes of equal revenue yield, but
rather taxes which have equal effects on aggregate demand.[64] His
justification is that, ". . . it is the economic function of a tax to reduce
private-sector real factor demand sufficiently to free a given quantity of resources for government use."[65]

Due also states that any change in factor incomes should not be
considered part of the incidence of a new tax:

> If in fact the introduction of a sales tax to replace an income tax reduces
> real factor demand to such an extent as to produce unemployment, those
> losing their incomes should not be regarded as bearing a portion of the
> tax, but rather as being adversely affected by the over-all deflationary fis-
> cal policy.[66]

Further, although a decrease in factor incomes should not be
considered a direct result of the tax, any price increases from mone-

---

[61]Ibid., p. 318.

[62]Most economists today would argue that a consumption tax is neutral in its
application to capital and consumer goods. Each good is taxed only once under, say,
a VAT.

[63]John F. Due, "Sales Taxation and the Consumer," *American Economic Review*
(December 1963), p. 1078.

[64]This is a highly unorthodox view which is not accepted today. It clearly begs the
question because if factor demand is unchanged, the factors, by definition, cannot
bear any of the tax burden.

[65]Due, "Sales Taxation and the Consumer," p. 1079.

[66]Ibid.

tary expansion should be considered as directly caused by the tax:

> The general intent of sales tax legislation is that taxes be shifted forward to consumers through higher prices; thus the appropriate assumption to make about monetary policy is that adjustments will be made in the money supply to permit the realization of this intent. Thus the tax, not the monetary adjustments, may be regarded as the "cause" of the general price level increase.[67]

Due concludes by restating his belief that a general spending tax will be borne solely by consumers. This is because firms will immediately raise prices and the government will accommodate those changes. Any change in real factor demand should not be attributed to the tax.[68]

Clara Sullivan, in a 1965 book on value-added taxes, summed up the view that a VAT would be borne solely by consumers:

> Under a purely competitive economic system, the tax will raise the marginal costs of private concerns, making some production unprofitable at current prices. To restore profits, the entrepreneur reduces output, thus freeing resources for government use. Given the employment of these resources by the government and therefore, probably the same aggregate demand for consumers' goods despite a smaller output, the average price level of consumers' goods will rise by the amount of the tax. Appropriate adjustments in the velocity of money or, if necessary, its supply are also assumed. Under imperfect competition, similar results are achieved through direct action by taxable vendors who, with the use of average cost techniques, are expected to raise prices by the amount of the tax. . . .
>
> Possible modifications in relative factor prices because of shifts in quantities demanded are treated as effects rather than incidence.[69]

In summary, the traditional view of incidence is dependent upon several factors. The first is that, for the most part, firms face sufficiently little competition that they can affect immediate price increases after the introduction of a new general spending tax. Second, the government must spend the proceeds to restore aggregate demand. There is a problem with this factor because under modern theories of differential incidence, two taxes of equal yield are compared holding government spending constant. Therefore, if an income tax and a consumption tax were being compared, it would be assumed that the level and composition of government spending

---

[67]Ibid., p. 1081.

[68]Ibid., pp. 1083, 1084.

[69]Clara K. Sullivan, *The Tax on Value Added* (New York and London: Columbia University Press, 1965), pp. 263, 264.

would be the same. The effects of government spending are to be ignored in order to isolate the tax effects. Third, it is assumed that monetary expansion is, itself, a tax effect which can accommodate price increases. The problem here is that, unless it is believed that a nominal increase in the money supply can change real demand and supply conditions, all the monetary change does is to affect the unit of exchange and cannot shift the real burden of tax from one place to another. Finally, the traditional analysis depends on assuming away any effects on factor demand that do occur. This would seem to fly in the face of most definitions of incidence.

4

IMPLICATIONS OF THE FORM OF VAT ON INCIDENCE AND OTHER FACTORS

by David G. Raboy

Chapter 3 presented, in some detail, two different views of the incidence of consumption taxes. The traditional view holds that consumption taxes are fully borne by consumers while the alternative view holds that consumption taxes result in a shared incidence where the tax is borne by individuals in three roles -- consumers, wage earners, and providers of capital services. In the latter view, the incidence is held to be qualitatively, though not necessarily quantitatively, similar to existing systems of taxes facing businesses (most notably the combination of the corporate income tax and the employer's portion of the Social Security payroll tax).

The discussion of incidence is of more than purely academic interest. The two analyses produce very different implications for a range of economic effects and, therefore, two entirely different sets of questions for policymakers.

This chapter briefly considers the different implications of the two incidence analyses which will be covered in detail in later chapters. It will serve as an introduction to later chapters which will identify the implications of the different analyses on exemptions and preferential treatment, transition rules, and trade effects.

In addition, some other issues need to be addressed which go beyond the debate on incidence. If enactment of a value-added tax (VAT) is considered in this country, one of the most important issues which will be debated is whether the method of computation, collection and administration will affect the ultimate incidence of the tax. Specifically, there is some feeling that, while a generic VAT (as generally represented by the subtraction method of computation) might well result in a shared incidence, an equal-yield invoice and credit VAT is more likely to result in a tax borne primarily by consumers. Such a debate involves issues beyond purely economic phenomena, and commentary on the issues will be provided in this chapter.

Other controversies addressed here include the savings/consumption issue, the VAT treatment of capital expenditures, and international experience with inflation following the introduction of a VAT. This chapter, addressing a variety of concerns, will in no way be definitive, but will attempt to shed light on each one of these issues.

First, a delineation of issues under the two incidence analyses is necessary.

THE EFFECTS OF A TAX ON CONSUMPTION UNDER THE TRADITIONAL ANALYSIS

Consider first a few of the implications of a multi-stage consumption tax from the point of view of the traditional analysis which concludes that the tax falls on the consumption of goods and services and is borne solely by consumers.

Regressivity

The regressivity of consumption taxes is an obvious economic, as well as political, issue which arises under the traditional analysis. To the extent that policymakers are forced to confront concerns that lower income households will bear an unjustified share of the economic burden, adjustments in the form of exemptions from the consumption tax or alterations to other taxes in the system would be hotly debated. This issue would command a substantial amount of attention. However, it would not appear to be of critical importance to business, except to the extent that remedies such as exemptions or zero rates would erode the tax base and increase the generally applicable tax rate. This potential problem is discussed in more detail in Chapter 5.

Exemptions/Lower Rates

Exemptions and lower rates *per se* should not be highly controversial subjects within the business community under the traditional analysis. Theoretically, it would be a matter of virtual indifference that manufacturers/sellers of certain exempt items would not have taxable receipts or would remit at a lower tax rate, since all taxable companies would be passing the tax on to consumers. There would be no distortion of the prices of capital or labor across industries and no question of horizontal equity among firms. However, it might concern some companies that non-taxable or tax-preferred goods would also be preferred by consumers because of the price differential, thus triggering shifts in consumer demand.

Offsets

Given that a consumption tax is a tax on goods, the only purpose for offsets for previously paid taxes -- e.g., allowing a credit for prior purchases in an invoice and credit VAT or a deduction in a subtraction method VAT -- would be to prevent cascading of the tax at each stage of production and distribution. There should be no concern about goods which are taxed after the effective date of implementation of the tax, even though significant amounts of value-added in such goods arose *before* the effective date. Since such taxes are passed on, the affected businesses should be indifferent. Presumably, the general rule would be that all goods sold after the effective date would be taxed, and only those inputs purchased after the effective date (and therefore subject to the tax) would be eligible for credits and deductions. Matters of transition are discussed in detail in Chapter 6.

Trade Effects

International trade implications are significantly affected by the traditional analysis of incidence, and importers and exporters have developed strongly held positions. Assuming that consumption taxes are reflected in price while income taxes and payroll taxes are not, there would be no effects on trade flows of substituting a VAT for an income tax or a VAT for a payroll tax. This subject is discussed in detail in Chapter 7.

IMPLICATIONS OF THE ALTERNATIVE ANALYSIS

Now, consider the implications of the alternative analysis which finds a value-added tax to be a proportionate tax on incomes for capital and labor services, the incidence of which is shared by providers of capital and labor, and by consumers.

Regressivity

The alternative analysis asserts that the incidence of consumption taxes falls only partially on consumers. If accepted, this should significantly reduce the magnitude of the regressivity debate because the problem would be diminished. However, as has been observed in recent income and payroll tax debates, the political sensitivity of even a minor regressivity issue cannot be ignored. Nonetheless, policymakers would be forced to consider the fact that the typical analyses based on the traditional perspective would substantially overstate the distributional impact of consumption taxes on lower income households. Efforts to redress regressivity based on typical distributional tables could overshoot the mark substantially.

Exemptions, Lower Rates, and Transition Issues

While regressivity as an issue of controversy would decline in importance, acceptance of the alternative analysis would elevate the importance of other issues, particularly within the business community. A new set of neutrality guidelines would be necessary, especially when exemptions, lower rates and transition rules were considered.

Exemptions, reduced rates or zero-rating for certain goods and services could mean that companies and entire industries would avoid a VAT altogether. This would be a matter of considerable importance to investors, lenders and labor in *non*-exempt/non-favored business sectors because of potential competitive consequences.

As for transition questions during implementation, companies with substantial value-added inputs acquired or developed prior to the effective date could be very sensitive to imposition of a VAT with no relief for pre-existing factors.

Horizontal equity and tax neutrality questions across industries and among companies within an industry become particularly crucial when considering partial or complete substitution of a VAT for existing business taxes. For example, under the current income and payroll taxes, is the effective tax rate on labor's value-added higher than that on capital's value-added? Any whole or partial substitution of a proportional tax on capital and labor for an existing tax on just *one* factor could change the respective burdens on capital and labor incomes significantly.

Trade Effects

The alternative analysis holds that, since so-called indirect and direct taxes bear qualitatively similar incidences, the substitution of a border adjustable tax for a non-border adjustable tax could have trade consequences. This complicated subject is discussed in detail in Chapter 7.

DOES THE VAT METHOD AFFECT INCIDENCE?

In studying the subtraction method VAT proposals by Senator Roth, Rep. Schulze and the Canadian government, some business executives and tax practitioners have begun to conclude that the method of computing and remitting a VAT may be a critical factor in determining incidence. In contrast to the invoice and credit VAT used in Europe, these North American varieties are perceived by some to have a greater impact on business.

These three proposals pose the following question, "Is there either a mathematical or a practical/psychological basis for concluding that incidence is affected by the structure of the tax?" Can a subtraction VAT (the "generic VAT" discussed in Chapter 2) and an invoice and credit VAT (a generic VAT with an additional collection option involving invoicing) of equal revenue yield have qualitatively different incidences?

To conclude that incidences are qualitatively different over a period of time for a subtraction VAT vis-a-vis an invoice and credit VAT, it seems essential to argue that the Distributive Law of Algebra does not apply. After all, the two methods are mathematically equivalent.[1] Yet, there is a strongly held belief that if the tax is explicitly stated on an invoice, it is more easily passed forward than one which is computed by simply using the subtraction method.

---

[1] The distributive law states that $A(B+C) = AB+AC$. If the VAT tax rate is t, output value is O and input value is I, then the tax paid under a subtraction method is $t(O-I)$. By the distributive law $t(O-I) = tO-tI$. The latter is the formula for the tax paid under the invoice and credit method.

Thus, under an invoice and credit VAT, consumers will bear more of the burden.

When assessing the impact on incidence of the VAT mechanism itself, it is probably prudent to differentiate between the short run and the long run. The long run would be the period in which firms have fully adjusted to the imposition of a new tax. But the "long run" in this case does not necessarily refer to some distant academic horizon which will never be reached within a relevant time span. Tax systems which are algebraically equivalent should produce the same incidence after some legitimate adjustment period. Therefore, this discussion will focus on the short-term possibilities which are much more likely to be influenced by business managers' perceptions and expectations than by pure mathematics and economics. These short-run effects may, however, influence long-run effects.

What follows is an attempt to identify the issues and internal company mechanisms which may affect the initial behavior of corporate decisionmakers when faced with two equal-yield VATs that have different computational mechanisms and different collection and administrative formats.

The first VAT to be considered will be a generic or subtraction method VAT. This tax would be based on books of account similar to those required for the corporate income tax. The tax department of the corporation would be charged with complying with the tax, and there would be no direct connection between tax remittance and the pricing mechanism.

One could envision the type of discussions which would have to occur concerning how to adjust the prices of output in the face of the new tax. In the first instance, the payor, the entity statutorily responsible for writing the check to the government, would be the corporation. Based on a period's receipts and purchases, the tax department would remit a check to the government. In order to shift the tax, a series of discussions and analyses would have to occur which would involve the marketing department, corporate planning, the tax department, and maybe other corporate officers. The situation would be similar to that of deciding how to price merchandise in the face of a corporate tax increase or a payroll tax increase.

After investigation by the various departments, in order to shift the tax forward in price, the relevant corporate executives would have to make a *conscious* decision to raise the price to recoup the tax. The tax is not shifted automatically. Once the decision is made on how much to increase prices, actual market forces will determine whether or not the decision was the right one. If sales weaken considerably, the decision may have to be revised.

The key points with a generic VAT are that the company is the payor, initial tax liability is independent of price, many different departments must debate the response to the tax, and ultimately a conscious decision must be made to increase prices if the tax is to be shifted. Then, in the final analysis, the economy will determine if the market will bear the increased price for if it does not, profits and payroll will be reduced as a result of declining sales.

Before contrasting this situation to an invoice and credit VAT, the case of a retail sales tax must be discussed. In this case, the initial payor is the consumer. Absent any conscious decision to the contrary, base prices remain as they were before and the tax is added on to the price. The economy then determines whether or not the market will bear the higher prices. If profits fall as a result of the higher prices, a *conscious* decision on the part of companies must be made to *lower* base prices.

Thus, there is an opposite direction in decisionmaking regarding shifting between a generic VAT and a retail sales tax. In the first case, where the company is the payor, a conscious decision must be made to *shift* the tax forward. In the latter case, when the company is not the payor, if companies are passive, the tax is automatically shifted and a conscious decision has to be made *not* to shift the tax. In either case, the market is the final arbiter. It is extremely important to note that shifting the tax forward in price is a necessary, but not sufficient, condition to have consumers bear the entire burden of a consumption tax. The second condition is that consumers must purchase the same quantity of goods at the higher price.

There are many who view an invoice and credit VAT as equivalent, in terms of the payor, to a retail sales tax. In this view, the company is merely a collector of a tax which accumulates up to the retail stage where the actual payor is the consumer. In this view, the tax is automatically shifted forward unless a conscious decision by companies to lower base prices is made.

The Tax-Exclusive and Tax-Inclusive VATs

There seems to be some confusion about the structure and mechanism of an invoice and credit VAT. In reality there are two types of invoice and credit VAT -- one levied on a tax "exclusive" base, and the other levied on a tax "inclusive" base. As will be shown, only the former approximates a retail sales tax where the tax is automatically shifted unless the company makes an *active* decision to lower base prices. With a tax-inclusive base, the company is still truly the payor and an active decision has to be made to shift the tax.

Both the tax-inclusive and tax-exclusive VATs contain the statutory presumption that the amount of tax will be stated on the invoice. The difference is the way in which the statute defines the tax base. The tax-exclusive VAT applies the tax rate to the base price only. The tax inclusive VAT applies the rate to a base defined as the base price *plus the tax itself*. This is an important distinction.

Consider the two alternative VAT systems employing a 10 percent rate. Assume that initially the base price of goods is $10. Under a tax-exclusive base, the tax base is defined by statute as $10 and when the rate is applied, $1 dollar in tax is yielded. The statute allows the taxpayer to sell his goods for $10 and recover the tax. In effect, the taxpayer sells his goods for $11. The invoice states a base price of $10 and $1 in tax for a total of $11.

Now consider a tax-inclusive base. The base price of goods is $10 and the rate is applied, yielding $1. But notice what happens if the taxpayer attempts to recover the tax. If he charges his customer $11, he has changed the base of taxation because the tax base is defined by statute as the base price *plus the tax*, i.e., the total amount collected from the customer. If the taxpayer tried to recover the tax by charging the customer $11, the tax base would increase from $10 to $11, and an additional 10 cents in tax would be owed.

To achieve an equal yield, the tax rate must be higher under a tax-exclusive VAT than under a tax-inclusive VAT. In case of these $10 base price examples, a tax-inclusive VAT with a rate of 9.09 percent raises the same amount of revenue as the 10 percent rate under the tax-exclusive VAT.

Effects on Pricing Decisions

Two examples will show the difference in company decision-making under the alternative tax regimes. Assume a three-stage production process where, in a non-tax world, Company A produces goods valued at $10, sells them to B which produces goods that are then sold to C for $20. C is the retailer which sells to the public for $30. Thus, each company produces $10 of value added, and the final price of the good is the sum of all value added or $30. If the tax-inclusive value-added tax rate is 10 percent, the equal yield tax-exclusive rate is 11.1 percent as will be shown below.

First, consider what happens under a tax-exclusive VAT at 11.1 percent.

Company A produces goods valued at $10 and sells them to B. A is liable for a VAT of $1.11 which it remits to the government. A actually charges B $11.11. The invoice states a base price of $10 plus a tax of $1.11. No marketing decision has been necessary to change the base price. Thus, in a totally passive manner, the tax has been fully shifted onto B, and A still receives $10 for its goods. B's *base* price to C will also remain at $20. It sends C an invoice for $22.22, with the base price listed as $20 and $2.22 stated in tax. B has a tax credit from A for $1.11, a liability of $2.22, and remits $1.11 to the government. No marketing executive has had to argue that the base price must be increased in order to recover the tax. All base prices remain as before the tax. C has paid $22.22 for inputs and sells them to the public. On the final sales tag is listed the base price of $30, the same as before, plus $3.33 in VAT. The retailer receives the $33.33, collects $3.33 in VAT, credits $2.22, and remits $1.11 to the government. A total of $3.33 in tax has been paid including the remittances of all three producers.

Under this tax-exclusive VAT example, the shifting was a purely passive operation. No decision ever had to be made by any officer of any company to change base prices. Firms have merely collected tax while receiving the same revenues after-tax for their products, and ultimately the consumer was the payor. Other than the multistage nature of the collection process, it is very similar to a retail sales tax. The tax is fully shifted unless some company makes an *active* decision to change its base price.

This is not the case with a tax-inclusive VAT. Now each company is facing a 10 percent VAT on a tax-inclusive base. Consider Companies A, B and C again. In the non-tax world, Company A's marketing executives have set the base price of its product at $10. If the company is passive, making no decision to change base price, the following occurs.

The tax rate is levied on the base price *which is assumed to include the tax*. Company A is liable for $1 in tax but can only charge a total of $10 to Company B (for if it charged more than $10, the tax base would increase and additional tax would be owed). Company B receives an invoice for $10 which includes a sub-line noting that $1 in VAT has been paid. After tax, Company A has only received $9. *If the company is passive, the tax is shifted backward, not onto consumers.*[2]

In order to shift the tax, the company, through discussions

---

[2]Note the difference between the tax-inclusive and tax-exclusive case. In the tax-exclusive case, the supplier is allowed to charge its customers the base price plus the tax. In the tax-inclusive case, the supplier can only charge the customer the base price and note what part of the base price is the tax.

between marketing and tax executives, must make a conscious decision to increase the base price. To fully shift the tax so that its after-tax receipts are the same as before the implementation of the tax, Company A must actively increase its base price to $11.11.

Once Company A makes the decision to fully shift the tax, it charges $11.11 to Company B and notes on its invoice that $1.11 of the base price is tax and therefore creditable. Company B now must also make an active decision to increase its base price to $22.22. It then applies the VAT rate to this sale, collects $2.22, credits the $1.11 from Company A, and remits $1.11 to the government. The retailer, Company C, buys goods for $22.22, including a $2.22 VAT credit. If Company C wants to fully shift the tax, it must increase its final sales price, consciously, to $33.33. *Depending on the country, the VAT may or may not be stated on the retail level sales tag.* At any rate, the retailer must actively increase the price in order to shift the tax so that after-tax revenues are intact.

The difference between the tax-inclusive and the tax-exclusive base case is similar to the difference between a generic VAT and a retail sales tax. In the cases of the generic VAT and the tax-inclusive invoice and credit VAT, a passive position on the part of a company results in the tax being shifted back onto the company (in reality onto the company's providers of capital and labor services). In order to shift the tax forward, an active decision has to be made to increase the base prices of products.

In the cases of either a retail sales tax or a tax-exclusive invoice and credit VAT, a passive position on the part of the company results in the tax being fully shifted in price. The company must actively lower the base price in order to not shift the tax.

Both systems are used around the world. But, for purposes of this discussion, an important comparison is between a generic VAT and a tax-inclusive invoice and credit VAT.[3] Before regarding the differences, it is worth repeating the fundamental similarities: in both cases the company is the payor, and in both cases an active decision has to be made to shift the tax in price.

Much has been made of the notion that an invoice and credit VAT is a transactions-based tax whereas a generic VAT is based on annual accounting mechanisms similar to an income tax. This distinction is largely erroneous. In no European VAT is an attempt made to trace the tax on a product-by-product basis by relating the tax on a specific intermediate component to the precise final pro-

---

[3]This is not to imply that a tax-exclusive VAT would not be considered in North America.

duct to which it contributes.

In fact, in any accounting period, total outputs are compared to total inputs, which may or may not have any relationship to each other in terms of final production. An annual, quarterly or monthly tax return is filed which has a line for total taxable sales in that period. The relevant tax rate is applied to those sales. A second line lists total taxable purchases over the same accounting period. The relevant tax credits related to these previously taxed purchases are claimed. The difference between the tax on outputs and the tax credits from inputs is then remitted to the government. In reality, there is no necessary difference between the tax form and accounting period for a generic VAT and one with an invoice and credit mechanism.

The only major difference between the two types of taxes is that one explicitly lists the tax on an invoice at the sub-retail level, and *possibly* at the retail level, and the other has no explicit invoicing mechanism. Two issues arise: (1) invoicing at the sub-retail level, and (2) explicitly stating the tax at the retail level.

It may be the case that explicitly stating the tax at the sub-retail level makes it easier for marketing executives to justify increasing their base prices in order to shift the tax. The invoice system, along with the knowledge that the purchaser will receive a "chit" in the form of an explicitly-stated VAT credit may afford a psychological advantage over the generic system in terms of tax shifting, given the internal workings of corporations. This may also vary from company to company depending on corporate culture and the relative positions in the corporate hierarchy of different departments and mechanisms for making pricing decisions. It is beyond the purview of this study to survey corporations on this psychological effect but it is conceded that, in this context, invoicing may make a difference.

The immediate goals and planning horizons may also be important. Is the company a short-term profit maximizer or is it more concerned with short-term gains in market share? The bottom line is that if marketing executives *perceive* that invoicing makes it easier to increase prices, then they will do so. And then it is up to the market to demonstrate whether or not that perception was correct.

This brings up the question of explicitly stating the tax at the retail level. Once again, if consumers are to bear the full burden of the tax, the tax must be fully shifted in price *and* consumers must purchase the same amounts (thereby drawing down wealth from sources such as savings or other assets). Thus, the success of passing a tax onto consumers depends on the market demand structure. If consumers refuse to purchase the same level of goods, then sales volume will drop, as will profits, and the owners of businesses will share some of the burden even though the tax was fully reflected in price increases.

Are consumers more apt to reduce purchases if prices merely increase or if prices increase by the same amount but part of the price increase is explicitly stated on the sales receipt as a tax? Will consumers buy the same number of bottles of shampoo if the price rises 50 cents due to a hidden tax or if the price rises because of a 50 cent tax which is stated on the price tag? Once again, the analysis has entered the realm of psychology. One viewpoint is that consumer demand is less elastic if the tax is explicitly stated than if consumers are faced with a price hike from an unknown source. This suggests altruistic feelings toward paying taxes. Tax protesters might argue the opposite.

Once again, it is beyond the scope of this study to draw conclusions, or even offer evidence, on this question. It is certainly one worthy of investigation. It may very well be the case that consumer demand is different for equally priced goods if part of the price is explicitly stated as a tax. Whether the response is positive or negative is unknown. At any rate, most VAT countries *do not* explicitly state VAT at the retail level. The only purpose of invoicing is to properly credit previously paid taxes and since consumers receive no input tax credits, in a tax-inclusive VAT system, there is no reason to explicitly state the tax at the retail level (originally the United Kingdom stated VAT at the retail level but has since dropped this practice).

The short-run results of a generic VAT versus a tax-inclusive invoice and credit VAT can be summarized as follows:

- In both systems, at any stage of the production process, the seller is statutorily liable for VAT payment and is considered the payor.
- In order to shift the tax forward in price, a conscious decision must be made to increase base prices in both systems.
- The periodic accounting mechanisms are similar in both systems.
- There may be a psychological advantage to explicitly stating the tax on an invoice at the sub-retail level.
- There may be a psychological difference affecting consumer demand if the tax is explicitly stated at the retail level although the direction of this effect, if it exists at all, is unknown.

Beyond the short-run implications of company decisionmaking, which merely begins the process by which incidence is determined, the market is the arbiter of final incidence. Market demand, competition among firms, and other factors become relevant. To see one possible adjustment path, an experiment can be performed where, at first, a generic VAT exists, which is then replaced by a VAT with a specific invoicing system. In this stylized experiment, it will be assumed that under the generic VAT, some of the burden falls on companies and, in fact, an equilibrium exists where all companies are just making a normal rate of return. Therefore, there is no incentive for entry or exit, nor to change the prices of output. Yet, managers believe that an explicit invoicing system would make it easier to pass on more of the tax to consumers.

Assume that an invoice and credit VAT replaces the generic VAT and that the reaction of all companies, initially, is to state the tax on invoices and fully pass it on. Prices to consumers rise and, depending on the elasticities in the various markets, quantities purchased will drop. In some markets where demand is highly elastic, companies will see an immediate drop in profits as the effects of a drop in quantities purchased dwarf the price increases. In such markets, companies will have an instantaneous incentive to cut base prices and absorb some of the tax.

In other markets, companies will also pass on the tax and will be making extra-normal profits. This is an unstable situation. All companies are making extra-normal profits, but any one company can increase profits still further by cutting prices and gaining market share. By the nature of the competition, it is impossible for companies to collude for very long. Individual firms, attempting to maximize their profits, will begin to cut prices. Competitors will respond, and prices will continue to fall until all firms are making a normal rate of return. Because the cost structure facing companies is the same under the old and new tax regimes, the competition will end when the after-tax prices in both systems are the same. This is the point where firms just make a normal rate of return.

Thus, if two tax systems produce identical cost structures for companies and if demand conditions are the same, the incidence results after an adjustment period should be the same.

This does not mean, however, that there would not be differences during the adjustment period. In the real world, there will never be a time where a pure subtraction method VAT is replaced by an invoice and credit VAT as described above. A more likely possibility is that part of the existing tax system will be replaced by a VAT.

Certainly it is plausible to expect businesses to price goods and services in a manner which covers higher costs, and such short-run effects are likely to be driven by managers' expectations and perceptions. Yet, adjustments to price increases are inevitable. The speed of adjustment, given highly imperfect information, and a fluid and unpredictable economy, may be different for two different types of

VATs. Further, the adjustment period may be fairly lengthy. But in the long run, the two different types of VAT should converge to the same solution because of their equivalent effects on companies' cost structures.

OTHER ISSUES

The incidence questions discussed in this chapter, and the last, technically do not extend beyond assessing the differential effects of one tax versus another on economic income. However, two other topics are often linked to incidence debates -- "tax neutrality" and inflationary impact.

Tax Neutrality

One of the criteria by which tax systems are judged is that of tax neutrality. Essentially, a neutral tax is one which does not distort the economic choices facing participants in the economy. No tax can be perfectly neutral, but VATs have generally received high marks for neutrality.

There are two aspects of neutrality which are of particular interest. The first concerns the way taxes affect the mix of factors of production -- capital and labor -- employed in the productive process. The second concerns tax-induced distortions in society's decision to save or consume.

It is generally agreed among economists that VATs are neutral with regard to the mix of productive inputs -- a VAT taxes both labor and capital only once and at the same rate. Yet, confusion continues. Many observers consider a VAT to be, in essence, a tax on labor and, therefore, non-neutral. This view derives from the observation that, under a subtraction method VAT, a deduction is allowed for all capital acquisitions while no deduction is allowed for labor expenses.

Single Taxation at a Single Rate. For a tax to be truly neutral, all payments to the factors of production must be taxed only once and then at the same rate. Under a VAT, physical capital has already been subject to one layer of tax when the capital supplier sold the capital asset to the capital user. The deduction for such a purchase prevents a second, punitive layer of tax. Because there is no head tax at birth, labor services have not been subject to a previous VAT layer. Therefore, no labor deduction is necessary in order to ensure that, economy wide, all factor payments are taxed at the same rate.

The rate of payment to labor is the non-wage inclusive compensation rate per unit of time. A similar concept exists for capital. The rate of payment to capital is the implicit rental rate. It is the equivalent lease payment which would exist if the capital owner leased to himself. The implicit rental rate includes both the return of and the return to capital. It is algebraically stated, in an expensing or non-tax world, as $c = q(r+d)$, where c is the implicit rental rate, q is the cost of a unit of capital, r is the after-tax rate of return required which includes payment to debt and equity holders and d is the rate of physical decay and obsolescence. For neutrality to occur, the economy-wide implicit lease payments and non-wage inclusive compensation rates must be taxed at the same rate. This requires a deduction for the capital user.

To see this, note that the present value of the implicit lease payments over the life of an asset equal the original price of the asset. Now, consider a subtraction method VAT. The capital user is allowed a deduction for the price of an asset which is equivalent to allowing a deduction for implicit lease payments in every period.

The capital supplier is taxed on the sale of the asset which is equivalent to taxing the supplier on implicit lease payments in every period. If the user did not receive a deduction, the implicit lease payments, the wage-equivalent for capital, would be taxed twice while the compensation rate for labor would be taxed once. This would clearly cause a bias against capital. The expensing deduction for capital results in a system where the economy-wide compensation rates for labor and capital are taxed only once and at the same rate.

Savings Versus Consumption. The second type of neutrality is neutrality over time, or "intertemporal" neutrality. A neutral tax will not alter the terms of society's decision to consume or save from those which exist in a non-tax world. Again, there is confusion concerning the intertemporal neutrality of a VAT. The term "consumption tax" has been presumed to mean that a VAT penalizes consumption. In fact, a VAT is intertemporally neutral.

To see this, begin with a non-tax world in which an individual must decide between consuming and saving. If the individual consumes, he or she is foregoing interest and therefore the consumption must be worth as much or more to the individual than the interest. Now consider what happens under an income tax. The individual pays tax and, out of after-tax income, has a choice whether to save or consume. If the individual chooses to consume, there are no further tax consequences. If the individual decides to save, however, taxes must be paid on interest income. Thus, the

terms of trade between saving and consumption have been altered
from those which occur in a non-tax world. Either allowing a deduction for current saving or exempting interest income from tax
restores the terms of trade to those which existed in the non-tax
world.

In a national accounting sense, a VAT, through its single level of
tax on capital, allows the equivalence of a deduction for current
saving. Therefore, rather than being a tax which discourages consumption, it is intertemporally neutral.

The belief that a consumption tax penalizes consumption, however, triggers a predictable pattern of responses from business
executives and economists who favor or oppose efforts to restrain
consumption and to encourage saving and investment. In fact, the
political support for and opposition to consumption taxes within the
business community is probably attributable more to reactions to
this one concern than to all other subjects combined. The fact that
consumption taxes are neutral diminishes these responses somewhat, but the issue is still relevant, especially if the neutral tax is
used to replace taxes that currently penalize saving. A further discussion of this issue and other macroeconomic implications occurs
in Chapter 10.

VAT and Inflation -- International Experience

Traditional analysis of VATs generally cite the European experiences with inflation following implementation of VATs to reinforce
the consumer-incidence conclusion. Evidence on the inflationary
effects of such changes does exist, but accurate interpretation is difficult.

Many things were going on simultaneously in the economies
adopting value-added taxes. Tax changes coincided with cyclical
changes, monetary and fiscal policy changes, and external shocks.
Therefore, it is not easy to isolate the effects of a VAT on prices. In
addition, the introduction of a VAT may have involved an equal-
yield substitution for another tax or the overall tax burden on the
private sector may have increased.

Alan Tait of the International Monetary Fund performed a study
which attempted to separate the price effects of a VAT introduction.[4] He studied the implementation of VATs in 31 countries and
in each case considered the external and internal economic condi-

---

[4]See Alan Tait, "Is the Introduction of a Value-Added Tax Inflationary?" *Finance
and Development* (June 1981), pp. 38-42.

tions in an effort to isolate tax effects. Four possibilities were considered. The first was a one-time only shift in the price level. Since inflation is defined as an increase in the rate of change of prices, a one-time shift is not evidence of inflation. The second possibility is an acceleration of prices or inflation. The third is a combination of inflation plus a one-time shift in prices. The fourth possibility is no effect.

Of the 31 countries surveyed, Tait found that there was no effect at all on prices in 21 of the countries. In 6 of the remaining 10 countries, there was a one-time price shift. Denmark's shift attributable to the VAT was a 5-percent increase in the consumer price index, but the VAT introduction involved a significant increase in overall tax liabilities. The price shift attributable to the VAT introduction in France was one percent or less, and in Germany it was 0.6 percent.

Three of the four remaining countries had accelerated inflation -- Italy, Peru, and Israel. In Israel, the VAT introduction was associated with "expansionist policies of a new government in the second half of 1977."[5] Tait believes that "a sharp increase in government expenditure and wages, and an exchange rate reform that increased the capital inflow and expanded the domestic credit base, seem to have had more impact on prices than the VAT."[6] The final country -- Norway -- had both a shift in prices and an increase in inflation. Tait concludes that for the four countries where there was inflation that it ". . . was associated in each case with expansionary wage and credit policies."[7]

Finally, Tait comments on the basic assumption governments should make concerning substitutions:

> Clearly it is possible to introduce a VAT (sometimes even to increase revenues) without shifting, or increasing the rate of change of, prices. If anything, the assumption should be that an equal-yield substitution will have no effect on the rate of change of prices and that even if an increased yield is derived and prices increase, it will not necessarily accelerate inflation.[8]

Further commentary on the inflation issue can also be found in Chapter 10.

---

[5]Ibid., p. 41.

[6]Ibid.

[7]Ibid., p. 42.

[8]Ibid.

CONCLUSION

This chapter has considered various issues relating to incidence. After outlining the policy issues posed by the two different incidence analyses, the chapter discussed at length whether the method of VAT computation affected the final incidence analysis. Although granting that, in the short run, psychological factors stemming from different computation methods may differentially influence internal company pricing decisions, in the long run the market will force equal yield, equal base, systems to converge to the same result.

5

PREFERENTIAL TREATMENT: THE IMPLICATIONS FOR HORIZONTAL EQUITY AMONG COMPANIES

by David G. Raboy

Pressures for exemptions and other preferential treatment under consumption taxes are intense, given the traditional incidence analysis which indicates that consumers bear the burden of such taxes. Regressivity then becomes a politically explosive issue which commands extensive attention. In addition, specific business sectors begin to complain about their administrative and competitive problems and seek redress. To date, there has been no implementation of a national consumption tax by an industrialized country which has not been accompanied to some degree by special treatment in the form of exemptions, "zero-rating" or reduced tax rates for certain goods and services.

After a brief review of foreign experiences, this chapter explores exemptions, zero-rating, and multiple rate devices and their implications for businesses. The discussion approaches these subjects first from the traditional incidence perspective where the tax is presumed fully shifted in price and borne by consumers. The latter part of the discussion considers the effects of providing special treatment from the alternative perspective where the burden is believed to be shared by capital, labor and consumers alike. A multi-stage VAT will serve as the example throughout.

Special treatment generally is enacted to address two categories of problems. The first and probably the most obvious is regressivity. Presuming that a larger share of income is devoted to consumption for less wealthy people than for more wealthy people, the burden of a VAT is found to vary inversely with economic income under the traditional analysis.

The second category consists of requests for preferential treatment for certain sectors of the economy, including small business, agriculture, non-profit organizations, the government sector, and the financial services industry. The requests generally are based either on administrative and compliance problems or on social policy objectives.

There are three means for providing special treatment under a VAT.

Exemption. An activity, firm, or sector is simply exempted from the tax, and the exempt entity is not part of the VAT system. In an invoice and credit VAT, this means that no tax is levied on the exempt sales, but no credits are allowed for VAT paid on purchased goods, since the entity is outside the system.

Zero-rating. An alternative treatment is applying a zero rate to the entity which remains *in* the system. No tax is levied on sales by the zero-rated entity, but input tax credits are allowed, because the entity is still within the VAT system.

Lower Rates. A third alternative is to apply lower rates for certain activities.

THE INTERNATIONAL EXPERIENCE

Most countries which have adopted VATs have afforded preferential treatment to various activities. Under the European Economic Community's 6th Directive, several financial/service activities (banking, insurance, and real estate) as well as education, medical services, and contributions to charitable organizations are exempt from VAT. Zero-rating is, in most cases, used only to remove the VAT from the cost of goods exported.

In Europe, the most common special treatment is to apply multiple rates of tax in combination with exemptions. France has a standard VAT rate of 18.6 percent (with a 33.33 percent rate on certain luxury items). However, a 7 percent rate applies to such items as hotels and public transportation, and only a 5 percent rate applies to food and to water bought from utilities. In addition, France adheres to the 6th Directive exemptions for several service sectors.

West Germany has a two-rate structure -- a standard rate of 14 percent with a 7 percent rate for such items as food, dental care, and local bus or train travel.

Italy has a four-rate structure with a standard rate of 18 percent, a rate of 2 percent on most foods, books, newspapers and building work, a 9 percent rate on selected foods, wines, records and telephones, and a 38 percent rate on luxuries.

The Netherlands has a normal 19 percent rate with a 5 percent rate for such items as food, newspapers, and transportation.

Norway has a flat rate of 20 percent with exemptions similar to other European countries (real estate, financial services, medical services, etc.), and applies a zero rate to many activities having to do with North Sea oil production.

The United Kingdom has a standard rate of 15 percent. The British VAT is unique in its widespread use of zero-rating. Besides exports, it zero-rates most foods, seeds and fertilizer, transportation, newspapers and books, fuel, clothes and footwear for children. Education and health care are exempt but not zero-rated.[1]

An effort is underway to further harmonize European VAT systems. If successful, this would include harmonization of both rates and exemptions. The purpose seems to be to broaden the various VAT bases and reduce the number of rates in order to achieve more neutrality among the systems within the Common Market.

Canada currently is considering substantial sales tax reform in the context of general tax reform legislation. A new value-added tax system is one of the major changes being considered. Government documents explaining the VAT options reflect a desire to hold special treatment provisions to a minimum. The government's preference is to address regressivity through adjustments in the income tax rather than through exemptions, zero-rating or multiple rates (although recent news accounts suggest that food will be exempt). In addition, the VAT will be extended to financial services, and there will, therefore, be fewer sector exemptions.[2]

There have been three comprehensive VAT legislative proposals in the United States in recent years. A general tax reform bill, H.R. 7015, included a VAT. The bill was introduced in 1980 by the late Rep. Al Ullman (D-OR), former Chairman of the House Ways and Means Committee. The VAT in H.R. 7015 included a single rate,

---

[1]See description of European systems from Graham Bannock, *VAT and Small Business: European Experience and Implications for North America* (Canada: Canadian Federation of Independent Business, 1986), pp. 79-90.

[2]Michael H. Wilson, *Tax Reform 1987, Sales Tax Reform* (Canada: Department of Finance, 1987).

but zero-rated food, medical care, and housing.[3] Senator William Roth's (R-DE) proposal for a subtraction method VAT, S. 1102, known as the Business Transfer Tax or BTT, was introduced in 1985. The bill contained several exemptions including those for retail sales of food and non-alcoholic beverages, sales or rental of housing, medical services and sale or rental of medical property, sale or rental of land, and exports. In 1986, Rep. Richard Schulze (R-PA), a member of the House Ways and Means Committee, introduced H.R. 4598 -- the Business Alternative Minimum Tax or BAMT.

SPECIAL TREATMENT UNDER THE TRADITIONAL ANALYSIS

Regressivity

Pressures to address regressivity arise as a result of the conclusion drawn from traditional incidence analysis that a VAT is a tax on goods and services which is in turn borne fully by consumers. Generally, the family is viewed as the relevant unit for comparing income distributions, and the family's tax as a percentage of *economic income* is the common distributional measure.[4]

The Treasury has estimated that, absent any adjustments, a broadbased VAT of 10 percent would impact low-income households far more than wealthier taxpayers. Specific estimates are shown in Table 5-1.

In short, a disproportionate percentage of economic income would be paid as value-added taxes by low income families facing the higher prices resulting from the VAT. This presents a very sensitive political issue, and remedial measures generally are considered essential.

A partial offset would automatically be provided by the many entitlement programs which are already indexed for price changes. Social security, food stamps, supplemental security income and government pensions are examples of indexed programs which would partially reduce regressivity. However, other programs such as

---

[3]Dan Throop Smith and Bertrand Fox, *An Analysis of Value Added Taxation in the Context of the Tax Restructuring Act of 1980* (Washington, D.C.: The Financial Executives Research Foundation, 1981).

[4]Economic income would include adjusted gross income for income tax purposes plus certain tax-exempt income.

Table 5-1

VAT IMPACT ON HOUSEHOLDS

Economic Income	Percentage of Income Absorbed by 10% VAT
under $10,000	14.2
$ 10,000 - 15,000	9.2
$ 15,000 - 20,000	7.5
$ 20,000 - 30,000	6.1
$ 50,000 - 100,000	5.0
$100,000 - 200,000	3.0

Source: U.S. Department of the Treasury, *Tax Reform for Fairness, Simplicity, and Economic Growth, Volume 3: The Value-Added Tax* (Washington, D.C.: U.S. Department of the Treasury, November 1984), p. 93.

unemployment insurance and Aid to Families with Dependent Children are not indexed. With current levels of indexing, the regressivity of a VAT would be reduced. Allowing for indexing of federal programs as contained in current law, a broad-based VAT would result in 9.6 percent of economic income under $10,000 being absorbed by the VAT (compared to 14.2 percent without indexing). For households with annual income between $10,000 and $15,000, 6.9 percent would go to pay value-added taxes (compared to 9.2 percent without indexing).[5] The cost of allowing such indexing would equal 11 percent of VAT revenues.

As mentioned previously, the suggested remedy for regressivity is to exclude certain necessities from the tax base. Targeted items could include food, clothing, medical care, housing and utility services. If all the items were exempted from the base, Treasury estimates that families with under $10,000 in economic income would pay 8.9 percent of such income in value-added taxes and families

---

[5]U.S. Department of the Treasury, *Tax Reform for Fairness, Simplicity, and Economic Growth, Volume 3: The Value-Added Tax* (Washington, D.C.: U.S. Department of the Treasury, November 1984), p. 93.

with incomes between $10,000 and $15,000 would pay 5.9 percent.

There are many problems with using zero-rating and exemptions to address regressivity, however. A major one is the high revenue loss. The Treasury projects 1988 personal consumption expenditures to be $3.1 trillion. If the value of owner-and-tenant occupied housing is deducted, the consumption tax base is eroded by $460 billion (although $170 billion must be added back to reflect the sale of new housing as well as the value of alterations). Removing medical care and health insurance costs reduces the base another $232 billion. Zero-rating of food would reduce the base by $349 billion and result in a new VAT base of $2.2 trillion. If new housing, drugs, and household utility services were also excluded from the base, the tax base would fall to $1.74 trillion. Thus, if most "necessities" were eliminated from the VAT base, the base would constitute only about 55 percent of personal consumption.[6] This would dramatically improve the regressivity situation but at a very high price and in a very inefficient manner.

This high price would include a VAT rate substantially above what would otherwise be necessary to raise equivalent revenues on a broader base. The inefficiency arises from the fact that the majority of consumption in the exempt categories is by families with incomes in excess of the poverty level who presumably are not the groups being benefited. About 90 percent of the base erosion from zero-rating of food, new homes and repairs, and from exempting energy, water and sanitation would benefit families with economic incomes greater than $10,000.[7]

It is this lack of cost efficiency which has led the Canadian government to recommend *against* exemptions for dealing with regressivity:

> . . . Exempting food and clothing from sales tax gives higher-income people a greater absolute tax benefit than those at lower income levels. This is because higher-income people spend more on food and clothing, in particular, more on expensive foods and clothing. Thus, tax is not collected from higher-income Canadians, resulting in substantial foregone revenue. This puts upward pressure on the overall tax rate paid by all.[8]

In addition to the revenue cost, exemptions and zero-rating involve complex distinctions between exempt and non-exempt items and severe administrative problems. If milk is exempt, what about soft drinks? How do supermarkets distinguish between food and

---

[6]Ibid., pp. 85-87.

[7]Ibid, pp. 97, 98.

[8]Wilson, p. 45.

non-food items and among various types of food items?

An alternative to exemption or zero-rating of necessities is to enact a broadbased VAT and make adjustments to the income tax, such as through a refundable income tax credit similar to the earned income credit. The Canadian government, after citing the problems with exemptions, prefers this route:

> Credits overcome this problem. They are flexible. They can be targeted directly to those in need and adjusted for family size. They can be paid regularly and in advance of expenditures by households.[9]

Currently the states of Hawaii, Massachusetts, New Mexico and Vermont have refundable credits to lessen the regressivity of state sales taxes.[10] Assuming a 10 percent VAT rate, the Treasury calculated that, for a family of four, a $971 credit would be necessary to remove the VAT from essential expenditures for those below the poverty line. The credit for a head of household would be larger than that for each dependent. The VAT credit could be targeted to whatever income group policymakers deemed appropriate. If the poverty level credit of $971 were available to everyone, it would absorb 25 percent of the tax revenue. If, however, it were phased out between the poverty level and 150 percent of the poverty level, only about 5 percent of revenue would be lost.[11]

If a credit of this type were based on 100 percent of the poverty level, Treasury estimates that 10.5 percent of economic income would be paid in value-added taxes by families under $10,000 and 7.8 percent by families between $10,000 and $15,000. This would cost the government 4.8 percent of tax revenue. If the credit were based on 150 percent of the poverty level, 8.7 percent of income would be paid as value-added taxes by families under $10,000 and 7.1 percent by families between $10,000 and $15,000. This would cost the Treasury 7.2 percent of VAT revenue.[12]

A refundable income tax credit appears to be a cost-effective way of dealing with regressivity and avoids the problem of distortion of consumer choices associated with exemptions or zero-rating. There are, however, several problems which would arise in other areas as a result of using a tax credit approach.

---

[9]Ibid.

[10]Treasury, p. 102.

[11]Ibid., p. 103.

[12]Ibid., p. 111. Not all the effects of the VAT are removed by the credit, according to the Treasury. First of all, low income families may borrow and spend beyond their incomes and, second, the credit is targeted to remove the effects of the VAT from essential consumption only.

One such problem is that an objective of the Tax Reform Act of 1986 was to remove low income taxpayers from the tax rolls. To receive VAT credit refunds, many low income families not currently filing income tax returns would once again have to file. A significant number of individuals who are eligible for a refund probably would fail to file.

There also will be timing problems with a tax credit. Expenditures on necessities occur throughout the tax year, but refunds presumably would be distributed after the end of the tax year. The equity of this timing seems questionable.

Another problem concerns the economic effects of any phaseout of the credit for higher income levels. A phaseout is necessary to properly target the credit and minimize the revenue loss. However, this produces some serious consequences for effective marginal tax rates similar to those which will occur under the phaseouts in the Tax Reform Act of 1986. If the VAT credit is phased out between the poverty level and 150 percent of that level, a family of four's VAT credit would be reduced by $154 for every $1,000 of new income over the phaseout range.[13] This is equivalent to an additional marginal tax rate of 15 percent. For families above the poverty line, the post-1986 marginal income tax rate is 15 percent. Thus, over the phaseout range, the effective marginal rate of tax would be 30 percent. This is a very high marginal tax rate which could have serious consequences in terms of labor supply among low income individuals.

Agriculture

One sector of an economy that is often given special treatment is agriculture. This is partially due to the perceived compliance problems and costs in the industry and partially due to the relationship between food costs and regressivity.

European systems generally offer special treatment to farmers. In Britain, a zero rate is applied to food, animal feeds, and livestock which ultimately end up as food for people. On the continent, there is a system of "global offset," which essentially results in a zero rate for the intermediate stage of agriculture. Farmers are exempt from tax, but to prevent a cascading of tax, those who purchase from farmers are allowed a "constructive input tax credit" which approximates the VAT contained in the inputs to farmers.[14]

---

[13]Ibid., p. 105.

[14]American Bar Association, *Report of the Special Committee on the Value-Added*

There will probably be considerable political pressure in the U.S. to afford special treatment to farmers, either independently or as part of a small business exemption. The Treasury states: "In general, it is not feasible to simply treat farmers and agricultural products in the same fashion as other segments of the economy."[15] It is often claimed that small farmers do not keep sales tax records (although they are subject to the income tax) and, therefore, there would be significant compliance problems if a VAT were applied to them.

In addition, the Treasury argues that a large portion of farm produce is exported (although in very few cases are exports a majority of an individual farmer's sales). Thus, the revenue potential from the farm sector is diminished to the extent of export activity from which all value-added taxes will be removed.

The American Bar Association's report disagreed with the Treasury's view:

> In the view of the Committee, neither the British nor the continental approach is proper for the United States. Because of our preference for a broader tax base, we believe food should be subject to tax. If the effect of including such necessities as food in the value-added tax base is considered to be regressive and is objectionable on that ground, we propose that such effect be overcome by a credit administered through the income tax system. We believe that the Continental approach is unnecessary in this country, since U.S. farmers are accustomed to paying income taxes and maintaining records which will permit them to collect value-added tax like other businessmen.[16]

With the exception of very small farmers who should be treated like other small businessmen, it is unclear why the agricultural sector should get special treatment. Still, the political pressures for preferential treatment may be great.

Small Business

It is common in countries that have a VAT to exempt small businesses from this tax. In Europe, the business income levels exempted are fairly low. In many countries, such as Sweden, the U.K. and Denmark, the exemption levels are for entities with less

---

Tax of the Tax Section of the American Bar Association (Washington, D.C.: American Bar Association, 1977), p. 61.

[15]Treasury, p. 61. The Treasury estimates the number of small farmers in the U.S., those with gross receipts under $25,000, to be 2.2 million of the 3.2 million farmers.

[16]American Bar Association, p. 61.

than $2,000 in annual sales. On the higher end are countries such as
Belgium which exempts firms with less than approximately $45,000
in sales from value-added taxes. Canada exempts firms with less
than about $40,000 in sales from its current manufacturers excise
tax. Throughout the world, only very small firms typically are
exempt from indirect taxes such as the VAT.[17]

The standard argument in favor of a small firm exemption is that
small businesses do not maintain adequate records and that there
would be serious problems with compliance. Indeed the position of
the American Bar Association is:

> We recognize that it may be necessary, for administrative convenience, to
> provide some VAT relief for small traders whose annual turnover from
> sales and services is below a statutory minimum. In order to minimize
> possible economic distortions resulting from this relief provision, we
> recommend that the minimum annual turnover be set at a low level.[18]

The Treasury argues that the small business exemption is not as
crucial in the United States:

> [T]he case for exemption of small firms is not nearly as strong in the
> United States. Regular retailers, no matter how small, have learned to
> keep records adequately for complying with income, social security, and
> state retail tax requirements. The states do not exempt small firms, per
> se, and state tax officials, in general, report that the problems of small
> firms without adequate records is not significant.[19]

As is the case with exemptions in general, exemption of small
business can cause economic distortions. As will be explained in a
later section, exemption at an intermediate stage under an invoice
and credit system can have the perverse effect of cascading the tax
to the point where the exempt firm is at a competitive disadvantage.
On the other hand, under a simple subtraction system, exempt firms
would be at a competitive advantage because, at the exempt stage,
one level of value added would escape taxation.

Other Potential Exemptions

Exemptions are also urged with respect to entities generally free
from other forms of taxation, including governments and non-profit
organizations. In some cases, these entities compete directly with
taxable entities, and distortions can occur when special treatment is
afforded. Special treatment decisions in these areas generally are

---

[17]Treasury, p. 59.

[18]American Bar Association, p. 209.

[19]Treasury, p. 61.

based on social policy concerns, technical issues, and maintenance of competitive balance between like activities.

Implications of Zero-Rating Versus Exemption

Within the confines of the traditional analysis, it is clear that there are major differences in the way in which different forms of preferential treatment affect the economy. Consider the difference between zero-rating and exemption in an invoice and credit system.

If a product is exempt, sales of the product are not taxed. Because the product is outside the VAT system, however, no credits are allowed for the inputs which were used to produce the exempt product. If the exemption occurs at the retail level, the effect is to remove the final layer of value added from tax. But because no input credits are allowed, all previous layers of the VAT are still imbedded in the price. Thus, an exempt product can still be subject to considerable amounts of tax.

If the exemption occurs at an intermediate stage, the anomalous result is that the tax burden is actually increased: "Tax-exempt sales lead to tax cascading -- some elements of the total value of a product are taxed twice."[20] The cascading occurs because of a break in the chain of credits:

> An exempt firm pays no tax on sales but can take no credit for taxes paid on inputs. Yet its customers must pay tax on the full amount of their sales and have no tax on inputs for which to take credit. Because of this break in the chain of credits, the total tax is actually increased by the exemption.[21]

This cascading of the tax puts exempt firms at a competitive disadvantage. Supplies from exempt firms contain some double taxation while supplies from taxable firms contain only one layer of taxation. The result of exemptions may be generalized economic distortions:

> Tax exempt sales lead to a discrepancy in the effective tax rate between a particular product and its competition by disrupting the uniform application of the multi-stage tax. Variable effective rates cause prices of comparable products to differ, distorting consumer perceptions of their respective values and giving some products and producers an unfair, tax-induced advantage.[22]

---

[20]Wilson, p. 39.

[21]Charles McLure, *The Value Added Tax* (Washington, D.C.: American Enterprise Institute, 1987), p. 73.

[22]Wilson, p. 39.

Thus, the problem with exemption is that, if applied at the retail level, it only eliminates the tax on the last layer of value added and, if applied at an intermediate stage, it results in tax cascading that can actually increase the overall tax burden.

The alternative to exemption is zero-rating. If a zero rate is applied to sales, then tax on inputs is creditable. All tax on all layers of value added is removed if the zero rate is applied at the retail level. If, however, the zero rate occurs at an intermediate stage, there is no economic change, at least under the traditional analysis. Since all tax is assumed to be passed forward, zero-rating at a given *stage* simply allows the tax to be picked up at the next stage. The tax will apply to the full price at the next stage and because the previous stage was zero-rated, there will be no input credits. Thus, all tax removed at the zero-rated stage is picked up at a later stage.

Under the traditional analysis, a zero rate at the retail stage removes all tax from the final purchase price. If the zero rate occurs at an intermediate stage, the final purchase price will be the same as if there was no zero rate at all.

There is a tradeoff between zero-rating and exemption under the traditional analysis relating to compliance costs. For a firm to be zero-rated, it must be registered and keep records. Once it is decided that preferential treatment is desired, the determination whether to zero-rate or exempt an activity depends on whether or not it is desirable to exclude firms from filing requirements, and whether or not it is important to fully free the good from the VAT or to only partially remove the tax.

The choice of the type of VAT can have some effect on the functioning of exemptions or zero rates, although problems associated with the subtraction method are often overstated. In its simplest form, where all purchases are deductible, there is no difference between zero rating and exemption. If a firm is exempt or zero-rated, the associated layer of value added is not taxed. There has been no serious proposal, however, that ever adopted this simplistic approach. (Senator Roth's Business Transfer Tax proposal disallowed deductions with respect to sales of exempt goods.)

It is clear that a subtraction VAT can be modified to accommodate zero rating. First, a distinction must be made between exempt or non-exempt supplies, and registration of taxpayers may be necessary for compliance purposes. A zero rate would be achieved by exempting sales receipts from the product in question, while allowing deduction of inputs from all registered taxpayers. Of course, the stricter the registration requirements, the more the subtraction method begins to function like an invoice and credit system:

Compliance with the sophisticated subtraction method might be slightly less onerous than compliance with the credit method. Under the credit method invoices or receipts for sales to registered taxpayers must identify VAT paid so that the purchaser must record credits as well as purchases. Under the sophisticated subtraction method the seller need only record whether tax has been paid on a given sale, since only tax-paid purchases are allowed as a deduction. The purchaser must, of course, record deductible and nondeductible purchases separately.[23]

Whereas both the subtraction and invoice and credit systems are capable of operating under exemptions and zero rates, only the invoice and credit system can readily accommodate multiple rates.

ECONOMIC EFFECTS UNDER AN ALTERNATIVE ANALYSIS

The alternative analysis concludes that a VAT is *not* a tax on goods and services which is borne only by consumers, but is a tax on factor incomes whose incidence is shared by the owners of capital, the suppliers of labor, and consumers. Under a broad-based VAT, income from capital and labor is taxed proportionately and at the same rate among all firms. Expensing costs of physical capital at an individual firm level is necessary to prevent a cascading of tax on capital. Viewed from this perspective, special treatments which erode the VAT base lead to differential rates of tax on capital and labor among industries, and predictable economic inefficiencies would follow. When a VAT is viewed as a proportionate tax on factor incomes, the analysis of different effective rates of tax is similar to the analysis of different rates of tax in an income tax.

Regressivity

Exempting or zero-rating the sales of necessities to address regressivity has much less merit as a socially/economically essential step from the alternative perspective. Since incidence is not considered to fall solely on consumers, the presumption of regressivity cannot be sustained as a general policy. Shared incidence would place a substantial burden on owners of capital (which tend to be middle and upper income households) and on labor (which spreads across all income levels), rather than solely on consumers in general and consumers of necessities in particular.

---

[23]McLure, p. 79.

Agriculture/Small Business

Removing or lessening the VAT liability for small businesses and for farmers also seems much less economically rational when a VAT is found to be a proportionate tax on capital and labor as well as on consumers. The complexities and administrative burdens of payroll taxes and income taxes have not been found to justify exemptions from those taxes. Furthermore, the link between farming and food is not relevant given that it is not "food" *per se* which is taxable, but rather the factors of production related to agriculture and food processing.

Neutrality and Equity

Instead of addressing these traditional issues, proponents of the alternative analysis argue that two basic economic concepts are critical -- tax neutrality/economic efficiency and tax equity among firms.

The underlying tenet of tax neutrality is that the market is the most efficient allocator of resources. When individuals and companies are free to make choices based on undistorted costs and rewards, such as rates of return and wages, economic well-being is maximized. When the relative costs or rewards facing economic actors are distorted by taxes, then decisions are based on tax consequences and not on underlying economics. The result can be less than optimal for society. One factor of production may be used excessively or investment may be greater than warranted in one industry so that resources are wasted.

For example, consider an investment in Industry A which yields a 10 percent return pre-tax and an investment in Industry B which yields 7 percent pre-tax. From society's point of view, it is better to invest a dollar in Industry A than in Industry B since A yields a higher return. But what if B is exempt from taxes entirely and A is subject to a 50 percent effective tax rate? B still yields 7 percent but the after-tax rate of return to A is reduced to 5 percent. To the private investor, Industry B is preferred to Industry A, even though A is preferred by society. The result of the tax system is to encourage over investment in B, resulting in less output than could be the case if the market were to decide where investment should occur.

In the context of a VAT, if incidence falls only on consumers, then exemptions or zero rating may distort consumer choices, but should have no bearing on the efficient allocation of the capital stock. But if shared incidence is the correct analysis, then allocative efficiency is as important in a VAT context as with any other tax.

If a firm is exempt from value-added taxes and all other market conditions are unchanged, that firm faces a lower cost of capital and a lower cost of labor than similarly situated firms not eligible for the exemption. In general, this would lead to over investment in exempt firms. Recall, however, that exemption at an intermediate stage results in a cascading of tax. Thus, even though an exempt firm has a lower cost of capital and labor, demand for its products will be lessened because purchasing firms will receive no input tax credits. Exemption at the retail stage will lower the cost of factors to the retailer and, to the extent that the tax is shifted forward, distort consumer choice as well.

Zero-rating has the effect of removing tax from the cost of capital and labor for the zero-rated firm, and all suppliers to the zero-rated firm. Zero-rating at the retail level, once it works its way back through the production chain, can clearly distort allocative decisions among entire sectors. For instance, if retail sales of clothing were zero-rated, the result would be over investment in all firms that supply the apparel industry.

This issue was one of the principal topics of debate during consideration of the Tax Reform Act of 1986. It was felt that elimination of differentials in effective marginal income tax rates for investments in different assets or industries would lead to a more efficient capital stock. One risk in accepting the traditional analysis on incidence is that the allocation effects of exemptions or zero rates may not be perceived.

The second issue is horizontal equity: firms in like situations should face the same tax consequences. If only consumers bear the burden of a VAT, the issue of horizontal equity among companies is non-existent. But if the VAT is partially borne by capital, the issue becomes crucial. During the 1986 tax reform debate, a split in the business community developed between "high" effective tax rate payers and "low" effective tax rate payers. A similar gulf could exist in a VAT world with exemptions and zero or multiple rates.

6

PROBLEMS OF TRANSITION TO A VALUE-ADDED TAX

by David G. Raboy
and Cliff Massa III

The United States has not had much recent experience with implementing a new tax system which required a significant degree of transition planning. The last major tax system to be introduced in the U.S. was the payroll tax enacted more than 50 years ago to fund the Social Security system. Imposing such a tax on limited amounts of wages and salaries beginning on a fixed date did not present substantial transition issues such as retroactive application of the tax or inequitable treatment of particular employers or employees.

Transition issues tend to be much more significant when taxes are imposed on capital or on income from capital which has been acquired prior to the imposition of the tax. The income tax on corporations and, to a lesser extent, on individuals is such a tax on capital. But the income tax was first introduced more than 70 years ago. If transition issues were of concern at that time, such considerations have long since faded from institutional memories, both within and outside government.

Attention to substantial transition issues has not been a routine matter in value-added tax (VAT) debates, probably as a result of the wide acceptance of traditional analysis. The presumption that a VAT is a tax on the sale of goods and services which is ultimately borne by the consumer avoids significant transitional issues. Goods sold after a certain date are taxed, and those sold before that date are not. As tax collectors and remitters, businesses are indifferent to all but a few transition questions involving sales which "straddle" the effective date of the tax and therefore could affect a company's ability to collect from the consumer what the company must remit to the government.

However, transitional relief issues are particularly important under the alternative analysis of the value-added tax. If a VAT is a tax on capital and labor services (which are the components of the value added of each firm), equity among taxpayers requires careful attention to the equitable application of the tax to value added arising after a certain date. Value added which is attributable to physical capital that was acquired before the implementation of the tax would be taxed more heavily than similar value added arising from physical capital which is acquired after the effective date.

This and related issues can be found in every industry to varying degrees, because physical capital is used in even the most labor-intensive businesses. But the problems are magnified for industries which have long-lived capital and/or which utilize resources for which the value added is created in small increments over very long periods.

This chapter will consider the transition issues which are posed by the implementation of a VAT under both the traditional and alternative analyses. The latter discussion will obviously be the longer of the two. The chapter will also present particular transition problems associated with certain industries which utilize natural resources and physical capital with long useful lives.

TRANSITION ISSUES

Since the VAT is an entirely new tax system for the United States, transition issues should be viewed differently from transition issues which arise during implementation of changes to the existing income tax system. There are few, if any, income tax transition issues which are decided on the basis of pure public finance theory. Income tax transition issues tend to be decided based on a combination of factors which generally include political power and "fairness."

For example, when cost recovery rules are revised, binding contract provisions are generally written to govern the treatment of newly acquired equipment. These transition rules are desirable as a means of minimizing the unfairness and inequities of changing the tax law after orders are placed for new equipment. Nonetheless, there is not much basis for arguing that tax theory requires such treatment.

When an entirely new tax system is introduced, however, transition issues deserve added analysis so that the inevitable political decisions are made in an informed environment. The box on page 106 lists a number of transition issues which could arise during the consideration of a VAT. The list has been divided into two groups. The "Straddle Issues" are relevant under both the traditional view of the VAT as a tax on goods and services and the alternative analysis of a VAT as a tax on each individual company's value added. But the more difficult issues are those which arise only under the alternative analysis. These are listed under the heading "Pre-Existing Value-Added Issues."

TRANSITION ISSUES FROM THE TWO ANALYTICAL PERSPECTIVES

These transition issues have differing impacts depending on the observer's analytical perspective of the VAT. Horizontal equity among companies is not a relevant issue under the traditional analysis, as has been discussed in some detail in Chapter 4. Therefore, differing remittance liabilities attributable to pre-existing stocks of inventory and capital are not sources of concern. However, such matters are of great concern under the alternative analysis. Before discussing the precise problems in more detail, a quick overview is offered.

The Traditional Consideration of Transition Issues

The traditional analysis generates relatively minor transition issues because it concludes that a VAT is a tax on goods and, therefore, is a tax which is borne by consumers. For example, imposing a VAT on the sale of widgets after December 31, 1990 would not create competitive inequities among producers and distributors of widgets because neither they, their shareholders nor their employees would bear any of the burden of the tax. The producer or retailer which had an ample inventory of widgets on December 31, 1990 would bear no additional tax burden when it sold those widgets in 1991 under a new VAT system. The company would simply increase its price to collect the VAT on its sales of pre-existing inventory, just as would the producer or retailer of widgets which acquires all of its inventory in 1991.

The general acceptance of this analysis likely explains the absence of extensive discussions of transition issues in the public finance literature. For example, the Treasury's volume on value-

VAT TRANSITION ISSUES

Straddle Concerns

- **Binding contracts which determine prices:** Contracts to sell goods for a specified unit price both before and after the effective date of a new VAT could prohibit a price increase which might take the VAT into account.
- **Cash basis seller/accrual basis purchaser:** A cash basis taxpayer sells goods to an accrual basis taxpayer before the effective date of a tax. The payments are made after the effective date. The seller is taxable on the receipt of payment, but the purchaser is not allowed a deduction (or credit) for its purchase, thereby creating a "cascading" effect which taxes the same goods/value added twice.
- **Accrual basis seller/cash basis purchaser:** An accrual basis tax-payer sells goods to a cash basis purchaser before the effective date. The purchaser pays for the goods after the effective date. The seller is not taxable on the sale of goods because such sale occurred before the effective date. However, the purchaser is allowed a deduction (credit) for which there is no corresponding taxable receipt in the system, thereby creating a benefit with respect to untaxed value added.
- **Prepaid/partially paid purchases:** Payment terms and business practices of a company or industry may require full or partial prepayments for goods, resulting in the payment falling before the effective date with acquisition or receipt of goods occurring after that date. Differences in accounting methods will produce differing results.

Pre-Existing Value-Added Issues

- **Capital assets acquired prior to the effective date:** Capital assets (e.g., equipment, structures, land, mineral rights, patents, etc.) acquired prior to the effective date of a new tax will continue to be used by a taxpayer after the effective date. Because such prior costs would not be deductible (creditable), post-effective-date value-added tax payments may be substantially overstated for affected companies.
- **Supplies and other non-capital assets acquired before the effective date:** Fuel, raw materials, components, spare parts and other such non-capital items acquired before the effective date will be included in the production and distribution of goods which will be subject to the VAT after the effective date. As with capital assets, the VAT will be imposed on the first taxpayer to use such items after the effective date, thereby overstating the taxpayer's value-added.
- **Inherent value of items involving long gestation periods or appreciation over time:** A substantial portion of the value added with respect to natural resources is either produced over a long period

of years, such as is the case for growing timber, or is inherent in the item itself due to appreciation over time, such as mineral deposits. For goods sold after the implementation of a VAT, substantial value added will be attributable to the years before the implementation of the tax.

added taxes does not address the subject at all. There appear to be no significant papers on this subject from European observers -- probably because the traditional analysis is generally accepted. Further, in most cases, the European VATs were replacing cascading turnover taxes which already imposed multiple levels of taxes on sales of goods.

The Canadian experience to date has included somewhat more attention to potential transition issues, although government documents still tend to be limited to discussions of "straddle" issues:

> Special rules will be required to ensure fair treatment of transactions which straddle the implementation date. For example, payment may be received prior to the implementation date but delivery of the goods or services may occur after that date. On the other hand, payment may be received on or after implementation but the delivery may be before. Rules will be developed to define clearly the application of the new tax to such transactions.[1]

These issues, plus the issue of rebates on previously paid manufacturers excise taxes, are the only transition issues acknowledged by the Canadian tax documentation. The documentation states, however, that ". . . no general exemption will be provided for existing contracts entered into prior to release of the implementing legislation. Given the considerable time that will elapse between the release of the legislation and the implementation date, most taxpayers should be able to arrange their affairs to take the new tax system into account."[2]

Thus, the transition issues which arise under the traditional analysis appear to be very manageable. The only policy decision to be made is how to treat transactions which straddle the effective date.

Transition Issues Under the Alternative Analysis

The alternative analysis of incidence raises substantially broader

---

[1]Michael H. Wilson, *Tax Reform 1987, Sales Tax Reform* (Canada: Department of Finance, 1987), p. 108.

[2]Ibid., pp. 107, 108.

transition issues in addition to the straddle concerns. This analysis considers a VAT to be a tax on the components of value added -- the payments for labor services and for capital services -- which results in *shared incidence* among consumers, employees and share-holders/lenders.

Horizontal Inequities. From this perspective, the imposition of a tax on value added after a specified date which does not replace equivalent tax structures poses problems with respect to the taxation of value added that is created by the use of capital assets which were acquired before the effective date. Absent a credit or deduction for the prior acquisition of capital assets, the company's post-effective date value added may be artificially increased in comparison to its competitors which made lesser capital acquisitions prior to the new tax.   Therefore, from the alternative perspective, it is likely that there will be substantial horizontal inequities, both among com-panies within an industry and particularly among industries which have differing investment patterns and useful lives for capital investments.

The potential impact of these issues was first identified when Senator Roth's Business Transfer Tax (BTT), introduced in 1985, was subjected to analysis by corporate tax executives.   This BTT proposal made no provision for transition rules. Many large corpo-rations were asked to estimate their remittance liabilities by using a simple tax form which took into account all of the features of the BTT. These estimates were based on a prior year's experience using information which was generally available from income tax compu-tations for that year.[3]

The results were stunning in many cases. Some capital-intensive companies reported very high liabilities while similar companies did not. Although these findings were not analyzed scientifically, dis-cussions with numerous executives suggested that the wide variance in tax remittance among ostensibly similar firms was almost cer-tainly the result of different patterns of investment. Absent any transition treatment, companies which were producing goods with the use of capital assets acquired before the base year were com-puting higher liabilities than companies which were deducting substantial new investments in capital assets under the BTT in the base year.

Executives' reactions to the BTT based on such rough computa-

---

[3]Clearly, such computations fail to take into account any adjustments in the economy and, therefore, are subject to criticism for "short cuts" as noted in Chapter 3. However, for purposes of illustrating the impact of acquisitions of capital occurring before and after the effective date, this static analysis was useful.

tions demonstrated that transition treatment can be extremely important, at least in the short run, under the alternative shared incidence analysis. Whether or not there would be a serious long-term effect was not clearly demonstrated.

Mismatching of Deductions and Receipts. Under the alternative analysis, another critical transition issue concerns value added which was created before -- and sometimes *long* before -- the effective date of the tax but which contributes to the value of goods and services sold after the effective date. Within any taxable year, an individual company's value added is defined as the value of goods sold minus the value of all inputs. The purchase of many inputs such as energy, component parts and/or raw materials occurs in the same year (or in an adjacent year) as the sale of the outputs which these inputs are used to produce. Any "mismatching" of deductions and receipts is relatively minor. Although there would be some problems in the year that a VAT is implemented because of the effects of purchases and sales which straddle the effective date, this would not appear to be a substantial problem for the economy as a whole.[4]

While overall effects might be minor with respect to inputs which are quickly used, this is not the case with capital assets such as structures, machinery, equipment, etc. whose contribution to a company's value added will generally occur over several years. Taxable value added in the first few years after enactment of a VAT will generally include amounts attributable to capital assets purchased years earlier. To the extent that this occurs, the users of such capital will pay tax on overstated value added, in comparison to users who acquire such assets after the effective date.

This problem is not limited to pre- and post-effective date purchases of capital assets. Taxpayers who *lease* capital assets would also realize an advantage over competitors who purchase assets prior to the effective date. Lease payments by the capital user would fall within the accounting period in which the capital is used to produce value added and would be deducted accordingly. However, *purchasers* of physical capital who paid for their assets years before the VAT would not be allowed a deduction for their use of capital equipment in adding value to their products.

---

[4]However, there might be a need to provide a type of "averaging rule" which could apply to particularly inequitable situations, such as when a company had acquired substantially more inputs in the year before the effective date of a VAT than was its historical pattern and than is continued in the first year or two under the VAT. Such a "bulge" could be allowed to be spread forward to compensate for the otherwise excessive computation of value added in the early years.

The differences in tax treatment arise solely from tax accounting constraints rather than from any underlying economic differences. Purchasing capital in a given taxable year for use over several years is equivalent to purchasing or "renting" capital services in each separate year. In theory, the acquisition price of a capital asset is equal to the present value of the lease payments which the company would pay over the life of the asset. Thus, there is an "implicit lease payment" by the capital purchaser which is the true price of capital services in any taxable year. Within that year, a firm's value added is defined as the value of sales minus the value of inputs, including the implicit rental price of capital.

Value added can also be correctly measured by allowing the expensing of capital in the taxable year of acquisition, with no further deduction in any subsequent year. Because the price of the capital asset is, by definition, equal to the present value of the implicit lease payments, the two methods are equal in present value terms. Expensing capital purchases would not, however, correct for pre- and post-effective date problems.

Consider the following example involving two identical firms which compete in the same market and sell their goods at the competitively determined price:

> Prior to a VAT implementation, Firm A and Firm B sell 20 units of a single good per year at $10 each. Raw inputs cost each firm $50 annually. Firm A leases capital assets at $50 per year. Firm B has purchased its capital assets and, since capital markets are competitive, bears an implicit lease price of $50 annually. Thus, before the VAT implementation, each firm is producing $100 of value added per year.

Horizontal equity requires that both firms should have the same tax liabilities *after* imposition of a VAT. Two cases will be explored in which a 10 percent subtraction VAT is introduced. The first case assumes that the VAT is fully shifted forward in the price of all goods.[5] The second case assumes that no tax is shifted forward. (Assumptions on tax shifting will not affect the qualitative results.)

> Case 1. The competitively determined price of goods sold by each firm increases to $11.11 as a result of tax shifting. For simplicity, it is assumed that each firm now sells 18 units annually.[6] The price of raw inputs increases to $55.56, and Firm A's lease payment increases to $55.56 because the lessor is subject to the VAT. Firm B still faces an implicit lease payment of $50 since its capital was purchased prior to the VAT

---

[5] In Chapter 3, it was shown that even a tax fully shifted in price can result in a shared incidence. Thus, even if firms fully shift the tax, an argument can still be made that the VAT should be viewed as a tax on company value added.

[6] Unitary elasticity is assumed.

implementation.

Firm A has actual value added of $88.86 (receipts of $199.98 less raw inputs of $55.56 and lease payments of 55.56). Firm A's taxable value added is also $88.86. It remits $8.89 in VAT.

Including the implicit lease payment of only $50, Firm B's actual value added is $94.42. But because it receives no capital deduction, its taxable value added is $144.42. It remits VAT of $14.44.

Thus, two identical firms have very different tax liabilities. The effective rate of tax, i.e., the ratio of tax liability to actual value added, is 10 percent for Firm A, but 15.3 percent for Firm B.

Firm B's "economic" capital cost of $50 annually represents value which was created before the effective date of the tax *by the producer who sold the capital to Firm B*, not by Firm B itself. The reason Firm B has a higher tax liability is that it is being taxed on its own value added, *plus* the value added attributable to its capital supplier but which it is not able to deduct. The horizontal inequity is a result of including in the tax base the capital supplier's value added which was produced before the effective date but is being included in the tax base of Firm B.

Case 2. Each firm continues to sell 20 units of output at $10 per unit and has raw input costs of $50. Firm A has a deductible lease payment for capital assets of $50 to produce actual and taxable value added of $100 per period. It remits $10 in tax. Firm B has nondeductible capital costs of $50. Thus, its actual value added is $100, but its taxable value added is $150. It remits $15 in VAT.

Firm A's effective tax rate is 10 percent, but Firm B's is 15 percent. Once again, the difference in effective tax rates is caused by the taxation of value added which was produced before the effective date.

If horizontal equity is important, then a theoretical answer to this problem would be to remove previously produced value added from the tax base. This would require an annual deduction for the implicit lease price of capital which was in service on the effective date of the VAT. Under Case 1, Firm B would still have a slightly higher tax liability than Firm A ($9.42 as opposed to $8.89), but the effective tax rates would be the same. Under Case 2 both tax liabilities and effective tax rates would be the same.

TRANSITION ISSUES AS A PRACTICAL MATTER

This type of transition issue exists any time inputs are purchased before the effective date and aid in the production of value added after the effective date. In some cases, however, the problem is less serious than in others. For example, quantities of components or raw materials purchased in a given time period probably will be relatively constant if production levels are relatively constant or follow a normal trend. Thus, if components or materials are used within a one-year lag following purchase, this year's sales will be includible in this year's gross receipts and purchases of next year's inputs (approximately equal to this year's inputs) will be deductible. After the effective date, the measurement of value added will be approximately correct even though inputs purchased before the effective date are not deductible. At worst, there will be a one-time loss of the time value of money associated with inputs purchased just prior to the effective date. Any time the supply of inputs is "smooth," as a practical matter, no major transition problem should exist.[7]

A more substantial transition problem exists when the supply of inputs is "lumpy," as is the case for purchases of capital assets in some industries. Company or industry factors may dictate that a large new capital expenditure is made, with only replacement purchases occurring in subsequent years. At a later date, a new "net" investment may be required. If the initial capital expenditure occurs before the effective date of a VAT, the company or industry will not be able to take a corresponding level of deductions until well after the effective date.

There are two general types of investments which occur in this pattern. The first involves large capital expenditures, principally in basic industries. For example, a steel company will build a basic oxygen furnace facility or a continuous slab operation. An oil company will build a refinery. Another affected industry could be the airlines which acquire new fleets of aircraft when new technologies and efficiencies are available. No company makes annual investments of this magnitude. If such large investments are made shortly before a VAT introduction, a severe transition problem will arise.[8]

A company may also make internal investments with very long gestation periods. For example, an energy company's acquisition of mineral rights may require that substantial investments be made for 5 to 10 years before the effective date of a VAT. Or a timber-producing company's planting and nurturing of trees is a process which

---

[7]For the extraordinary situations, some averaging rule might be appropriate. See Footnote 5 above.

[8]The problem arises only when sales continue to grow at a reasonably steady rate while investment occurs in uneven spurts. If sales flatten or fall in conjunction with reduced investments, then the problem is minimized or eliminated.

involves continuous production of value added over even longer periods. If a VAT is implemented without transition treatment, it would be possible, in effect, to retroactively tax timber producers for up to 30 years of value added.

PATTERNS OF INDUSTRY INVESTMENT

To develop a sense of the industries potentially affected by transition effects, it is necessary to observe the data on industry investment. However, while this data will present a general picture of affected industries, it may be misleading because individual firm investments can vary within an industry. Therefore, it is also instructive to look at these particular company situations.

As a practical matter, companies which have steady or increasing levels of investment likely would not be viewed by policymakers as hardship or inequity cases, as long as annual investment is at or above previous levels of investment. Large current deductions for new investment after the effective date would offset receipts from sales, even if the costs of capital assets which produced the goods were nondeductible. Thus, even if value added were not properly measured due to a lack of deduction for pre-existing capital, such companies would not be disadvantaged.

The problem would be most acute for companies whose previous capital investments greatly exceed investments after the effective date. Large amounts of sales receipts generated from pre-existing capital assets would be fully taxable in the absence of sufficient deductions associated with correspondingly large new investments. It is these situations which are likely to draw the most sympathetic political attention.

The Appendix to this chapter provides data on investment and economic activity on an industry by industry basis. The results of this analysis suggest that, while for most industries transition is not a problem, there have been industries that could have faced severe problems if a VAT were implemented at certain crucial times in their history.

Probably the most extreme example of an industry which would have faced a serious transition problem is that of the petroleum production industry. This industry was characterized by massive plant and equipment expenditures in the mid- to late-1970s. Investment has fallen off in the 1980s, but the capital previously put into place continues to produce massive amounts of value added. This is depicted in Figure 6-1 below. If a VAT had been imple-

Figure 6-1

**CAPITAL EXPENDITURE AND VALUE ADDED IN THE
PETROLEUM PRODUCTION INDUSTRY**
($ billions)

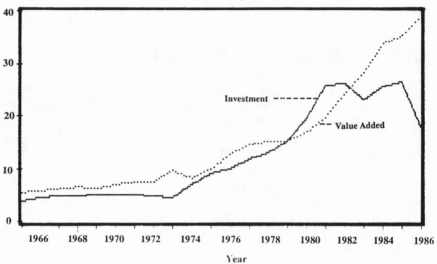

Source: Value added is GNP by industry as reported in the *Survey of Current Business*. Investment data is
           also from the Commerce Department.

mented in the mid-1980s, this industry as a whole would have encountered serious transition problems as indicated by the wide
divergence between the continuing increase in value added and the
flat or declining capital expenditures in the decade.   Similar
problems of a lesser magnitude would have existed for the airplane
manufacturing industry and the stone, clay and glass manufacturing
industry, as illustrated in the Appendix.

PROBLEMS FACED BY REGULATED SECTORS

To this point, transition issues have been considered for companies whose prices are generally set in a market environment. An
entirely separate area of concern involves companies whose output
prices are set by regulatory agencies. In addition, there are many
cases in which new unregulated entrants will compete with large
former monopolies which still yield considerable price-setting power
and are still subject to price regulation.

Utilities often have their prices set by public utility commissions
(PUCs). Such companies are allowed to recover all costs and earn a

specified rate of return. Generally, taxes are included in the costs of providing services and tax changes trigger rate changes after the utility files a request for a rate adjustment to the PUC. Intrastate rates are set, generally, by state PUCs. Interstate rates may be set by the Federal Energy Regulatory Commission. A company operating in many states will have to file a rate case in each separate jurisdiction. The PUC's response often will depend on local economic and political considerations.

Thus, if a federal VAT were implemented, a regulated utility would have to file for rate increases in all states in which it operates. The response of PUCs may vary, and each PUC's perception of the incidence of the VAT may affect the outcome. It is by no means certain that the responses will be consistent. The lag between VAT implementation and PUC action may also vary from state to state.

An industry which is in a state of disequilibrium due to recent deregulation is another important special case. The former monopolist typically still enjoys market power and is the industry leader. In some cases, where the former monopolist's prices are still set by regulation, the set price may be lower than that required to maximize its profits. The new entrant, on the other hand, may have to sell at a discount in order to be competitive. (In many cases, the new entrant's price will be set by the market, not by regulation.) Customer loyalty, technological difficulties, and other factors facing new entrants may result in consumer demand which is more sensitive to price changes than is demand for the leader's products or services. As a result, the new entrant may discount its price to maximize short-term profits (or minimize losses) by increasing its sales volume.

When a VAT is implemented, the industry leader likely will seek a rate increase. Because its prior price is suboptimal, it can successfully recover the tax. The new entrant, however, may not be able to pass the tax forward in price because of its more elastic demand. Thus, one possible consequence would be a disruption of the competitive balance in a newly deregulated industry. This may not be grounds for transition rules, but policymakers should be aware of the special problems of regulated and newly deregulated industries when a new tax is introduced.

GENERAL RULES AND PRACTICAL ANSWERS

This chapter has considered transition problems associated with a VAT when it is viewed as a tax on company value added with a shared incidence.   In general, transition becomes an issue when there is lumpiness in the purchase of inputs -- most notably capital assets and investments involving long gestation periods such as natural resources.

From the perspective of the alternative analysis, a set of theoretical, if not necessarily practical, guidelines for taxation during an implementation period might include the following:

- **Value added should be taxed only once:** A first principle should be to structure offsets in a manner which taxes value added once, but *only* once. This is an obvious anti-cascading principle. It also is essential to developing a VAT system which does not artificially encourage business arrangements motivated solely by a desire to avoid multiple taxation along the production distribution chain. (For example, a firm might vertically integrate from raw material production through final sales to consumers solely to avoid overlapping VAT payments.)

- **A new VAT system should not apply retroactively:** Imposing a new tax system such as VAT on a specific date, preferably with substantial advance preparation, would give ample notice to taxpayers and would represent the fair and equitable means of initiating such a dramatic change. To impose a VAT on value added which arises *before* such date would be undesirable. Therefore, a second principle governing transition rules should be to avoid retroactive taxation of value added.

- **A VAT should result in horizontal equity among firms:** Since the economic incidence of a VAT may be illusive and will likely remain the subject of debate, the compliance mechanisms in a VAT should focus on the initial or remittance incidence in a manner which provides some equity among taxpayers without regard to long-term economic incidence. A general rule would be that the remitting business should be taxed only on its own value added and not on the elements of value added created by its suppliers. Therefore, a third general principle should be to treat all taxpayers the same by requiring them to remit VAT only with respect to their own value added, no matter how large or small a proportion this constitutes of the total value of the goods and services they sell.

Of concern to policymakers should be the retroactive nature of a VAT on long gestation, lumpy investments.   Simply applying the first principle and ignoring the second and third principles would result in severe retroactive taxation of previous value added. Totally relieving prior value added from tax, however, raises obvious practical problems. If all three principles were applied literally, it is conceivable that the VAT would raise little or no money during the transition period.   For instance, a literal application would allow deductions equal to the entire value of the existing capital stock on the date of VAT implementation. Such a result is clearly ludicrous.

The political problems associated with relieving some companies from a sizable tax liability because of pre-existing assets could be difficult. Still, within the traditions of transition treatment in this country, these three principles are tenable. If a deduction for pre-existing capital is unworkable, compromises in certain industries might be warranted. Within the realm of political reality, it may be possible, for instance, to amortize a percentage of existing capital over a period of years. In some industries, or for some firms, a partial deduction for existing capital may be warranted.

APPENDIX: INDUSTRY DATA AND TRANSITION PROBLEMS

This chapter has explored the theoretical implications for transition treatment under the traditional and alternative views of incidence. The chapter implies that, under the alternative analysis, transition is an issue of at least theoretical concern. Potential problems exist when capital acquired prior to the effective date of the new tax, and therefore not deductible, contributes to taxable value added after the effective date.

There is a particular type of pattern which would produce a practical problem of transition. For instance, if an industry undertook massive capital investment, followed by a period of low investment, *and* the rate of output remained high during the lull in investment, *and* a VAT was implemented directly after the capital spending binge, the firm would face a serious transition problem. This confluence of events is necessary to produce a capital transition problem.

Companies which have relatively steady rates of investment, or whose investment levels vary directly with economic output or activity (providing a fairly stable ratio of investment to gross sales), will not have serious transition problems. Companies at risk will be those with steady rates of output but lumpy levels of investment.

In order to see if the type of investment pattern which would produce a transition problem exists in the real world, it is necessary to study industry data on investment and output. Data on capital expenditures by industry comes from the Bureau of Economic Analysis of the Department of Commerce. No data on gross sales by industry exist, so each industry's contribution to GNP was used as a proxy.[9] This is labeled "Value Added" in all the figures. The value

---

[9]An industry's contribution to GNP is its total value added in any year.

added correlates with gross output data and is a good proxy to judge economic activity. GNP data by industry also comes from the Department of Commerce as reported in the *Survey of Current Business*.

Figures 6A-1 through 6A-20 compare trends in capital expenditure to levels of output as measured by contribution to GNP, by industry, from 1965 through 1986. Most industries do not display the peculiar pattern necessary to trigger transition problems. In some notable cases, however, such a pattern is apparent.

In the primary metals industry (Figure 6A-1), investment and output track fairly closely together. As economic activity falls off, so does investment. There is no point during the time series displayed that a VAT implementation would trigger an obvious transition problem.

This is also true of the fabricated metals industry (Figure 6A-2). Here, again, output and investment are highly correlated. When investment drops off after a period of rapid capital expenditure (as in the period 1981-83), output falls off as well. Therefore, even if a VAT were implemented in, say, 1981, no transition problem would have occurred.

Investment in the electrical machinery industry moves with output. There is no obvious pattern that would trigger transition concerns in Figure 6A-3. The same is true of non-electrical machinery in Figure 6A-4.

Investment and output in the motor vehicle industry move cyclically and in tandem. There is one period, between 1978 and 1981, where output is falling dramatically while investment is rising. If a VAT were implemented at the beginning of this period, companies, rather than worrying about inequitable transition burdens, could conceivably have been receiving tax refunds from the government (see Figure 6A-5).

The airplane manufacturing industry (Figure 6A-6), may have encountered some transition problems if a VAT were implemented in, say, 1980. There was a very rapid period of investment between 1977 and 1980. Investment then remained constant or fell from 1980 to 1983. For all intents and purposes, however, investment levels have been flat between 1980 and 1986. Output over the same period, however, has increased rapidly and steadily. Clearly, large amounts of value added are being produced with capital acquired prior to 1980. If transition problems exist, however, they are probably relatively small. Annual investment in this industry is on the order of $3 billion dollars a year while value added is between $30 to $55 billion. Capital investment as a percentage of value added is thus low in this industry, relative to other industries.

A more severe problem exists over the same time period for the stone, clay and glass industry (Figure 6A-7). Investment, in general, is larger in relation to value added then that for airplane manufacturing. Investment expanded rapidly between 1975 and 1980 and has fallen rapidly ever since. After a brief decline during the early 1980s, output expanded rapidly. There is a much wider gulf now (and over the 1980s) between value added and investment than existed historically for the industry. Thus, had a VAT been introduced during the early 1980s, this industry could have exerted pressure for transition relief.

For most of the time period, investment and output have tracked closely in the food production industry (Figure 6A-8). There was a brief dip in investment between 1980 and 1982 but this industry does not seem to be at risk in terms of transition problems. The same holds, in general, for the textile industry (Figure 6A-9). Paper manufacturing (Figure 6A-10) exhibits the same general characteristics as the food production industry with investment and output moving in tandem, except for a brief decline in capital spending between 1980 and 1982. No apparent transition problems are displayed in the history of the chemical manufacturing industry (Figure 6A-11).

On the other hand, the potential for severe transition problems exists in the petroleum production industry (Figure 6A-12). If a VAT had been implemented in the 1980 or 1981, this industry would have faced severe transition problems. Massive new investment was made in petroleum production from 1973 to 1981. In some years, capital expenditures actually exceeded value added. (Capital spending was in excess of $20 billion in some years.) Thereafter, capital spending leveled off and then fell dramatically. In 1986, spending was about two-thirds of what it was in 1980. Large amounts of value added were being created by a capital base put in place during the late 1970s. Over this period, this industry was more at risk for transition problems than any other industry over 21-year time series.

In the rubber manufacturing industry (Figure 6A-13), investment has been more erratic than output. For brief periods of time, investment has been falling while output has been increasing. Still, the type of peculiar investment pattern necessary to cause concern is not evident. In the mining industry (Figure 6A-14), investment and output move in tandem. The same holds true for railroad transportation (Figure 6A-15). Neither industry seems to be at risk.

Investment in the air transportation industry (Figure 6A-16) is a little more erratic, but patterns which would cause transition problems are not evident after 1976. The utilities industry (Figure 6A-17) does not appear to display any suspicious patterns, although investment has flattened slightly since 1982 while output continues to grow steadily.

There is no evidence of potential transition problems in either the wholesale and retail industry (Figure 6A-18) or the financial services industry (Figure 6A-19). This is also true of the communications industry (Figure 6A-20), although there was a brief decline in investment between 1980 and 1982.

Of the 20 industries surveyed, only three displayed the type of investment/output pattern which could have triggered substantial transition problems. These are the airplane manufacturing; stone, clay, and glass; and petroleum production industries. Each would have been at risk if a VAT had been introduced in the early or mid 1980s. Each had experienced a rapid buildup of investment prior to the 1980s, followed by a decline in investment that coincided with rapidly accelerating output (or levels of value added).

These patterns occurred only once in the 21 year history of each industry, and each such occurrence may have been a fluke. Still, the data show that it is possible for entire industries to be at risk to transition problems at given points in time. It is beyond the purview of this study to investigate the investment/output histories of individual firms to check for intra-industry variance, but it is to be expected that individual firms might be caught in a transition trap if a new VAT is introduced in this country.

Figure 6A-1

PRIMARY METALS
(\$ billions)

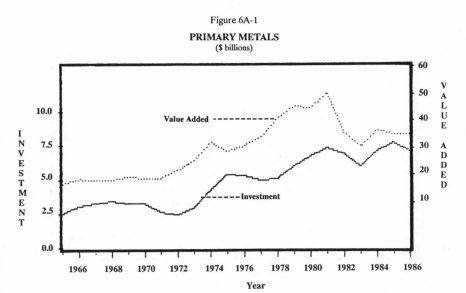

Year

Figure 6A-2

FABRICATED METALS
(\$ billions)

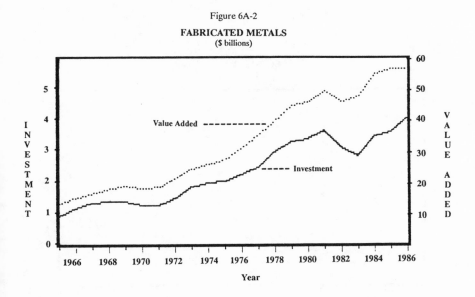

Year

Figure 6A-3

ELECTRICAL MACHINERY
($ billions)

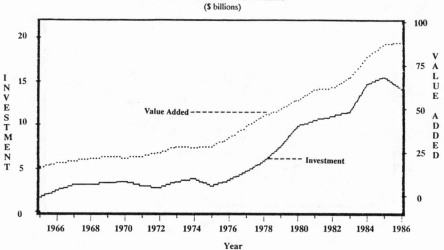

Year

Figure 6A-4

NON-ELECTRICAL MACHINERY
($ billions)

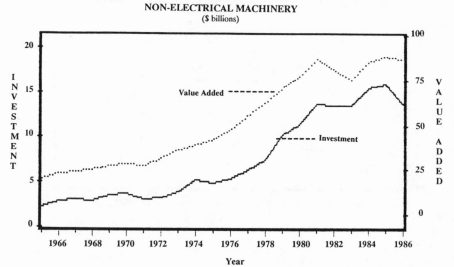

Year

Figure 6A-5

MOTOR VEHICLE MANUFACTURING
($ billions)

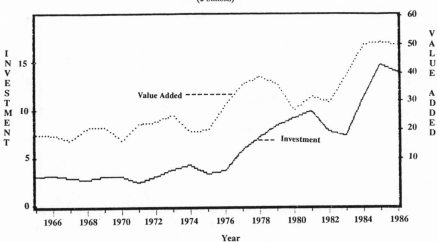

Figure 6A-6

AIRPLANE MANUFACTURING
($ billions)

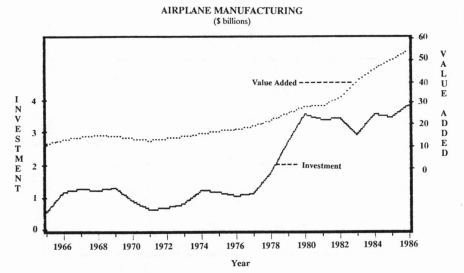

Figure 6A-7

STONE, CLAY AND GLASS
($ billions)

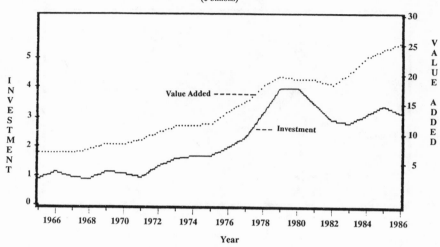

Figure 6A-8

FOOD PRODUCTION
($ billions)

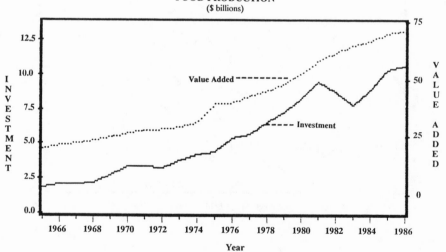

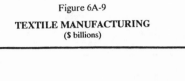

Figure 6A-9

TEXTILE MANUFACTURING
($ billions)

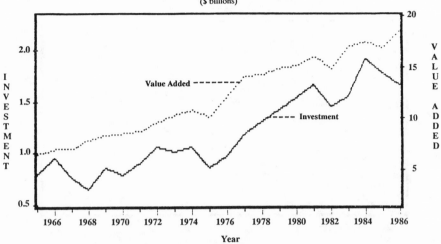

Figure 6A-10

PAPER MANUFACTURING
($ billions)

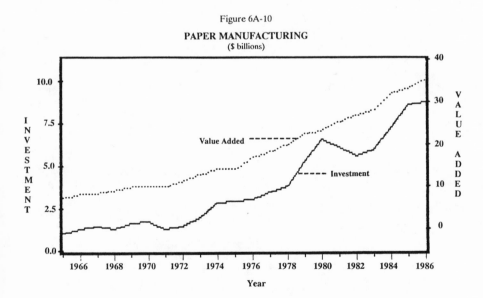

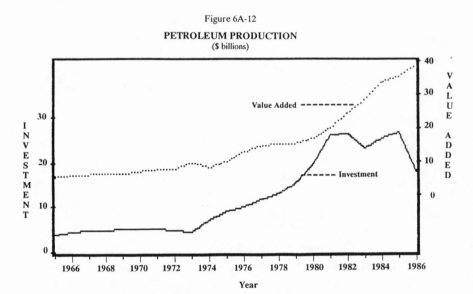

Figure 6A-11

CHEMICAL MANUFACTURING
($ billions)

Figure 6A-12

PETROLEUM PRODUCTION
($ billions)

Figure 6A-13

RUBBER MANUFACTURING
($ billions)

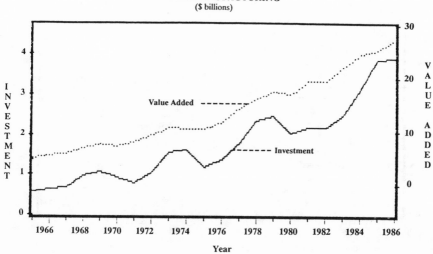

Value Added

Investment

Year

Figure 6A-14

MINING
($ billions)

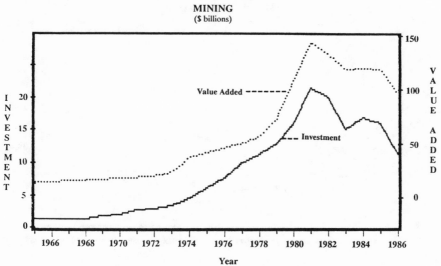

Value Added

Investment

Year

Figure 6A-15

RAILROAD TRANSPORTATION
($ billions)

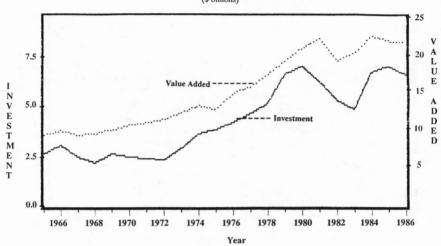

Year

Figure 6A-16

AIR TRANSPORTATION
($ billions)

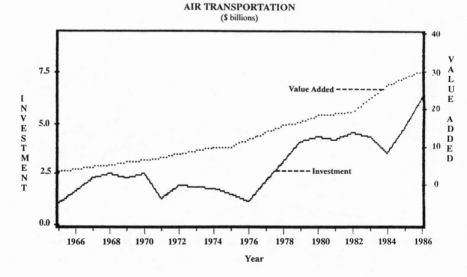

Year

Figure 6A-17

ELECTRIC, GAS AND OTHER UTILITIES
($ billions)

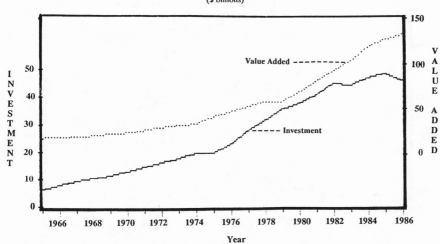

Figure 6A-18

WHOLESALE AND RETAIL
($ billions)

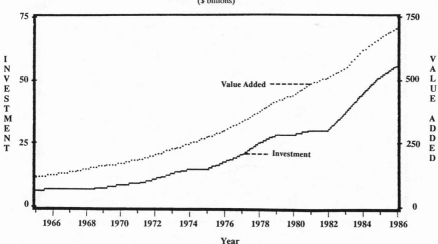

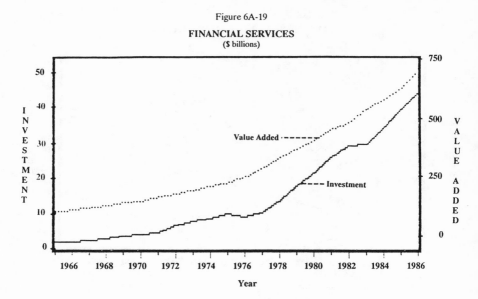

Figure 6A-19

FINANCIAL SERVICES
($ billions)

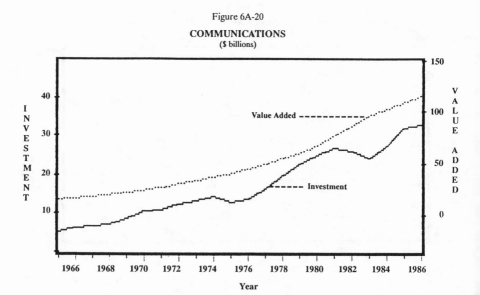

Figure 6A-20

COMMUNICATIONS
($ billions)

7

INTERNATIONAL IMPLICATIONS OF VALUE-ADDED TAXES

by David G. Raboy

Support for enactment of a federal value-added tax (VAT) in the United States is attributable to a substantial degree to the belief that significant international trade benefits would arise from such a change in tax policy. The imposition of a VAT on imports and the rebate of a VAT on exports -- the "border tax adjustments" -- are widely perceived within the business community to be an effective means of making imports more expensive in the domestic markets and exports more attractive in foreign markets. This assumes that a VAT is substituted for existing domestic taxes which currently are not paid by foreign producers or consumers. The expected result is an increase in exports and a reduction in imports. Given persistent trade deficits in excess of $100 billion annually, the border tax adjustment features of a VAT are seen as at least a partial remedy for the problem.

However, these trade implications of a VAT are controversial. While some proponents of a VAT contend that implementation will benefit U.S. trade, other observers argue that there would be no effect on trade flows whatsoever. Dan Throop Smith and Bertrand Fox have argued that substituting a VAT for a "direct tax" (i.e., an income tax or payroll tax) would improve the U.S. competitive position:

> It is increasingly recognized, however, that corporate income taxes do to a considerable but imprecise extent constitute costs and that they are reflected in prices of products. More clearly, at least part of the payroll taxes are costs of production, as much as are the wages to which they are

related. And even individual income taxes to some extent influence both wages and the cost of capital. . . .

All taxes rest ultimately on people. Some taxes fall on them primarily as receivers of income and owners of property; others reach them indirectly as users of income and of property, that is as consumers and savers. The distinction [under GATT] implies a difference that does not exist in real terms.

To the extent a VAT which is rebated on exports takes the place of income and payroll taxes which cannot be rebated [it] in the long run would improve the international competitive position of U.S. exports.[1]

At the opposite end of the spectrum, Jane Gravelle argues that there would be no trade effects:

This analysis suggests that the trade deficit can only be altered if tax policies alter capital flows. Any direct price effects which occur due to initial effects of corporate income taxes on prices will be offset in the aggregate by an adjustment in the exchange rate. . . . This analysis also suggests that the practice of rebating indirect taxes also has no effect on trade. Indeed, a uniform indirect tax (such as a tax on value added) will have the same general consequences for trade regardless of whether it is rebated at the border.[2]

A view from the middle of the spectrum is provided by the U.S. Treasury:

The substitution of a value-added tax for either of these direct taxes [the corporate income tax or the employer's portion of the Social Security payroll tax] could improve the U.S. trade balance only if the domestic price level remains unchanged, or at least increases by less than the full amount of the value-added tax. This would occur if one of these taxes is shifted to consumers and would be "unshifted" if reduced. Under these circumstances, the export rebate would reduce the price of U.S. exports, and the import tax would increase the price of imports relative to those of domestically-produced goods. In this instance, there would be a tendency for the U.S. trade balance to improve. Even this conclusion, however, requires some important qualifications.

First, it assumes that exchange rates are fixed, or at least are not allowed to adjust fully over time. Exchange rates, of course, have been allowed to adjust since 1971. Thus, any expansion in net exports resulting from the substitution of the value-added tax for the corporate income tax would be

[1]Dan Throop Smith and Bertrand Fox, *An Analysis of Value Added Taxation in the Context of the Tax Restructuring Act of 1980* (Washington, D.C.: The Financial Executives Research Foundation, 1981), pp. 20, 21.

[2]Jane G. Gravelle, "Corporate Tax Reform and International Competitiveness," Congressional Research Service Report No. 86-42E (Washington, D.C.: Library of Congress, February 25, 1986), pp. 1-2.

dampened by an appreciation of the dollar relative to other currencies.[3]

The potential trade effects of a VAT would depend on several factors including the legality of border tax adjustments under the General Agreement on Tariffs and Trade (GATT), the substitution versus add-on nature of the VAT, the traditional versus alternative analysis of incidence, and the effects of exchange rate fluctuations. It should not be surprising to find that opinions about trade effects of a VAT are affected by the divergence in views about incidence analysis. But the exchange rate factor apparently has not received substantial attention beyond the professional economics literature, so opinions on the effects of a U.S. VAT on trade are less well developed.

This chapter will address each of these trade-related factors. A discrete discussion of each would not be particularly instructive because the factors interact with one another. For example, the incidence analysis affects one's views about the effects of a VAT as a substitute tax, while the GATT distinctions affecting border adjustments are implicitly based on the traditional incidence conclusions. Therefore, the following commentaries cover overlapping factors.

Following presentations relating to incidence, the legality of border adjustments and substitution of a VAT for other taxes, the remainder of the discussion in this chapter is devoted to a summary of views on the exchange rate issue. A detailed account of the determinants of exchange rates is provided by the Appendix to this chapter.

VALUE-ADDED TAXES AND BORDER ADJUSTMENTS UNDER THE GATT

The trade benefits which are usually attributed to a VAT are perceived to be linked to the border tax adjustments that are standard features of the VAT systems used in Europe. These adjustment mechanisms impose the applicable tax rate on goods which are imported into the country and rebate an amount equal to the applicable rate applied to goods exported from the country. Proponents of a VAT argue that such adjustments subject imports to the same tax burdens which are borne by domestically-produced goods while

---

[3]U.S. Department of the Treasury, *Tax Reform for Fairness, Simplicity, and Growth, Volume 3: The Value-Added Tax* (Washington, D.C.: U.S. Department of the Treasury, November 1984), p. 22.

relieving exports of such burdens. The combination of more expensive imports and more competitive exports is expected to increase domestic production and reduce trade deficits (or increase trade surpluses).

For countries which are signatories to the GATT, border tax adjustments are allowed only with respect to taxes which meet certain requirements. As the United States discovered in the case of the former Domestic International Sales Corporation (DISC) provisions of the Internal Revenue Code, the GATT countries can be unrelenting in their insistence that each country's domestic tax structures affecting exports (and imports) must be "GATT-legal."

To facilitate orderly trade in goods, the GATT sought to prevent double taxation by harmonizing tax systems. This was to be accomplished by adopting a standard which would determine the country that could tax goods which are traded across borders. The two available options were taxation in the country of production (the "origin principle") or in the country of consumption (the "destination principle"). The GATT opted for the destination principle requiring that goods be freed from transaction taxes in the country of production.

The ability to make border tax adjustments under GATT is governed by the agreement's provisions which distinguish between taxes based on transactions (which are deemed to be "indirect" taxes) and taxes based on flows of income (which are deemed to be "direct" taxes). GATT assumes that direct taxes such as corporate and individual income taxes and payroll taxes are not readily identifiable with respect to the goods and services produced in the economy. Therefore, such taxes cannot be accurately imposed on imports or rebated on exports. However, indirect taxes such as sales taxes and VATs are explicitly identifiable. Implicit in this distinction is an acceptance of the traditional incidence analysis which concludes that a VAT (or other indirect tax) applies to the goods themselves and is included in the consumer's purchase price.

Some U.S. producers believe that the GATT provisions place U.S. corporations at a competitive disadvantage. They argue that the distinction is artificial, that all taxes are costs of doing business, and that direct taxes are just as likely to end up in product prices as indirect transactions taxes.[4] From this perspective, the GATT dis-

---

[4]On a more formal level the corporate income tax is not a tax on pure economic profit since the normal rate of return is taxed as well as any excess over the normal rate. Since the normal rate of return is imbedded in the firm's variable cost structure, the corporate income tax is *ad valorem* in nature and therefore qualitatively similar to transactions-based *ad valorem* taxes.

tinction both creates an artificial bias against U.S. exports in foreign markets and favors imports in the U.S. market. Supporters of the GATT distinction would argue that it is economically sound because the traditional analysis of incidence is correct.

Clearly, the incidence question continues to influence the VAT debate, and this will be reviewed again below. As a practical matter, U.S. displeasure with border tax adjustment rules, particularly those based on the direct versus indirect tax distinctions, is not likely to generate sympathy from foreign officials who could properly observe that the distinction has been clear since GATT was negotiated. If the United States is unhappy with its inability to make border tax adjustments which are GATT-legal, why does the U.S. continue to rely on tax systems which have not been eligible for such adjustments from the inception of GATT?

Beyond the direct/indirect tax distinction, there are other legal questions that have come to light recently with respect to GATT border tax adjustments. During consideration of Senator Roth's Business Transfer Tax and a proposed VAT to finance the environmental Superfund, it became clear that the method of VAT calculation, and certain combinations of VAT/direct tax replacements, might raise questions concerning the United States' eligibility for border tax adjustments. These questions were raised by GATT scholars and might be raised by trading partners of the United States. It is beyond the scope of this work to address such concerns, but the reader should be aware that the subject is quite complex.

A BORDER TAX ADJUSTMENT AND THE RELATIVE PRICES OF TRADED GOODS

The issue of the effects of a border tax adjustment on the terms of trade is an extension of the discussion of incidence in Chapter 3.[5] Whether or not the relative prices of traded goods will change with the introduction of a VAT is dependent first upon whether the VAT is an add-on tax or a substitute tax. If a substitution is intended,

---

[5]When discussing "terms of trade," it is important to focus on the real as opposed to nominal prices of goods being traded. Of interest is the number of units of one good which are required to be exchanged for a number of units of another good. If, initially, three bottles of French wine bear equal value to a pound of Wisconsin cheese and then, after some event, four bottles are required in exchange for the same pound of cheese, then the terms of trade have changed. However, if the prices of the wine and cheese are increased to amounts which still bear a 3-to-1 ratio, then the terms of trade have not changed. Therefore, it is the relative levels of real values of goods and services which are important, not their nominal prices.

terms of trade will be affected by whether or not the taxes being replaced have an incidence similar to the VAT.

In the case of an add-on VAT, both the traditional and alternative analyses of incidence would predict no change in relative prices. The traditional analysis concludes that all of a VAT is reflected in the price of goods and services and ultimately is borne by the consumer. An add-on tax would increase the prices of domestic goods and incoming imports in exactly the same proportion. Thus, there would be no change in the competitive structure of foreign versus domestic goods in the domestic market. Similarly, although exports would be free from the domestic VAT, this would not *reduce* export prices below pre-VAT levels. Furthermore, the goods would continue to be subject to tax in the country of destination, the same as goods produced in that country. Thus, there would be no change in the relative prices of traded goods.

The alternative analysis concludes that a VAT is borne by shareholders and employees as well as by consumers, rather than totally by consumers. Given the border adjustment applied to imports, the tax would increase the costs and prices of both foreign and domestic producers. The export rebate would simply allow exports to maintain their pre-tax costs and prices. Therefore, an add-on VAT would not change the relative prices of foreign versus domestic goods.

The two analyses do *not* agree about the effects on relative prices of traded goods when a VAT is used to replace existing direct taxes such as the corporate income tax or a payroll tax. Under the traditional analysis, removal of the income or payroll tax would *not* affect prices because such taxes are not considered to be imbedded in prices. A VAT would therefore increase the price of domestic products and imports equally, as in the case of the add-on tax, rather than replace an existing tax element in prices. Similarly, a VAT would first increase the price of domestic goods and then rebate that increase when the goods are exported. Export prices would remain the same before and after the implementation of the tax. Thus, no change in the terms of trade would occur.

Both a VAT and the taxes it would replace bear qualitatively similar incidences under the alternative analysis. If a VAT with a border tax adjustment were to replace taxes which are *not* subject to a border tax adjustment, there would be an adjustment in the relative prices of foreign versus domestic goods. In the domestic market, an existing tax which enters into costs (by increasing labor and/or capital costs and therefore pricing strategy) would be replaced with a new tax which has qualitatively similar effects.

Therefore, there would be no change in the prices or costs of firms which are domestic producers. However, imports would face an entirely new add-on tax. Costs for foreign firms which import into the U.S. market would rise relative to their U.S. competitors.

In foreign markets, there would be a similar change in relative costs. Total costs to U.S. exporters would drop because the existing tax would be diminished and the new tax would be rebated upon export. However, the costs facing foreign firms selling in their own domestic markets would remain the same. In relative terms, costs to U.S. exporters would be lower after the VAT introduction than before. Presumably, exporters would attempt to increase their volume of exports by reducing prices to reflect reduced costs.

The alternative analysis would view the substitution of a VAT for U.S. income and/or payroll taxes as a step toward international tax neutrality and a reduction of the distortions in the terms of trade, rather than bestowing an unfair advantage on U.S. firms. From this perspective, the GATT distinction between direct and indirect taxes for border tax adjustments is considered an arbitrary distinction, which provides an unfair advantage to countries employing consumption taxes and artificially distorts the terms of trade.

FLOATING EXCHANGE RATES AND THE TERMS OF TRADE

Within the business community, consideration of trade effects generally has been limited to the substitution and incidence issues. However, the role of the current international financial structure in determining the effects of border tax adjustments on trade has received much attention from the economics profession. Many observers will concede that at least part of the corporate income tax is shifted forward in price but will then argue that floating exchange rates eliminate any benefit from a substitution of a VAT for the corporate tax.

Simply stated, the price advantages and penalties which are created by export and import adjustments will be eliminated by exchange rate changes which arise from changes in the demand for goods as a result of the immediate price effects of the adjustments. This view has been expressed strongly by Jane Gravelle and is cited in some of the literature on tariffs, such as the following:

> In a large class of macroeconomic models with flexible exchange rates the tariff also has no impact on the current account, because an exchange rate appreciation will immediately offset all changes from higher tariffs. ...

[I]f a tariff is to reduce a current account deficit it must have the effect of decreasing the country's international borrowing.[6]

If this analysis is correct, the international trade arguments supporting U.S. enactment of a VAT would be undermined.

In reaching its conclusion, the "no trade effect" analysis focuses only on the nominal dollars in the "current account" (described below) rather than the actual volume of real goods and services which are traded. In addition, this analysis assumes a system of instantly adjusting, freely floating exchange rates.

These issues require a detailed exploration. The first issue to be addressed is the impact on real trade flows of a new border tax adjustment, assuming for the moment a system of instantly adjusting exchange rates. Beyond this, however, a thorough analysis of the exchange rate market and the determinants of exchange rates is necessary. This will be accomplished later in the chapter.

Definitions and Explanations

The international accounts of the United States are separated into two basic accounts. The first is the balance on *current account* and is popularly referred to as the balance of trade. This account is the net balance resulting from export and import flows, investment income flows, military transactions, transfers, and income from the provision of services. Transfers include pension payments and international relief efforts. Table 7-1 shows the current account between 1981 and 1985.

The second basic account is the *capital account*. The components of this account are essentially capital inflows and outflows. These include private investment, purchases of government securities by governments and private entities, and shifts in official reserve assets. In addition, a small component is the International Monetary Fund (IMF) allocation of Special Drawing Rights (SDR).

Under a system of floating exchange rates, it is assumed that the international accounts of a country must balance in order for the exchange market to clear. Thus, the capital account and the current account for the United States *should* offset each other.

However, measured net capital inflows are never close to the amount that is necessary to finance the current account deficits. Similarly, these accounts never balanced during the years when the current account was in surplus. It is assumed that measurement

---

[6]Charles Engel and Kenneth Kletzer, "Tariffs, Saving and the Current Account," National Bureau of Economic Research Working Paper No. 1869, March 1986, p. 1.

Table 7-1

THE U.S. CURRENT ACCOUNT FOR 1981-1985
(millions of dollars)

	1981	1982	1983	1984	1985
Merchandise Trade					
Exports	$237,085	$211,198	$201,820	$219,900	$214,424
(Imports)	(265,063)	(247,642)	(268,900)	(332,422)	(338,863)
Net Surplus/ (Deficit)	$(27,978)	$(36,444)	$(67,080)	$(112,522)	$(124,439)
Investment Income					
Receipts	$86,411	$83,549	$77,251	$86,221	$89,991
(Payments)	(52,329)	(54,883)	(52,410)	(67,469)	(64,803)
Net Surplus/ (Deficit)	$34,082	$28,666	$24,841	$18,752	$25,188
Net military transactions	$(1,183)	$(274)	$(369)	$(1,827)	$(2,917)
Net travel and transportation receipts	$144	$(992)	$(4,227)	$(8,593)	$(11,128)
Other services net	$8,699	$8,829	$9,711	$9,881	$10,603
Balance on goods and services	$13,764	$(215)	$(37,124)	$(94,308)	$(102,694)
Remittances, pensions and other unilateral transfers	$(7,425)	$(8,917)	$(9,481)	$(12,157)	$(14,983)
Balance on current account	$6,339	$(9,131)	$(46,604)	$(106,466)	$(117,677)

Numbers may not add to sum due to rounding.

Source: *Economic Report of the President -- 1987.*

techniques simply fail to pick up a large amount of capital flows. Thus, a "statistical discrepancy" is added to balance the international books. This number is quite large -- $23 billion in 1985 -- and is generally assumed to be comprised of unmeasured net capital inflows, generally associated with private investment by foreigners in U.S. assets. Table 7-2 shows the components of the capital account for 1981 to 1985.

Post-War History of Exchange Rates

The post-war history of the international financial system began with the Bretton Woods Conference of 1944. At this conference, the major trading countries agreed to fix currency exchange rates in order to limit exchange uncertainty.

Under a system of fixed exchange rates, a country's international books, known as the balance of payments, need not balance. A trade imbalance is not necessarily offset by net capital flows, given a set of relative prices, relative rates of return and an exchange rate. If a country is exporting less than it is importing, interest rates may be such that not enough foreign capital is attracted to offset the trade deficit, resulting in a balance of payments deficit. At the given exchange rate, the supply of the country's currency exceeds the demand. Balance is restored when the country's central bank buys up the excess currency by shifting reserves abroad. If the central bank did not act, the currency would depreciate because supply exceeded demand. This is what happens when exchange rates are allowed to float.

After World War II, the U.S. ran large trade surpluses, due in part to the devastation in other countries from the war. This surplus was funded by U.S. foreign aid, lending, and transfers of foreign reserves from foreign central banks to the U.S. The latter was necessary to finance the U.S. balance of payments surplus.

By the end of the 1950s, the U.S. trade surplus had fallen while capital outflows continued at a speedy rate, resulting in overall balance of payments deficits. Over the period, the dollar became the *de facto* world currency due to its ability to be converted into gold and the political stability of the U.S.

Large capital outflows in the 1960s resulted in further balance of payments deficits as these outflows dwarfed the balance of trade surplus. During the Kennedy Administration, direct controls were placed on capital outflows and monetary policy attempted to increase interest rates to attract capital inflows.

By the end of the 1960s, the U.S. trade surplus had shrunk to

Table 7-2

THE U.S. CAPITAL ACCOUNT FOR 1981-1985
(millions of dollars)

	1981	1982	1983	1984	1985
Capital Outflow					
U.S. official reserve assets	$(5,175)	$(4,965)	$(1,196)	$(3,131)	$(3,858)
Other U.S. government assets	(5,097)	(6,131)	(5,005)	(5,523)	(2,824)
U.S. private assets	(100,758)	(110,177)	(43,821)	(14,986)	(25,754)
Total	$(111,031)	$(121,273)	$(50,022)	$(23,639)	$(32,436)
Capital Inflow					
Foreign official assets	$4,960	$3,593	$5,968	$3,037	$(1,324)
Other foreign assets	78,362	90,486	79,527	99,730	128,430
Allocations of SDRs	1,093	-	-	-	-
Total	$84,415	$94,078	$85,496	$102,767	$127,107
Balance on current account	$6,339	$(9,131)	$(46,604)	$(106,466)	$(117,677)
Statistical discrepancy*	$20,276	$36,325	$11,130	$27,338	$23,006

*Statistical discrepancy = Capital Outflow + Capital Inflow - Balance on Current Account

Numbers may not add to sum due to rounding.

Source: *Economic Report of the President -- 1987.*

zero -- actually becoming negative in 1968. By 1971, the U.S. had a balance of payments deficit of $29.8 billion. The demand for imports coupled with increasing inflation placed downward pressure on the dollar. Propping up the dollar meant massive transfers of reserves from the U.S. to foreign central banks. The U.S. gold stock shrank from $15 billion in the mid-1960s to $10 billion in 1971.

In 1971, the Nixon Administration unilaterally devalued the dollar in terms of gold and foreign currencies, placed a tariff surcharge on imports and ended the commitment to sell gold for dollars to central banks. For a while, central banks continued to purchase dollars to maintain its value. Speculators sold dollars believing a collapse was imminent. Finally, in 1973, central banks ceased attempting to prop up the dollar and the Bretton Woods System ended. The dollar was allowed to float.[7]

This specter of floating exchange rates leads some analysts to the conclusion that a border tax adjustment is irrelevant. Their analysis begins with the proposition that the currency markets instantly and efficiently restore the balance of payments to equilibrium. The implicit assumption is that the flow of cause and effect runs from the components of the international balance sheet to the exchange rate, thus rendering the exchange rate merely a residual which restores balance. As will be discussed later, there is substantial evidence that currency markets do not follow that pattern and that the flow of cause and effect may be in the opposite direction.

For the moment, however, it will be assumed that exchange rates are freely floating and adjust immediately to restore equilibrium. This assumption is necessary to explore the consequences of the traditional view of exchange rate determination -- that *only* if there is a change in the capital account can there be a change in the current account. This follows from the basic accounting identity that exports minus imports must equate to capital inflows minus capital outflows. (This identity supposedly specifies all the components of the supply and demand for a currency, but as will be shown later, this model is somewhat oversimplified).

Ultimately the supply of dollars must equal the demand for dollars. When the U.S. exports goods, foreign purchasers buy goods with dollars. Thus, the dollar value of exports represents one component of the *demand* for dollars. Similarly when foreign entities invest in the United States, they must convert their currencies into

---

[7]This history comes from Jeffrey A. Frankel, "International Capital Flows and Domestic Economic Policies," National Bureau of Economic Research Working Paper No 2210, April 1987, and William H. Branson, *Macroeconomic Theory and Policy* (New York: Harper and Row, 1979).

dollars to purchase assets. Thus, capital inflows constitute the other component of the demand for dollars.

When goods are imported into the United States, U.S. importers must convert dollars into foreign currencies. Thus, the dollar level of imports is one component of the *supply* of dollars. The other component is capital outflows. U.S. investors must convert dollars into a foreign currency to purchase foreign assets.

As with any good, if the supply of dollars exceeds demand, the price will fall (i.e., the currency will depreciate). Once the currency is sufficiently devalued, supply will equal demand.

As mentioned previously, the determination of exchange rates is more complicated than is suggested by this simple accounting identity, but it is instructive to view the effects of a border tax adjustment under even this simple view of exchange rates. Assume that a VAT replaces part of the corporate income tax and that the corporate tax is shifted forward in price. Since the VAT is rebated on exports and levied on imports, this tax change would decrease the price of U.S. exports relative to goods produced in the foreign market and increase the price of imports relative to domestic goods in the United States.

As a result, U.S. consumers would demand fewer imports (thereby lowering the supply of dollars) and foreigners would demand more U.S. exports (thus increasing the demand for dollars). At this point, the demand for dollars would exceed the supply of dollars. If there is no change in the capital account, balance could only be restored if the dollar appreciated until the dollar amounts of exports and imports were equal.

Assuming this analysis is correct, it nonetheless overlooks a seemingly critical factor -- the *real volume* of goods exported and imported would change. It is the *value of exports and imports* expressed in the producer's own domestic currency that is of concern to the firms involved, not the fact that the current account balances. By focusing only on nominal values, the real effects of the border tax adjustment are ignored.

Consider a hypothetical example of trade between the United Kingdom and the United States. In this example, capital inflows equal outflows and there is no change in capital flows, so that the effects on the current account can be isolated.

The initial exchange rate is $2/£1. The price of the American export is $10 (£5), and one million units are exported for a total of $10 million. The price of the good imported from Britain (a different product) is also $10, and one million units are imported. Thus, both the current account and the capital account are balanced.

A direct tax extracts from the exporters an amount equal to 10 percent of export sales. No border adjustment is allowed. The government replaces this tax with an indirect tax of equal yield which is eligible for a border adjustment. Based on static revenue estimates, the rate is set at 10 percent.[8]

It is assumed that both the direct and indirect taxes are fully reflected in price. One plausible adjustment to the tax change is as follows.

After the tax change, American exporters cut their price to $9.00. Simultaneously, in American currency, the price of the British import increases to $11.00 (£5.50) as British companies attempt to shift the border tax to consumers.

British consumers will desire to purchase more American goods, and American consumers will desire fewer British goods. Initially, the British may want to purchase, say, 1,200,000 units of the American good, and Americans will desire only 900,000 units of the British good. This is not a stable situation because at the existing exchange rate the dollar level of exports would be $10,800,000 and the dollar level of imports would be $9,900,000. Since there is no change in the capital account, 900,000 more dollars are demanded than supplied. Upward pressure on the dollar exists.

As the dollar strengthens, U.K. consumers will desire fewer American goods than would otherwise be the case and U.S. consumers will demand more imports. Based on demand elasticities, an equilibrium will be reached eventually. In this case, a plausible equilibrium would be that the dollar strengthens to $1.895/£1.00, U.S. exports are 1,100,000 units and 950,000 units of the British good are imported. The dollar value of exports, at $9.00 a unit, is $9,900,000. At the continuing price of £5.50 per unit, the dollar price of imports is $10.42 and the value of imports is also $9,900,000. The supply of dollars equals demand and the international account is balanced.

In this example, the rapid change in the exchange rate of dollars for pounds produces a balance in the current account. But the actual *quantities* of goods traded has changed dramatically. Therefore, it would be incorrect to argue that there has been no effect of the VAT on trade. The number of units exported has increased from 1 million units to 1.1 million units. The import level has dropped from 1 million units to 950,000 units. The export sector undoubtedly is better off because after-tax revenues have increased from $9,000,000 to $9,900,000. Furthermore, the decreased level of imports might be made up by increased domestic production.

---

[8]Based on the existing current account, the rebate on exports exactly equals the new tax on imports.

(Domestic producers' costs have not changed, and so it would be possible for them to undercut the British price and make up the difference in the domestic market.)

The actual level of exports and imports is a function of the demand elasticities for the respective goods and the extent to which the dollar appreciates. But there does not appear to be a basis for assuming that the dollar would appreciate to the point where unit volume does not change at all.

If the exchange rates adjusted to eliminate the effects of border tax adjustments, it seems plausible that the same result would occur with changes in other factors. For example, a technological breakthrough resulting in a better or cheaper domestic product presumably would increase exports and decrease imports of competing products. However, if the changing rate of exchange were to result in an appreciation of the dollar to the point that the efficiency or quality of the new product was no longer the better value, the breakthrough would not improve the terms of trade.

This seems intuitively illogical, and it can be challenged in terms of economic theory. Real changes in the economy such as technological advances and tax reforms should produce real effects. Monetary phenomena should not permanently mask changes in fundamental factors affecting the terms of trade. A border tax adjustment would be such a fundamental change. The actual costs of imported and exported goods and services would be altered. It would not appear logical to argue that such real changes can be eliminated by purely monetary events.

Assuming freely floating and instantly adjusting exchange rates which are only a function of trade and capital flows, it may be correct to conclude that only a change in the capital account can cause a change in the nominal current account. However, this does not appear to require the subsequent conclusion that a border tax adjustment will have no effect on the *volume of goods and services traded.*

THE DETERMINANTS OF EXCHANGE RATES

The preceding simple analysis considered a scenario in which exchange rates were solely a function of trade and capital flows and instantly adjusted to restore balance among international accounts. In essence, the exchange rate was treated as a residual equilibrating factor involving trade flows and capital flows. In the more complicated real world, economists have dismissed this simple notion.

Exchange markets are highly complex structures where substantial profits can be made by arbitrating currencies. The currency markets have developed identities of their own, and it is possible that exchange rates are determined by factors other than trade and capital flows. If so, trade and/or capital flows themselves may adjust to restore equilibrium following shifts in exchange rates, rather than the other way around. What follows is a summary of the current thinking on the determinants of exchange rates. A more detailed account is contained in the Appendix to this chapter.

No subject has proven to be more puzzling to economists in recent years than currency markets and exchange rate determination. Econometricians have been uniformly unsuccessful in their attempts to explain movements in exchange rates. In their report for the National Bureau of Economic Research, Frankel and Meese write:

> [T]he proportion of exchange rate changes that we are able to predict seems to be not just low, but zero. ... [N]either models based on economic fundamentals, nor simple time series models, nor the forecasts of market participants as reflected in the forward discount or survey data, seem able to predict better than the lagged spot rate. Second, the proportion of exchange rate movements that can be explained *after* the fact, using contemporaneous macroeconomic variables, is disturbingly low.[9]

Thus, changes in underlying economic fundamentals that are supposed to be the explanatory factors have not been able to forecast changes in the exchange rate. Further, with all the tools and theories at hand, economists have not been able to explain exchange rate changes even after they have occurred. Many feel that currency markets are entities with minds all their own. Frankel and Meese conclude:

> [T]he widespread feeling is that exchange rates have turned out to be more volatile than necessary. Many practitioners believe that exchange rates are driven by psychological factors and other irrelevant market dynamics, rather than by economic fundamentals.[10]

During the 1960s, economic theory held that the supply and demand for a currency was a stable function of exports and imports. It was assumed that in a system of floating exchange rates, exchange rates would move gradually and predictably in response to changes in the relative prices of goods.

---

[9]Jeffrey A. Frankel and Richard Meese, "Are Exchange Rates Excessively Variable?" National Bureau of Economic Research Working Paper No. 2249, April 1987, p 1.

[10]Ibid.

The 1970s, however, revealed currency markets which displayed all the volatility of financial markets.   Then, the theory was advanced that exchange rates were primarily a monetary phenomenon which responded to changes in a nation's money supply. In the face of more or less inflation, induced by monetary policy, exchange rates would adjust to restore purchasing power parity.[11] This theory also was difficult to defend empirically.

Finally, the role of capital flows has been noted, as well as the prospect that foreign exchange markets are profit-making investment centers. Money could be made by betting against the forward market or arbitraging in spot rates. Thus, a "portfolio" theory of exchange rates was developed to suggest that exchange rates were primarily determined by investors and were a function of relative rates of return in different countries as well as investor expectations of exchange rate changes.[12]

There appears to be some truth in each one of these theories, but currency markets have become so complex that one set of authors has commented that, ". . . no set of macroeconomic variables that has been proposed is capable of explaining a very high percentage of the variation in the exchange rate."[13]

The scope of the foreign exchange marketplace is massive and has grown by leaps and bounds. In 1986, the daily turnover for banks in New York's foreign exchange markets was $50 billion a day, and the turnover for non-bank institutions was $26 billion a day. These amounts respectively were 92 percent and 84 percent higher than in 1983. The daily turnover in London was even higher -- $90 billion per day.[14]

More important than the increased levels of trading is the composition of exchange rate transactions.   Previously, most transactions involved customers who needed foreign exchange to participate in the trade of goods and services or in the purchase of foreign capital assets. Today, such transactions comprise a very

---

[11]Purchasing power parity is a concept which states that, after adjusting for transportation costs, only one world price can exist for a given good. This is because differences in price would be arbitraged away. The function of the exchange rate, in this view, is to adjust so that, after inflation, the real prices of goods and services would be the same in two countries. If one country is suffering from increased inflation due to expansionary monetary policy, its currency would depreciate until purchasing power parity is restored.

[12]This synopsis of exchange rate theory is based on William H. Branson, "The Dynamic Interaction of Exchange Rates and Trade Flows," National Bureau of Economic Research Working Paper No. 1780, December 1985.

[13]Frankel and Meese, p. 21.

[14]Frankel, p. 11.

small percentage of foreign exchange dealings -- as low as 5 to 10 percent. The rest involve investors who are simply trying to profit from arbitrage possibilities. Foreign exchange trading among banks and other financial institutions has become a major profit-making economic activity. Foreign exchange transactions are many times greater than that which would be necessary to cover activity involving international trade and international investment.[15]

If the exchange rates are set by the laws of supply and demand, then a very small part of this supply and demand involves economic fundamentals concerning trade and investment. Even more than the stock market or commodities market, most of the supply and demand pressures in the foreign exchange market stem from profit-seeking investors who view foreign exchange holdings as assets themselves. And it is the formulation of these investors' expectations which is crucial to the determination of the exchange rate.

A body of recent research has concluded that most exchange traders do not pay much attention to economic fundamentals but rather play on market psychology. The result of this has been extreme volatility in exchange markets and long periods of exchange rate misalignment. When the British pound was "over appreciated" between 1979 and 1982, many explanations were offered. But after exhaustive analytical attempts, much of the appreciation remained unexplained. The same is true of the dollar "misalignment" of 1980 to 1985. Serious misalignments have persisted for five years or more.

Previously, economists believed that exchange rates adjusted to preserve purchasing power parity -- the belief that international arbitrage would guarantee a single price for any good throughout the world. Exchange rates were supposed to adjust to reflect changing global inflation conditions.

Recent empirical research has shown, however, that when exchange rates, due to some shock, deviate from purchasing power parity, there is only a slow tendency, if any, for rates to return to the norm. Exchange misalignments continue to exist for five years or longer. The empirical evidence suggests that the *fastest* speed of adjustment to normalcy is on the order of 15 to 25 percent per year and much empirical research has been unable to reject the hypothesis that there is little or no adjustment at all. This has led many researchers to conclude that exchange rates follow a "random walk."

---

[15]Rudiger Dornbusch and Jeffrey Frankel, "The Flexible Exchange Rate System: Experience and Alternatives," National Bureau of Economic Research Working Paper No. 2464, December 1987, p. 22.

In the short run, exchange rates are extremely volatile and not reflective of economic fundamentals. They only move toward equilibrium in the very long run.

There are many factors which will affect exchange investors expectations. One of these is monetary policy. Monetary policy, whether in the form of domestic policy or direct foreign exchange intervention, will affect the supply and demand for a nation's currency. It will also affect the expectations of currency market investors. If investors perceive that the Fed will expand the world supply of dollars either through a domestic open market purchase to "stimulate" the economy, or through an exchange intervention (swapping dollars indirectly for foreign securities) geared to devalue the dollar, their expectations will be that the dollar will depreciate in the future and, therefore, investors will sell dollars currently.

This effect on expectations will occur any time investors perceive a change in Fed domestic or international activity, and it would be especially important in the context of a VAT introduction. Conventional wisdom holds that if a VAT were introduced in the United States, the Fed would accommodate the VAT with an expansion of the money supply. Such an action would exert downward pressure on the dollar both through the real expansion of the worldwide supply of dollars and the triggering of expectations of a dollar depreciation among currency traders. Even if the Fed never instigated the expansion, investors might act on the conventional wisdom that an expansion will follow a VAT introduction and sell dollars.

Thus, rather than a new border-adjustable tax triggering a dollar appreciation, both real and perceived monetary phenomena might lead to exchange trading which mitigates, and potentially even dwarfs, any pressures towards appreciation. Given the power of expectations and the levels of trading which are not motivated by trade flows, it is conceivable that the value of the dollar would be lower, not higher, after a VAT introduction.

Other factors which might affect exchange rates include the fact that the dollar is the *de facto* world reserve currency and changes in trends concerning capital flows. Without going into a great deal of detail, it is worth noting that changes in long-run capital flow trends can affect the speed of adjustment of exchange rates. For instance, foreign investment in the United States historically had been almost entirely portfolio investment. Such investment is relatively fungible and can move easily from country to country. There has, however, been an increasing trend towards more foreign direct investment in this country, which is much less mobile.

When U.S. investors purchase assets overseas, they supply dollars to the world which results in downward pressure on the dollar. When foreign investors invest here, they demand dollars, which exerts upward pressure on the dollar. Long-run changes in capital flow trends are not directly relevant to a VAT introduction but such trends can be of sufficient magnitude to dwarf other effects and, therefore, must be considered. In addition, unrelated tax policy changes can also affect capital flows.

CONCLUSIONS

This chapter has considered the international trade implications of the introduction of a VAT. Two basic questions were asked. The first concerns the prospects for a relative price change following the substitution of an indirect tax for a direct tax. The second asks whether or not any prospective relative price or cost changes would be eliminated by the effects of floating exchange rates.

The prospect of relative cost changes depends on whether or not one accepts the traditional or the alternative view of the incidence of consumption taxes. For analytical purposes, this chapter assumed that there were some relative cost consequences of substituting a VAT for all or part of the corporate income tax and then devoted considerable time to the second question.

Some analysts have claimed that any border tax adjustment effects are eliminated by floating exchange rates. This position is derived from a view that the exchange rate is a residual variable which adjusts easily to restore a nation's international books to balance. Given recently developed evidence and analysis, this view seems questionable at best and probably highly unrealistic.

First, the overwhelming preponderance of empirical evidence suggests that the speed of adjustment of exchange rates to underlying economic factors is extremely slow. Much econometric analysis suggests that changes in exchange rates can be quite random and that misalignments can be long-lived. This is because exchange rates are slaves to the expectations of multitudes of investors who view foreign exchange as an asset to be traded like stocks and bonds. It is obvious that investors' expectations are governed by much more than economic fundamentals. There is no available empirical evidence which suggests that investors' expectations exert pressure that would confirm the view that exchange rates are an equilibrating factor.

Even if investors responded in the way required by the traditional analysis, there is no guarantee that a border tax adjustment would result in a currency appreciation. The "no effects" analysis appears to ignore the effects of monetary policy. A rational response on the part of investors would be to expect that a VAT introduction would be accompanied by a monetary expansion. Therefore, it would be rational for foreign exchange investors to sell dollars in advance of a depreciation of the dollar induced by an accommodating monetary policy. Clearly, there would be countervailing forces in the exchange markets. Given a border tax adjustment under a VAT, less imports would be demanded by U.S. citizens and more exports would be demanded by foreign consumers, thus placing upward pressure on the dollar. But the expansionary monetary policy (if initiated or even if merely expected) would result in downward pressure. Depending on the strength of speculators' expectations, the net result would certainly be less dollar appreciation than the "no effects" analysis predicts, and could even be a dollar depreciation instead.

Numerous other influences would be felt simultaneously, such as trends in long- and short-term capital flows. These trends presumably enter into investors' expectations. Given all these countervailing factors and the severe variability and slow speed of adjustment in foreign exchange markets, a sound case can be made for rejecting the notion that the exchange rate would adjust quickly to eliminate the border tax effects. In the real world, a safer assumption is to take the exchange rate as a given rather than as an equilibrating device. Certainly within the time horizon of five or six years, this appears to be reasonable. It is possible that other aspects of the balance sheet, notably the capital account, serve as the equilibrating device.

To the extent that the "no effects" analysis is wrong, the trade effects of a border tax adjustment will not be eliminated by exchange rate changes. To what extent the terms of trade and the flow of goods will be affected is an empirical question beyond the scope of this study. It would be unrealistic to expect that the trade effects would be massive, but, on the other hand, they would not be trivial.

APPENDIX: THE DETERMINATION OF EXCHANGE RATES

The following discussion will explore in detail the issues involved in the determination of exchange rates. The first issue to be considered is the role of monetary policy and its effects on exchange markets. The impact of central bank actions on exchange rates through direct intervention and day-to-day activities in the domestic econ-

omy will be considered. Second, there will be a consideration of the
exchange markets themselves and the investors who participate in
those markets. Exchange rate variability and misalignment will be
discussed as will be the formulation of investor expectations that
govern their investment decision-making. Finally, the role of capital
flows will be considered.

Before this discussion begins, however, a collateral fact should be
noted. There is an aspect of the dollar which makes it unique
among all currencies and affects its demand and supply. The dollar
is the *de facto* reserve currency. Small countries issue dollar-
denominated bonds, and the majority of bank lending to less-
developed countries is U.S. dollar denominated. In 1985, 60 percent
of international bond issues were denominated in dollars.[16]

Monetary Policy and Exchange Rates

During the inflationary 1970s, a great deal of emphasis was
placed on the role of central bank (e.g., the Federal Reserve Board,
or Fed) activity in controlling inflation through domestic monetary
policy. During the mid-1980s, a great deal of emphasis was placed
on central bank activity in influencing exchange rates. In fact, central bank domestic policy is inseparable from policies geared to
affect the motion of exchange rates.

The Fed can conduct open market operations in order to control
the domestic money supply. If it wishes to contract the money
supply, the Fed can sell Treasury securities in the secondary market.
Financial institutions acting as intermediaries or in their own behalf
draw down reserves in order to purchase securities, thus transferring
money from their accounts to the Federal Reserve. Because
reserves are reduced, less money can be lent and the money supply
contracts. If, on the other hand, the Fed desires to increase the
money supply, it will buy Treasury securities in the secondary
market. The net result is that checks drawn on the Federal Reserve
are deposited in financial institutions to pay for the bonds. This
expands reserves, lending can be increased, and the money supply
expands.

The similarities between exchange intervention and domestic
open market operations can be seen through the exchange intervention process. Central bank exchange intervention occurs when the
Fed buys or sells foreign currency assets. The Fed holds its foreign
currency reserves in the form of interest-bearing, foreign currency

---

[16]Frankel, pp. 11, 12.

denominated securities. If it wishes the dollar to appreciate, it sells foreign securities in some secondary market, and then uses the resulting foreign currency to buy dollars. This increases the demand for dollars and should cause the currency to appreciate. If the process stops here, it is known as non-sterilized intervention. Foreign securities have been swapped for dollars. But note that this is virtually identical to a domestic open market sale designed to contract the money supply. The only difference is that in the domestic case, U.S. securities are swapped for dollars, and in the exchange intervention case, foreign securities are swapped indirectly for dollars. In an international economy, both domestic and foreign investors will be holding U.S. and foreign denominated assets. As such, both domestic and foreign investors are involved in both domestic open market operations and in foreign exchange intervention. Unless further action is taken, both activities shrink the money supply.

The Fed can take an additional step by using the dollars it has purchased to buy U.S. securities. This would be known as sterilized intervention and in reality is simply a swap of foreign securities for U.S. securities. It clearly has no effect on the domestic money supply, and, not surprisingly, has little effect on exchange rates:

> To date, however, there is no evidence that sterilized intervention can affect exchange rates. . . . On the basis of existing evidence, therefore, it is difficult to justify using sterilized intervention to carry out exchange rate policy.[17]

Therefore, non-sterilized intervention is required to affect exchange rates. As long as foreign bonds and U.S. bonds are substitute investments, the net result of open market operations and direct exchange interventions will be similar. In both cases, both foreigners and U.S. investors will be, directly or indirectly, swapping dollars for securities. In an open economy, any open market operation will affect worldwide supply and demand for dollars:

> There is virtually unanimous agreement among economists that non-sterilized intervention can affect exchange rates, just as more conventionally-defined monetary policy can undoubtedly affect exchange rates. . . .
>
> If sterilized intervention is ineffective, a second conclusion follows: to pursue active exchange rate management, there is no substitute for monetary policy. Monetary policy can be pursued either through traditional domestic instruments or with non-sterilized foreign exchange interven-

---

[17]Richard C. Marston, "Exchange Rate Policy Reconsidered," National Bureau of Economic Research Working Paper. No. 2310, July 1987, pp. 26, 27.

tion. Whether the latter is called monetary policy or not is of little importance.[18]

In a worldwide economy, there is no isolated monetary policy. If the Fed expands the money supply, it increases the worldwide supply of dollars. If the Fed contracts the money supply, it decreases the world-wide supply of dollars.

This has important ramifications for expectations concerning exchange rate motions during a VAT introduction. Expansionary domestic monetary policy will exert downward pressure on the dollar regardless of the intent of monetary authorities. Similarly, contractionary monetary policy will exert upward pressure on the dollar, even if the goal is simply a domestic anti-inflation fight. Some economists have argued that today's exchange rate is simply a reflection of the present value of the entire future path of monetary conditions:

> For example, if far-sighted agents expect an increase in the money supply to take place four years in the future, it will have an effect on the exchange rate today. The reason is that they expect the currency to depreciate (whether in terms of goods or foreign currency) in four years and thus expect that agents in three years will seek to move out of domestic currency in anticipation of capital losses, causing a depreciation in that period. Agents in two years will in turn seek to move out of domestic currency, and so on. The depreciation is passed all the way back to the present.[19]

The fact that current, or even anticipated, changes in domestic monetary policy can affect current exchange rates is of importance when considering the exchange effects of an implementation of a border tax adjustment. Seemingly unrelated monetary changes, governed by a macroeconomic agenda, could swamp any apparent effects on exchange rates from the new border tax adjustment. But more importantly, a money change related to a new VAT could cause exchange rates to move in a direction opposite to that predicted by traditional analysis.

Many analysts would predict that the Fed will accommodate a new VAT by expanding the money supply. This increase in the worldwide supply of dollars could cause the dollar to depreciate, the opposite of the appreciation conventionally predicted. Thus, it is equally plausible to predict that there would be not only a relative cost change in favor of U.S. exports and against foreign imports, but a currency depreciation from monetary expansion that enhances this

---

[18]Ibid., pp. 22, 27.

[19]Frankel and Meese, p. 30.

trend due to monetary expansion which mitigates, and maybe dwarfs any pressures towards appreciation.

The Foreign Exchange Markets

Exchange rates have been allowed to float for only about fifteen years. That period has seen dramatic growth and innovation in foreign exchange markets. These markets have developed into a huge, multinational entity with investors arbitraging in exchange markets all over the world. As speculators became more important in these markets, foreign exchange prices have behaved more like the prices of other financial instruments:

> One of the lessons learned from the voluminous literature on exchange rate behavior written in the 1970s is that exchange rates behave like asset prices, displaying much more volatility than most macroeconomic variables such as output or the prices of goods and services. This is not surprising given the dominance of asset trades in the determination of exchange rates.[20]

Bilateral exchange rates, which were previously thought to be reflective of purchasing power parity, turn out to be more than twice, and sometimes five times, as volatile as the relative price levels for the countries in question. This volatility is thought by many to be a serious problem. But of even greater concern than short-run volatility, is long-term misalignment.

Although it is difficult to define the "proper" exchange rate, there is a good deal of opinion to the effect that currencies have gone through lengthy periods of misalignment. In other words, all the economic fundamentals and theories have suggested that an exchange rate should be at one level, when in reality it was at another level. In addition, such misalignment, ". . . may persist for five years or more."[21]

Certainly some of the misalignment can be explained by economic fundamentals or government policies. Yet the best econometric results leave most exchange rate motion unexplained. And, most important, when exchange rates deviate from what economic fundamentals dictate they should be, they exhibit a very slow speed of return to normalcy.

Previous theory held that exchange rates served to preserve purchasing power parity. If the relative inflation rates changed, then exchange rates would adjust so that, after inflation, only one price

---

[20]Marston, p. 5.

[21]Ibid., p. 12.

would exist for a readily-traded good. Research has shown, however, that when exchange rates deviate from purchasing power parity, there is only a very slow tendency, if any, for exchange rates to readjust to the norm. There is no apparent tendency in nominal exchange rates and only a slow adjustment in real exchange rates. It appears that the most optimistic estimate is that, following an exchange rate deviation, the speed of return to the "proper" exchange rate may be only 15 to 25 percent per year.[22] This means that exchange rates take four to six years to adjust to economic changes. The implication is that even if exchange rates behave as Jane Gravelle and others have predicted in the face of a VAT introduction, the empirical evidence suggests that the adjustment would be very slow.

Misalignments and volatility occur because exchange rates are actually set by the multitude of profit-motivated investors in the exchange markets. These exchange markets have developed and changed rapidly since the failure of the Bretton Woods system. Of key interest is the fact that the volume of trading is no longer related to either trade flows or capital flows. One study estimates that only 11.5 percent of exchange trading by banks in the domestic market was with non-banks and that only 4.6 percent was with nonfinancial customers. Only 14.3 percent of brokers transactions involved a non-bank.[23] Similar percentages existed for exchange markets around the world. The fact that these transactions were not the result of customers needing foreign exchange to engage in trade or invest in capital assets is shown by the revelation that, "[t]hese totals are not only many times greater than the volume of international trade in goods and services; they are also many times greater than the volume of international trade in long-term capital." This leads to the proposition that ". . . trading among themselves is a major economic activity for banks and other financial institutions."[24] Such trading is consistently profitable for banks. More important, traders do not base their transactions on any model involving economic fundamentals but rather ". . . on the basis of knowledge as to which other traders are offering what deals at a given time, and a feel for what their behavior is likely to be later in the day."[25] It is this characteristic of exchange trading that negates the equilibrating nature of the exchange markets:

---

[22]Frankel and Meese, p. 49.

[23]Dornbusch and Frankel, p. 22.

[24]Ibid.

[25]Ibid., p. 24.

The result is that economic fundamentals do not enter into most traders behavior, even if fundamentals must win out in the long run . . .

But if most of the . . . investors in the market ignore fundamentals, and instead use technical analysis, or form expectations in any other way so that small exchange rate movements become self-confirming, then the rate may drift far away from its appropriate level. As with any other bubble, it does a single investor little good to recognize that the market is incorrectly valuing the current rate if the market is likely to be making the same mistake six months later when he wants to sell.[26]

The prices investors will be willing to pay for currency depends on their expectations concerning future trends. Understanding investor expectations is crucial to the determination of exchange rates. Theoretically, investors will incorporate all the information concerning future economic events and government policies when formulating their expectations. But they will also employ guesses about motion in the exchange markets including current trends in the spot market and the forward market. Profits are made by currently guessing trends in advance and acting accordingly.

One view is that the forward exchange rate discount measures the expectations of speculators regarding future exchange rate changes. When forward prices are compared, after the fact, to the spot prices which occurred when forward contracts matured, however, the forward market has been consistently wrong, both in magnitude and in sign. During the strong dollar period, the forward market consistently predicted dollar depreciation when in fact the dollar was generally appreciating. This has led two authors to conclude that, ". . . the implication is that one could expect to make money by betting against the forward discount whenever it is non-zero."[27]

A second view is that the expectations of investors are that the rate of depreciation is close to zero, regardless of what is going on in the economy. Current spot rates are expected to continue, despite changes in monetary policy or fiscal policy (including a VAT introduction). There is substantial empirical evidence for this view with one survey stating that, ". . . [a] variety of econometric approaches seem to end up at the same conclusion, that the exchange rate follows a random walk."[28] This empirical view is consistent with the view that exchange rates are very slow to adjust to economic phenomenon:

---

[26]Ibid., p. 25.

[27]Frankel and Meese, p. 24.

[28]Ibid., p. 10.

If the exchange rate follows a random walk, then there is no tendency to return to purchasing power parity and seemingly no limit on how far out of line one country's prices can get from another's.[29]

A final view is that if investors see the dollar currently appreciating or depreciating, they will expect the dollar to continue in the same direction in the future, regardless of economic fundamentals. This is known as a bandwagon effect and could result in exchange rates which do not respond to underlying economic changes. This approach is not necessarily irrational on the part of investors:

> [I]f everyone expects the dollar to appreciate, even if for a reason unrelated to fundamentals, they will buy dollars and drive up the price, so that the expectation turns out to have been rational.[30]

Thus, at least in the near term, the bandwagon effect can become a self-fulfilling prophecy. This prospect is exhibited by many financial markets but may be more obvious in exchange markets. One way to investigate the expectations of investors is to ask them via a survey. Such a survey was conducted and resulted in surprising results:

> It is immediately evident that the shorter-term expectations -- one week, two weeks, and one month -- all exhibit large and significant bandwagon tendencies.[31]

Long-run expectations, on the other hand, were of the stabilizing type; untoward appreciations led to expectations of currency devaluation towards a more normal value. The combination of these short-run and long-run countervailing expectations results in the very slow speed of adjustment to economic forces. The bandwagon effect can be strong. Econometrically, it has been estimated that a 10-percent appreciation in the present time triggers an expectation of a further 0.78 percent appreciation one month hence.[32] Compounded over several months, it is easy to see a currency can remain out of line for some time.

The exchange markets have been characterized by volatility and long periods of misalignment from exchange rates which would be justified by underlying economics. At best, exchange rates have been slow to adjust to economic changes; at worse, exchange rates

---

[29]Ibid., p. 11.

[30]Ibid., p. 31.

[31]Jeffrey A. Frankel and Kenneth A. Froot, "Short-term and Long-term Expectations of the Yen/Dollar Exchange Rate: Evidence from Survey Data," National Bureau of Economic Research Working Paper No. 2216, April 1987, pp. 1-2.

[32]Frankel and Meese, p. 54.

are described by a random walk. This characterization is in stark contrast to the belief that the exchange rate is an instantly adjusting equilibrating mechanism which brings a country's international accounts into balance.

Capital Flows and Exchange Rates

When American investors purchase assets overseas, they must convert dollars into the foreign currency, thus increasing the supply of dollars. When foreign investors invest in the U.S., they increase the demand for dollars. Economists have been in agreement that such capital flows influence exchange rates.

As was discussed earlier, no specific set of macroeconomic variables has been described to date which successfully explains exchange rate movements, but capital flows certainly are important. One economist has argued that the exchange rate, ". . . by the 1980s has become overwhelmingly determined by flows of capital rather than flows of goods."[33] It is important to understand the long-run trends and the short-run factors affecting capital flows in order to judge what might happen when a border tax adjustment is put in place in the context of a complicated world with substantial, coincidental, capital movements. This is especially important if long-run trends in capital flows affect speculators' perceptions of the exchange markets.

The composition of investment is also important when determining whether capital is committed to a country over a period of time or is completely fungible. Portfolio investment can be directed relatively quickly towards any country with a higher rate of return. But a peculiarity in the composition of U.S. investment abroad, which has become the model for the world, illustrates how trends in capital flows can exhibit staying power which is not subject to easy reversal:

> The U.S. has been unique among the major investing countries in that the principal form of its investment has been, from the earliest times recorded, direct rather than portfolio investment. That is, it has typically involved control of foreign operations rather than simply the lending of capital to foreign-controlled firms or to governments.[34]

U.S. investment abroad has been associated with total packages

---

[33]Frankel, p. 2.

[34]Robert E. Lipsey, "Changing Patterns of International Investment in and by the United States," National Bureau of Economic Research Working Paper No. 2240, May 1987, p.1.

including technology, management systems and physical plant. Such investments are long-term in nature and are not subject to quick reversals due to the arbitrage possibilities which exist for portfolio investment.

U.S. direct investment abroad (DIA) expanded rapidly in the 1950s and 1960s because of advances in communications and transportation. Most DIA was in the production of goods although there has been a shift towards the trade and services sector.[35] Recently, DIA has leveled off decidedly:

> Real DIA in 1984 is only 2% higher than it was in 1950. . . . DIA was consistently 20% or more of net investment in the 1960s and 1970s but has collapsed to 11 percent or less since 1981.[36]

Such a dramatic reversal in a trend affecting long-run capital outflows has relevance for exchange rate determination. But possibly more important is the model that DIA created for the world, the recent foreign response, and the implications of that response for long-run trends in capital inflows.

Previously, virtually all foreign investment in the United States was portfolio investment or U.S. bank liabilities. Foreign corporations, however, have realized that they, too, can exploit economies of scale by adopting the multinational form of organization, and, as a result, foreign direct investment (FDI) has become a larger component of capital inflow. This is a natural progression starting with redevelopment following the devastation of World War II. As Europe and Japan reindustrialized and began looking beyond their domestic markets, the U.S. model became very attractive. Still, although Europe and Japan invested overseas, FDI came to the United States only recently.

Before World War I, 80 percent of the long-term investment in the United States was portfolio investment. In the 1960s, less than 3 percent of FDI came to the United States. Between 1977 and 1982, however, there was a large increase in FDI in the United States. The ratio of FDI to U.S. DIA increased from less than 25 percent to 60 percent over this period.[37] By 1980, FDI had reached $17 billion, which was equal to 22 percent of net domestic fixed investment.[38] The majority of this new direct investment is in manufacturing.

---

[35]Ibid., p. 65.

[36]Michael J. Boskin and William G. Gale, "New Results on the Effects of Tax Policy on the International Location of Investment," National Bureau of Economic Research Working Paper No. 1862, March 1986, p. 8.

[37]Lipsey, p. 47.

[38]Boskin and Gale, p. 1.

Two-thirds of FDI is controlled by European firms, with 24 percent from the United Kingdom and 20 percent from the Netherlands. Japan controls 10 percent.[39]

This trend towards FDI as an increasing portion of capital inflow should result in more inflows than otherwise would be the case. FDI is not as fickle as portfolio investment which is more subject to short-run changes in monetary policy.

Factors Affecting Capital Flows

As noted above, long-run trends in industrial development and marketing and the natural evolution of a world economy result in long-run changes in the direct investment component of capital flows. There are also other government policies and economic phenomena which can affect short- and long-term capital movement, and therefore the exchange rate.

One factor which will affect capital flows, and therefore the exchange rate, is direct capital controls. These, however, have been virtually eliminated around the world.

If direct capital controls are no longer a factor in exchange rate determination, it should be noted that domestic tax policies can also exert indirect influence on capital flows, and therefore exchange rates. Previously, many countries had special taxes on the capital incomes of non-residents. Even after their removal, factors such as the issuance of nonresidential "bearer" bonds in the U.S. can trigger capital inflows through the expected tax consequences.

More importantly, tax policies which affect domestic investment will affect both inflows and outflows. Tax changes which lower the cost of capital to domestic investment relative to opportunities overseas can stimulate domestic investment and trigger new inflows:

> We estimate that a tax policy which raises the after-tax rate of return enough to lead to a dollar of increased domestic investment in the U.S. brings with it between eight and twenty-seven cents of FDI.[40]

The converse is true as well; policies which increase the cost of capital domestically relative to that overseas will affect domestic investment, capital outflows, and capital inflows. Thus, sweeping tax reform, such as that in the United States in 1986, can affect exchange rates even though the 1986 Act was not intended to address international economic issues. Domestic tax policies can

---

[39]Lipsey, p. 55.

[40]Boskin and Gale, p. 16.

inadvertently lead to unintended changes in exchange rates through
capital influences.

Some economists have argued that tax changes can occasionally
produce perverse results:

> Tax measures which stimulate investment but do not affect savings will
> inevitably lead to declines in international competitiveness as long as
> capital is freely mobile internationally. The economic mechanism is
> simple. Measures which promote investment attract funds from abroad
> leading to an appreciation in the real exchange rate and a reduction in the
> competitiveness of domestic industry.[41]

The implication is that, in a world economy, all of a government's
policies -- whether international or domestic in scope -- can exert
influence on exchange rates. Coupled with fundamental dynamic
change in the world economy, such policies can profoundly affect
the movement of capital in a way which dwarfs, either positively or
negatively, a change such as the substitution of an indirect tax for a
direct tax.

---

[41]Lawrence H. Summers, "Tax Policy and International Competitiveness,"
National Bureau of Economic Research Working Paper No. 2007, August 1986, p. 2.

8

VALUE-ADDED TAXATION OF FINANCIAL SERVICES

by Harry D. Garber and David G. Raboy

One of the most difficult subjects concerning value-added taxes is the imposition of such taxes on the financial services sectors. Conventional wisdom has held that, for a variety of reasons, financial services are not conducive to value-added taxation. In the overwhelming majority of countries which currently impose a VAT, most financial service activities are exempt from the tax.

INTRODUCTION

In considering the possible application of a VAT to financial services, it is important to recall that existing invoice and credit VAT systems usually impose taxes on gross revenue with credits for previously taxed inputs. The purpose of the credits is to avoid the effect of a cascading of taxes on previous levels of production. This approach would represent a reasonable approximation of a tax on value added for a typical manufacturing firm -- if there were no exemptions in the system and the same tax rate applied to all suppliers. Given the many exemptions and the multiplicity of rates present in a typical European VAT system, it is difficult to describe it as a tax on value added. Because the traditional view of a VAT assumes that the tax is shifted forward to consumers, however, the distorting effects of these structures have not been apparent and have not constituted serious issues to the business community.

These European-type invoice and credit VAT systems cannot be extended directly to financial services without creating several serious problems. First, the simple notion of focusing on monetary flows (as the manufacturing model does) is misleading for financial services. Monetary flows of financial services entities often are simply *transfers* of funds which do not represent an actual change of value. For example, payments made under property and casualty or term life insurance contracts represent, primarily, simple transfers of money and not increases in value. In order to apply a value-added tax structure to financial services, it is necessary to identify and to measure the value of the *services* provided by financial institutions, rather than the simple transfer of money. The single most important factor to understand is that, in terms of structuring a VAT (as opposed to traditional accounting), gross receipts, conventionally defined, are not the same for financial services entities as for a manufacturer. Gross receipts for a financial company must be defined to reflect only those revenues which are derived from the price of the service rendered by the financial institution.

A second problem is inherent in the nature of the VAT structure which focuses only on gross transfers of funds. The credits under the invoice and credit method are designed to avoid a cascading of the tax burden. In the case of financial services, however, many of the payments made by the intermediary (for example, payments by the insurance company from the insurance pool) are made to individuals, and the financial intermediary would receive no credit for these payments. The failure to allow a credit for these payments would constitute a material distortion -- if the intent is to tax value added.

Because of the real difficulty of encompassing these realities in an invoice and credit VAT, the general solution for existing VAT systems has been to exempt most financial services activities from the general levy and to impose separate (and usually gross receipts) taxes on financial services.

Given the size of the financial services sector in the U.S. economy, it is unlikely that any VAT structure would exempt this sector without imposing a separate (gross receipts) taxes. In these circumstances, it is in the interest of all concerned to consider carefully the various possible VAT structures and the possible theoretical and practical measurements for value added of the several financial services activities. The purpose of this chapter is to present material which will aid in these considerations.

The treatment accorded financial services could affect the selection of the basic VAT structure for the economy as a whole. As indicated above, the adoption of an invoice and credit European-style VAT must, of necessity, exclude most financial services activities.[1] This exclusion produces certain cascading tax effects and, in many cases, additional taxes on financial services which may or may not be comparable in economic impact to those imposed under the VAT. The adoption of a VAT structure which seeks to measure value added would permit appropriate inclusion of financial services, but is without precedent in any of the existing VAT systems. This would be a fundamental decision in the design of a VAT structure for the United States.

The next section of this chapter describes the theory which should be applied in determining value added for financial institutions. By and large the measurement theory is straightforward and non-controversial.

This is followed by a more detailed discussion of the effects of exempting financial services under a VAT. It is clear from this material that the exemptions and border tax adjustment practices of most countries with respect to financial services create a patchwork of unintended and undesirable consequences.

After considering exemptions, the next section of this chapter describes in more detail the treatment of financial services in existing VAT systems, including, where available and of interest, the reasons why a particular treatment was selected in a particular country. In some cases the nature and size of the particular taxes imposed on financial services is identified.

Following that section, the proposal being considered by the Canadian Government for the taxation of financial services under a VAT is described. This proposal addresses many of the relevant measurement issues but, by and large, fails to address the cascading question for the users of financial services.

After the discussion of the Canadian proposal, some practical concepts and methodologies are presented which would permit the application of the theory for taxing financial services under a VAT. These suggestions are practical but not unique, and they offer considerable promise as means for determining value added by financial services companies and the appropriate adjustments of VAT income for clients and customers of the financial services entities. It

---

[1]If gross receipts were properly defined as the value of services rendered, rather than as gross monetary flows, it is theoretically possible to apply an invoice and credit system to financial services. The administrative problems, however, would probably prove prohibitive. Consider a premium bill from an insurance company to a customer. The bill would have to state the total premium, the portion of the premium which represents the actual price of the service rendered (the true gross receipt), and then apply the VAT to only that portion. On a transaction-by-transaction basis, as would be required, the system would probably collapse under its own weight.

is important to note that these methodologies could most readily be employed only for a basic subtraction method VAT in which the value-added amounts from vendors are treated as deductions in determining the VAT base.[2] These methodologies could not easily be applied in a typical invoice and credit VAT system, although such an approach is not impossible.

Another important issue is the treatment of leasing and real estate under a VAT. Both present somewhat different issues, but both can be addressed within the theory and practical methodologies presented earlier.

The final section discusses briefly some of the issues involved in the determination of border tax adjustments for financial services.

APPLICATION OF A VAT TO FINANCIAL INSTITUTIONS -- THE THEORY

The underlying principles in the design of a VAT structure including financial services are equity and tax neutrality among companies and industries. As defined by economist Malcolm Gillis, neutrality in the value-added taxation of financial institutions has four components:

- Neutral treatment of financial services, relative to other goods and services;

- Neutrality among all types of financial institutions;

- Neutrality among firms that specialize in financial services and other firms which provide financial and other services; and

- Neutral treatment between foreign and domestic financial institutions.[3]

These concepts will be important when judging various proposals to apply, or not to apply, a VAT to financial institutions.

There are three basic types of financial institutions to be considered: depository institutions (e.g., banks, savings and loan entities, credit unions), insurance companies, and brokerage and investment houses. (Leasing and real estate may also be considered "financial services" and will be discussed later in the chapter.) One common thread runs through the fabric of services provided by

---

[2]See note 1.

[3]Malcolm Gillis, "The VAT and Financial Services" (mimeo: The World Bank, February 1987), pp. 12, 13.

these institutions; financial services companies serve as *interme-diaries* to the actual parties of a financial transaction. This interme-diation service has value which an institution's customers are willing to pay for, either directly or indirectly. It is this value which must be isolated for consumption tax purposes.

Value Added by Depository Institutions

First, consider the lending institution example as represented by a typical bank. The core activities of a bank might be described as follows:

> Financial intermediation brings depositors and borrowers together. In effect, depositors lend money to borrowers through the institution of the bank in order to pool both risks of default by borrowers and to economize on the transactions costs of bringing the parties together. The provision of these services requires the services of capital and labor inputs (value added) and other material inputs.[4]

Whereas the price or value of a good sold by a manufacturer is explicit, the price of the bank's financial intermediation service is not. Explicit fees may be charged for some bank activities (e.g., checking account transactions, safe deposit boxes, etc.), but more often the price of the principal intermediation service is implicit in lending and borrowing rates of interest:

> In practice there is not a real market for these services because they are paid in part or full from investment income. The fair market value, then, must be estimated as what would be charged if the services were sold independently at a price that would cover all costs including a normal profit.[5]

Interest received by banks is not gross revenue to the bank, for VAT purposes, in the way that sales receipts are gross revenue to a manufacturer. The bank is arranging a financial transaction between a lender and a borrower. A substantial portion of a bor-rower's interest payment represents the amount necessary to com-pensate a lender for postponing consumption, or alternatively, represents the amount a borrower is willing to pay in order to have funds earlier than the borrower could otherwise accumulate those funds. This portion of the interest received from a borrower is being transferred by the bank to the lender/depositor and does not

---

[4]Lorey Arthur Hoffman, S. N. Poddar, John Whalley, "Conceptual Issues in the Tax Treatment of Banking Under a Consumption Type, Credit Method, Destination Basis VAT" (mimeo, September 1986), p. 2.

[5]G. Brannon, "VAT and Financial Institutions" (mimeo, April 12, 1985), p. 5.

represent any value added.

It is the second component of interest that is critical to the computation of value added, i.e., the "spread" between the rates which banks pay to lender/depositors and the higher rates charged to borrowers. In essence, a depositor is willing to accept a lower interest rate than that paid by a borrower so that he or she does not have to search for a borrower, bear the full risk of default, handle the paperwork and so on. Similarly, a borrower is willing to pay a higher interest rate than the depositor received in order to avoid a costly search for a lender. It is this difference between borrowing and lending rates, with one further adjustment, which represents the gross revenue to the bank that is equivalent to the gross revenue from sales for a manufacturer.

The adjustment which is needed to compute the gross value of intermediation services concerns risk. A lender would ordinarily seek a higher rate of interest from a potential borrower with a higher risk of default. And this process exists indirectly when banks serve as intermediaries. This risk premium component of interest rates is, in reality, compensation to lenders for risk, and not part of intermediation services. Therefore, it should be accounted for when measuring the gross value of services from intermediation. This can be accomplished by deducting bad debts from the gross intermediation revenue measured by the difference of interest cost and interest income.[6] When loan losses are deducted from the revenue derived from the interest spread, the result is the equivalent of the revenue from sales for a manufacturer.

In the case of the manufacturer, the value of previously taxed inputs is deducted from sales to arrive at value added. The process should be the same for the bank. Previously taxed inputs (e.g., furniture, computers, paper, utilities, outside services, etc.) would be deducted from the value of intermediation services (net of default expense) as measured by the interest spread, to arrive at value added for the bank.[7]

There are a few other factors which must be added to this basic definition. First, not all financial intermediation is debt-related. Some intermediation is between suppliers of equity capital and

---

[6]Lorey Arthur Hoffman, S. N. Poddar, and John Whalley, "Taxation of Banking Services under a Consumption Type, Destination Basis VAT," *National Tax Journal* (December 1987), p. 547.

[7]Under an invoice and credit method VAT, the "gross revenue" to the manufacturer is the tax base. Tax is computed on this gross revenue and tax credits on previously taxed inputs are claimed. Under a basic subtraction VAT, previously taxed inputs are subtracted from gross revenue to determine taxable value added.

users of equity capital. Thus, some accounting must be made of the cost of equity capital because part of the payment to equity holders is for postponement of consumption, analogous to the payment given to a saver. Second, in some cases banks charge explicit fees for services such as safety deposit boxes and checking accounts. It is clearly appropriate to include such fees as revenue in the value-added calculation.

Value Added by Insurance Companies

Focusing on monetary flows would also be misleading in the case of an insurance company. Total premium income is *not* the equivalent of gross sales for a manufacturer. As is the case with interest charged by banks, the majority of the premium is merely a transfer and involves no value added.

The business of insurance is, in its most basic form, the business of pooling risks. This is most obvious in the case of pure single period insurance such as auto insurance or property and casualty insurance:

> Consider a very simplified insurance arrangement under which 10 people cover their risks of accidents by each paying a "premium" of $100 into a common pool. The arrangement provides that a total of $950 will be paid to the first one of the ten who suffers an accident. It is clear that neither the premium nor the payment of the claim represent the value of the service. Rather both are transfers of money. The value of the service in this case is the cost of administering the pool: the cost of getting the money to the victim where it is most needed.[8]

For the insurance company, gross revenue is not premium income, but rather that portion of premiums associated with administering the pool. Stated another way, gross revenue is the charge for intermediating between policyholders. In the example above, the gross revenue is $50, or $5 per policy. In insurance parlance, the value of the intermediation service is "... the portion of each premium over and above that required to cover losses -- the loading."[9] Thus, with some adjustments, the insurance company's counterpart to a bank's interest "spread" is the difference between premiums received and claims paid.

In the case of whole life insurance, annuities and certain other coverages, the actuarial structure involves the accumulation of funds to provide for future claims. The portion of the premium set aside

---

[8]Gillis, p. 16.

[9]Brannon, p. 5.

for this purpose does not constitute value added and should not be included as part of gross revenue under a VAT. In addition, this "savings component" of the contract will be invested, will earn an investment return and part of this return will be credited to the funds set aside under the contract. With respect to the "savings component" of these contracts, the life insurance company is performing essentially the same intermediation function as that provided by banks to depositors and borrowers. Therefore, for the "savings component" of insurance contracts, the value added is the spread between the investment income earned and the interest credited; it is this value-added amount which should be included in revenue for consumption tax purposes.

In general, the insurance company's equivalent of sales revenue for manufacturers is derived for the core activities as follows -- premiums minus claims minus the portion of premiums set aside for future claims plus the "spread" on the savings component. Value added by the insurance company then is calculated by subtracting previously taxed inputs from the value of intermediation services as defined above.

Value Added by Brokerage Firms

The definition of value added for brokerage and investment houses is generally clearer than that for other financial intermediaries. There are various ways that brokerage houses function. They can buy and sell securities on behalf of clients, in which case they charge an explicit fee for services rendered. They can underwrite the issuance of a security, thereby giving the issuing company easier access to capital. The profit which is derived from underwriting activity is the payment for the service provided to the issuing company.

If financial intermediation is to be subject to value-added taxation, the gross revenue of brokerage houses would be essentially fee income plus the profit from underwriting activities. To the extent that brokerage houses serve as investment bankers, the value of intermediation services would be included, as is the case with commercial banks. Previously taxed inputs would be subtracted from gross revenue to arrive at value added.

In summary, it is possible to define value added for the three basic types of financial institutions in a manner which is analogous to value added in the manufacturing industry. But the difficulty of designing and administering a value-added approach for financial services within a typical (gross receipt) invoice and credit VAT, as well as historic reasons, have led most VAT countries to exempt financial services. Exemption, however, creates its own set of serious problems. Before discussing some practical methods of determining the value added of financial services entities, the problems created by exemption are explored in the next section.

PROBLEMS WITH AN EXEMPTION OF FINANCIAL SERVICES ACTIVITIES

In Chapter 5, the issue of preferential treatment was discussed. It was shown that an exemption at an intermediate stage of production could lead to a cascading of tax rather than a single tax on value added. No credit is given for taxes paid on inputs before the exempt stage under an invoice and credit VAT nor in a sophisticated subtraction VAT. When the exempt firm sells products to a company further along the production chain, the purchasing company pays tax on its own value added. But because there is no credit for inputs from the exempt stage which include previously paid tax, value added from previous stages is taxed again. Thus, due to this cascading effect, the overall tax burden is higher than if there had been no exemption.

Many financial services are provided as intermediate inputs to other businesses. This is particularly true of banking and insurance. To exempt such intermediate services would thus cause a substantial cascading problem, particularly if a VAT could be fully shifted forward.

> The ultimate consumers of the goods and services produced by taxable businesses purchasing insurance would pay a price which in some degree included a double tax, since VAT paid by an insurance company on its purchases of goods and services would not be creditable but would be passed on in the price of the insurance. As a result, the price of goods and services furnished by policyholders and others downstream in the distribution chain would similarly reflect such VAT and the VAT thereon. The further result would be a tendency on the part of insurance companies to integrate vertically and a tendency of business to self insure.[10]

Exemption for financial firms would result in anamolous "... incentives to produce intermediate goods themselves (in-house computing, printing, and advisory services) rather than purchasing

---

[10]American Bar Association, *Report of the Special Committee on the Value-Added Tax of the Tax Section of the American Bar Association* (Washington, D.C.: American Bar Association, 1977), p. 67.

these inputs from specialized firms with consequent loss in efficiency."[11]

Besides the issue of tax cascading, there are other competitive
problems which would arise from an exemption. These are mainly
in the international arena.

Choice of treatment of financial services under a VAT can
greatly affect the competitiveness of domestic enterprises, vis-a-vis,
foreign financial institutions. Most European countries zero-rate
the export of financial services at the same time that domestic
activities are merely exempted. This zero-rating eliminates any cascading. *If zero-rated foreign services are competing with exempt
domestic services in the domestic market, the domestic services will be
at a competitive disadvantage, given the ". . . difficulty of applying VAT
to imports of all financial services which may be easily concealed."*[12]
Thus, the cascading of tax on domestic financial services, plus the
possible difficulty of taxing financial imports, render domestic services unattractive.

The cascading of tax is not a trivial matter, empirically. As has
been discussed, the value of intermediation services can be defined
for the core activities of financial institutions. This value covers the
cost of intermediate inputs, profit, labor compensation and other
taxes. The last three components make up the firm's value added.
But the value of intermediate inputs, on which tax would cascade
under exemption, is sizable. It has been estimated that 20 to 30 percent of the value of intermediation services goes to purchases from
other firms.[13]

If preferential treatment is desired, the alternative to exemption
is zero-rating which would eliminate all taxation of financial institutions. However, the size of the potential tax base indicates that the
zero-rate option would cost substantial amounts of revenue. One
estimate put the potential VAT base in 1982 at $22 billion for life
insurance carriers, $18 billion for property and casualty insurance
carriers, $16 billion for insurance agents and brokers, $70 billion for
banks, $6 billion for credit agencies, $16 billion for commodity and
securities brokers and $2 billion for other investment companies -- a
total tax base of $150 billion.[14]

---

[11]Gillis, p. 29.

[12]Ibid.

[13]Brannon, pp. 8, 9.

[14]Ibid., p. 8.

FOREIGN EXPERIENCE WITH FINANCIAL INSTITUTIONS

Almost all VAT countries exclude financial services from the VAT. This nearly universal exemption has both historical and practical roots. In Europe, most VATs were enacted to replace transactions-based taxes on goods, generally gross turnover taxes. Since the turnover taxes did not apply to financial services, it was logical not to subject financial services to the new VAT either. Furthermore, most European countries had separate taxes on financial services. To apply a VAT to financial services would have resulted in double taxation. Therefore, it was easy to conclude that the administrative and theoretical complexities in defining value added in the financial services sectors outweighed the benefits of broader VAT coverage.

Although most VAT countries exempt financial services, there are interesting differences in treatment. To date, the world model has been the experience of the European Community (EC) countries.

In general, EC countries exempt specific financial activities, rather than institutions, while six out of nine EC countries tax such banking activities as safe deposit box rentals, check printing and foreign exchange transactions.[15]

The United Kingdom provides a list of exempt transactions which apply regardless of the character of the business. These include transfers of money regardless of form (securities, notes, or orders), advancement of credit, issues of securities, and the operation of deposit or savings accounts. The provision of insurance is also exempt.[16]

Germany also exempts specific financial transactions, regardless of the type of business. Because of the possibility of cascading tax due to exemption, firms can waive exemption.[17] Germany exempts the provision of insurance but applies an excise tax on insurance premiums.[18]

France is different in that exemption depends on the character of the business. Transactions or businesses subject to specific financial services taxes are exempt from VAT. These taxes include the Tax on Financial Activities (TFA), the Tax on Insurance Contracts, and

---

[15]Gillis, p. 6.

[16]Gordon Insley, "The Value-Added Tax and Financial Institutions," *Tax Policy* (October-December 1978), p. 73.

[17]Ibid.

[18]Ibid., p. 74.

the Tax on Commodities Exchange Transactions. The normal or core business of banks, brokers, exchange dealers and discount houses are subject to the TFA. If these activities are the principal business activity of a company, then they are exempt from the VAT.[19] The TFA is not creditable under the VAT. Insurance is generally exempt from the VAT but subject to a 4.8 percent excise tax on premiums.[20]

A particularly interesting case is Belgium. When the legislature was discussing the coverage of financial institutions under the VAT, several possible justifications for exemption of banking were offered: (1) technical difficulties due to the complexity of banking transactions; (2) cost of administration; and (3) the increase in the cost of credit to non-registered customers.

The first reason was rejected as not being qualitatively different than in other sectors and in any event ". . . were shown by experience to be of quite minor proportions and quite easy to overcome."[21] It was pointed out that banks were covered under direct taxation.

The second argument concerning costs was also rejected:

> Indeed the implementation of any tax whatever involves levying charges and administrative costs shared between the community and those owing the tax or intervening at some stage of its application or collection. This argument was therefore valid only if it could be shown that these costs were excessive and constituted an impediment or were discriminatory against the banking sector. This was obviously not the case.[22]

The legislature did, however, accept the third justification for preferential treatment of banking. There was much concern ". . . not to cause a rise in the cost of credit at the crucial moment of the introduction of the VAT, which would be felt significantly by non-registered persons, principally the consumers."[23] Exemption was, therefore, granted to a broadly defined group of credit transactions. Of course, considering the previous analysis of exemption, this was the wrong thing to do:

> In view of the economic aim put forward this measure was the worst of all possible solutions and the only one which was totally inadequate, in that it

---

[19]Ibid.

[20]Gillis, p. 6.

[21]Jean Pardon, "Banks and VAT -- Lessons from Belgium," *Banker* (August 1974), p. 878.

[22]Ibid.

[23]Ibid.

was the only solution to create the very disadvantage it was hoped to avoid.[24]

Besides credit activities, securities and currency sales are exempt from the Belgian VAT but are subject to a special stock market transactions tax. As with the United Kingdom and Germany, it is the financial transactions themselves which are exempt, not the institutions. Insurance is exempt from VAT, but it is subject to a 4.4 percent excise tax on premiums.[25]

This same tension between a desire to free financial services from tax and the anamolous result of exemption existed during New Zealand's consideration and implementation of a VAT (known there as a Goods and Services Tax or GST). The Ministry of Finance originally proposed exemption for most financial services (general insurance and reinsurance were to be taxed while life insurance was to be exempt). Business reacted adversely to the possibility of exemption without credit for intermediate inputs. A special advisory panel offered a counter-proposal that the VAT apply to all financial services including life insurance, but with an exemption of the savings elements of life insurance. If the panel's recommendation proved unacceptable, the panel suggested zero-rating instead of exemption. The government rejected the panel's suggestion and went with the original exemption proposal. Zero-rating was applied only to exports.[26] This treatment of exports is also standard in EC countries.

Other countries generally follow the EC model. Korea exempts financial services while zero-rating exports. Most of Latin America follows the same pattern.[27] Zimbabwe and Ireland apply a retail sales tax to insurance, and Finland, Austria, and Peru are the only countries to tax insurance under their VATs.[28]

Israel attempted to apply a special 12 percent addition method VAT to financial institutions. No input tax credits under the normal VAT were allowed, so cascading remained a problem. After much opposition, this tax was abolished in 1981 and replaced with a sepa-

---

[24]Ibid.

[25]Gillis, p. 6.

[26]Ibid., p. 8.

[27]Ibid., p. 9.

[28]Vicky Barham, S. N. Poddar, John Whalley, "The Tax Treatment of Insurance Under a Consumption Type Destination Basis VAT" (mimeo, September 1986), p. 1.

rate tax of equal coverage which was completely divorced from the VAT.[29]

The Canadian government has announced its intention to implement a VAT with full coverage of financial institutions. This proposal, the most ambitious in any country to date, will be discussed in the next section.

TAXATION OF FINANCIAL SERVICES UNDER THE CANADIAN PROPOSAL

The current proposal for a credit-method VAT by the Canadian government includes an explicit plan for taxing certain financial services. The details of that plan are briefly summarized in this section.

Only certain "financial institutions" would pay tax on value added from financial services. These financial institutions are those ". . . whose principal business is the lending of money, or accepting deposit liabilities such as banks, trust companies, credit unions and loan and acceptance companies. As well, the definition will include traders or dealers in securities and insurers."[30] Holding companies in corporate groups are not financial institutions. An arms-length rule for financial dealings will produce this result. Dealings in financial instruments by non-financial companies ". . . represents their savings and investment activities rather than financial intermediation."[31] Therefore, under a consumption tax, such dealings will not be taxed.

The tax will be based on the financial flows of institutions based on a periodic tax accounting period. Leasing is not treated as a financial service and will be subject to the general rules of the VAT.

It is understood that not all financial services are debt-based:

> Financial institutions, however, also use equity funds in their provision of financial services, such funds being derived from share issues, retained earnings or other surplus. . . . [A]n examination of the balance sheets of financial institutions demonstrates that there is substantial variation in the sources and uses of funds, both within a particular type of institution and among different types. Equity funds may be used to purchase financial assets and borrowed funds may be used to purchase non-financial assets. It is therefore essential that further steps be taken to ensure neutrality in the treatment of debt and equity capital under a comprehensive sales tax.

---

[29]Gillis, p. 7.

[30]Michael H. Wilson, *Tax Reform 1987, Sales Tax Reform* (Canada: Department of Finance, 1987), p. 120.

[31]Ibid., p. 9.

This neutrality will be achieved by allowing a deduction not only for the interest cost of debt capital but also for an allowance for the use of equity capital in the business of a financial institution.[32]

One possibility for an equity allowance is a dividend deduction. There is a fear, however, that this could lead to tax avoidance among related parties. In addition, the cost of capital associated with retained earnings would not be accounted for under the dividend deduction plan.

Another suggestion is to apply a prescribed rate representing the cost of capital to the equity base as defined by financial data. This would involve a government determination as to the numerical value for the cost of capital. The Canadian government has not decided yet on which approach to use.

When a manufacturer is taxed under a VAT on goods sold, the user of the good in the next stage of production is allowed a credit or deduction to avoid cascading of tax. A similar principle presumably should apply to financial services. Value added which is taxed at the level of the financial institution should produce an offset to the user of the financial service. Except for property and casualty insurance premiums, however, the Canadian proposal allows no credits for the users of financial services. The proposal gives four justifications for this result.

First, a total interest deduction is unwarranted because banks are taxed only on the intermediation margin. Second:

> ... [F]inancial intermediation services performed by financial institutions involve, in essence, the bringing together of borrowers and lenders. ... The service performed by financial institutions -- intermediation -- is supplied to both borrowers and lenders, not just borrowers. Consequently, it would be inappropriate to allow a full input tax credit in respect of tax paid by financial institutions to borrowers alone, since the tax accrues on a service provided to both borrowers and lenders."[33]

Third, the proposal argues that it is impossible to calculate the financial margin on a transaction-by-transaction basis. Fourth, it is argued that "... any cascading of tax resulting from the denial of a credit should not cause significant economic distortions."[34]

The restriction on input tax credits applies to brokerage fees and commissions, as well as other insurance and banking-related intermediation charges. The only exception, other than property and casualty premiums, is for explicit fees for such things as safety

---

[32]Ibid., pp. 127, 128.

[33]Ibid., p. 121.

[34]Ibid., p. 122.

deposit boxes.

It must be recognized that the Canadian proposal will double-tax virtually all financial services to the extent that they are used by registered taxpayers. This must be viewed as a serious problem with the proposal.

The financial margin for banks (equivalent to the output sales of a manufacturer) is defined as follows:

> Banks, trust and loan companies and financial co-operatives will be required to include in the calculation of their sales tax base the amount of interest income derived from loans and mortgages, amortization of issue premiums or purchase discounts on debt obligations, dividends received on equity securities, foreign exchange gains, and gains or income arising from the disposition of financial instruments.

> In computing the margin for this activity they will be able to deduct the costs involved in attracting funds -- mainly interest expense and the return to shareholders, either deemed or actual -- together with losses on the sale of securities, amortization of purchase premiums or issue discounts on debt securities and foreign exchange losses.[35]

This margin is the tax base for banks. Banks are then eligible for input tax credits on previously taxed-business inputs (furniture, equipment, supplies, etc.).

The margin for insurance companies is basically premium income less claims paid. Recognizing that some premiums contain a savings element which results in lower future premiums, an increase in the surrender value of policies, or in policy dividends, an adjustment is made. "Thus, the margin for an insurance company will be, basically, premiums plus investments income, less claims, policy dividends and the increase in policy reserves."[36] These policy reserves will be equal to the maximum allowed under income tax law. In practice, the system works as follows:

> For each taxation year under the new system, the increase or decrease in the reserves will be deducted from or added to the sales tax base of the life insurer, by adding in the opening reserves and deducting the closing reserves. Transitionally, in the first year of the system, there will be included the amount which these reserves would have been at the end of the immediately preceding taxation period. Claims paid after the commencement of the system, and subsequent increases in reserves, will then be deductible.[37]

There are special rules for property and casualty insurers. Such

---

[35]Ibid., p. 130.

[36]Ibid., p. 134.

[37]Ibid.

insurers will be allowed special reserves for "unearned" premiums which relate to future coverage, as well as a provision for the present value of unsettled claims. A business taxpayer will receive an input tax credit for the full amount of premiums paid. When claims are paid to a business, they will be fully taxable. If such claims are used to pay a third party, they will then be taxable to that party, and creditable to the insured.

The treatment of brokerage houses is standard. Fees, commissions, and profit from underwriting transactions will determine the intermediation margin and will be taxed. As with other financial institutions, intermediate inputs purchased from manufacturers will be creditable. To the extent that brokerage houses act as investment bankers, they will be subject to the same treatment as banks.

SOME PRACTICAL SUGGESTIONS

A previous section has described the theoretical approach to measuring value added for the three types of financial services activities -- lending institutions, insurance companies and brokerage and investment houses. This section describes some practical approaches which might be used in determining value-added revenue.

These suggestions are designed to meet the tax-neutrality criteria specified by Gillis. In addition, the following two vital matters are addressed in these proposals:

- Any VAT system affecting financial services should be neutral as between the several types of investments. In particular, debt investments should not be favored over equity investments, real estate should not be favored over financial instruments, etc. In addition, the system should not favor rental or lease over purchase.

- In determining the tax base for financial institutions, the rules should not treat income or credit items derived from individual customers (who, presumably would not be included in the VAT system) differently from the treatment accorded corporate customers (who, presumably would be included in the VAT system). Thus, for example, the value added from the "spread" between the investment income earned on assets and the amounts paid on deposits for banks would be determined in the same manner for individual and corporate depositors and borrowers.

The two areas (identified in the previous section) which require special treatment for financial services entities are the "spread" on the intermediary investment services and the "loading" on the intermediary insurance pooling services. These issues are discussed in the following two sections.

Determination of Spread

The determination of the "spread" income and credits[38] is not just an issue for the financial intermediaries. It is also a concern for companies and other entities which deposit funds with such intermediaries or which borrow funds from such intermediaries. These entities would have to include in their VAT tax returns the "spread" income or credits which are reflected in the return of the intermediary because these financial services are a previously-taxed input. This inclusion is necessary to avoid tax cascading effects. Therefore, these amounts must be separately determined by the intermediary for their customers or there must be a process in which the customers can determine these amounts independently. The latter would be a more effective and practical approach, wherever possible.

A method which would permit such determinations by financial services company customers is to assume that there is an underlying rate of return on all invested or borrowed funds and to determine the spread or value added as the difference between the rate earned (or paid) and this underlying rate of return. For this purpose, the underlying rate of return would be based on some general index such as the intermediate period Applicable Federal Rate (AFR) specified in the Internal Revenue Code. The underlying rate of return used would not vary by type of asset, except, possibly, according to the maturity of the investment. For example, if a corporation borrowed $1,000,000 from a bank at an interest rate of 10 percent and the underlying return rate was 7 percent, the amount which could be considered as the "spread" paid to the bank and deductible on the VAT tax return of the corporation would be:

$$\$1,000,000 \times (.10 - .07) = \$30,000.$$

This $30,000 is the amount the corporation is paying to the bank for its intermediation services. It is an input in the production process just as surely as the purchase of raw materials.

For banks, insurance companies and other financial services

---

[38]Spread income refers to the revenue taken into account to determine a financial intermediary's tax base. Spread credit refers to the amount the customer would be able to use as an offset against his own VAT liability because it would represent intermediation services used as intermediate inputs in the customers production process.

companies, the spread would be determined as the excess of investment income earned over investment income credited less the product of the underlying rate of return and the excess of financial assets over customers' funds (including insurance liabilities). The effect of the latter is to remove an amount equal to the underlying rate of return on invested capital from spread income. For this purpose, financial assets would include all financial assets (cash and short term investments, mortgages, insurance policy loans, securities, investment real estate, etc.). It is necessary to include all financial assets in this determination in order to avoid favoring or disfavoring certain types of investments. For if certain investments were excluded (such as municipals or U.S. Treasuries) because it was assumed that there was no spread, this exclusion would affect the prices and markets for these securities.

For corporate or entity customers of depository institutions, the amount of funds deposited with these institutions will be known. This will also be the case with individual insurance contracts purchased by such corporations. For group and corporate casualty coverage, however, the insurance company will have to advise the customer company as to the amounts retained as unearned premiums or for future claim payments. This would be an end-of-the year amount or an average fiscal year amount. The key is that the same amount should be used by both the casualty company and the customer company. (Note that this is not an issue for group life and health insurance or pensions. Employee benefits would not be deductible in VAT calculations and therefore the "spread" associated with the accumulation of funds under such contracts is not taken into account in these calculations by the customer companies -- although they would be reflected in the determinations of the financial services company.)

Revenue from Insurance Pooling Services

For the insurance company, the determination of revenue from insurance pooling services is relatively straightforward. Such revenue is the amount of the earned premiums less the claims paid and the increase in claim liabilities. In the case of life insurance and other coverages which involve a build-up of reserves for future benefits, the portion of the premium added to reserves also would have to be deducted from premiums. All of these numbers are required, in effect, for the company's federal income tax return and their determination would not add significant administrative burdens.

Note that the determination of the revenue from insurance

pooling will necessarily be unbalanced in the overall tax system -- if the goal is to measure the value added by the insurance company. The system is unbalanced because some of the revenue and deductions recognized by the financial intermediary are not offset by deductions and revenue in other components of the system. This will occur because many of the transactions will be with individuals or with companies which are exempt or where the transaction (e.g., employee benefit costs) is not a deductible expense. If the intent is to measure the value added by the intermediary, this imbalance is not an improper result.

In the cases of companies and entities taxed under the VAT system, there are two key issues in determining the amount of insurance pool service charges which they can deduct in determining their VAT base. These are:

- Should the amount of these charges be determined by taking into account the actual experience of the company under the contract?

- If the answer to the first question is "no," should the client companies or entities determine the amount of these charges, or should they be supplied by the insurance company in a manner which reflects an allocation of its actual experience?

If the answer to the first question was "yes," the client companies would be able to determine policy service charges as the excess of their premiums over the claims payments received. This approach has several basic flaws. It would produce a large assumed level of intermediation service charges in years in which claims are low and the reverse situation when claims are high. It would violate the underlying premise that insurance is basically a pooling operation and that neither contributions to the insurance pool nor receipts from such a pool constitute VAT income.

If the client company cannot determine the amount of deductible insurance pooling charges directly from its financial flows with the insurer, what should be the basis for these charges and how would the client company obtain this information? There are two possible approaches.

The first approach would be to require each insurer to determine the total amount of pooling charges for the several types of coverage (based on its VAT return) and to allocate these amounts among the client companies. A second approach would require the Treasury Department to determine average pooling service charges for the various coverages as a percentage of premium and to publish these for use by client companies.

The first approach would be more accurate and, if all clients were subject to the VAT, would assure that the pluses and minuses in the system balanced out. As indicated earlier, however, for various reasons many clients would not be subject to the VAT so that overall balance is not a necessary condition. In these circumstances, one must weigh the more accurate but less timely *first* method with the less accurate but more timely *second* method. Either would be possible, but the second may be a more practical way of assuring more stable and timely information for VAT tax estimates and the filing of client company tax returns.

Summary

It should be clear from this discussion that it is possible and practical to include financial services in a VAT system which is based on a measurement of real value added. On the other hand, if the basic VAT system established were to be a typical invoice and credit system, it would be difficult to decide how to handle financial services. The fundamental problem is that the gross revenue of a financial service entity (deposits, insurance premium, investment income) is not at all comparable to the revenue from manufacturing and other service activities because financial services firms are, by and large, intermediaries.

Furthermore, the several intermediation services are very different from one another so that no simple approach such as a percentage of gross revenue could be used for all financial services without introducing significant distortion. It is theoretically possible to separate the value of intermediation services via the methodologies described above, define such amounts as "gross revenue" and state them separately on an invoice from the gross transfers or gross premium income that is traditionally defined as gross revenue to an insurance company. Then tax could be applied to only this amount and stated on the invoice. The administrative burden would be enormous, and it is hard to imagine such intricate decisions being made in the American political environment.

The danger in this political environment is that the Congress, if contemplating an invoice and credit VAT, will define all gross transfers as gross revenue, rather than separating out the *true* price of services and defining only that portion as gross revenue. Thus, the invoice and credit methodology is fraught with political pitfalls, although in a perfect world, it could be applied to financial services. These facts must be borne in mind in the selection of the basic VAT approach to be used.

The discussion in the preceding sections covered depository institutions, insurance companies and brokerage and investment banking functions. There are two other financial service functions -- leasing and real estate -- which require separate discussion. These functions are undertaken by specialized companies and entities or might be carried out within traditional financial services entities. The principles and practices which might be applied in taxing these activities under any VAT system are described in the following section.

REAL ESTATE AND LEASING -- THEORY AND PRACTICE

The fundamental principles which should be applied to these activities are the same as those applied to other financial services activities. These principles call for neutrality among different types of institutions, among different types of investments and between purchase and rental or leasing. They also call for the same treatment to apply to the financial service entity regardless of whether the services are being supplied to corporations or other entities taxed under the VAT system or to individuals who are not taxed under the VAT system. The problem with real estate, and to a lesser extent, leasing is that the property involved has characteristics of both operational assets and financial assets.

The treatment of operational and financial assets under a VAT system would be as follows:

Operational Assets - When the asset is purchased, the full amount is deducted in determining the firm's VAT income for the year. If the asset were sold later, the sale price (not the gain on sale) would be included in the firm's VAT revenue.

Financial Assets - The purchase of a financial asset is an investment and has no effect on the VAT revenue or charges. While the asset is held, the owner may exclude from VAT revenue an amount equal to the product of the underlying rate of return and the amount of the financial asset. At the time of sale, the gain or loss on sale relative to the amount of the financial asset is taken into account in determining the taxpayer's VAT base. (In general, the amount of the financial asset will stay constant during its period of ownership by the financial institution, but amortization of principal on mortgages and redemptions of bonds or stocks will be treated as repayment of investment and not as income for VAT purposes.)

It can be demonstrated mathematically that the present value (determined at the underlying rate of return) of the tax treatment of operational and financial assets would be equal.

There are two models which a leasing company could employ --

an operational asset model or a financial asset model. If the operational asset model were to be employed, the leasing company would treat the equipment as an operational asset, deduct the cost of that asset and then include all lease payments in its VAT base. The lessee would deduct the full amount of the lease payments in determining its VAT income. Under the financial asset model, the leasing company would treat the equipment as a financial asset and the lessee would be able to deduct only the excess of the lease payments over the underlying rate of return on the financial asset.

The operational asset model seems preferable. The reasons are that it maintains balance within the system because the credits to the leasing company buyer offset the revenue to the manufacturer. In addition, the assets leased are usually more like operational assets and, finally, the ability of the lessees to receive credit for the full amount of lease payments simplifies their accounting. The operational asset model is the model which, in effect, would apply if the lessee purchased equipment directly. Therefore, requiring leasing companies to use the financial asset model would violate one of the neutrality principles.

Real estate has both operational and financial asset characteristics. In this case, as well, either model could be used but the choice is much less clear-cut than for leasing. First, real estate is an asset which will usually increase in value over time. Second, unlike leasing, it usually involves relatively small numbers of relatively large assets.

In general, the financial asset model seems to be more appropriate for real estate companies. This is particularly true for property purchased as an investment by a financial services company such as an insurance company. If this model were to be used, the real estate owner could reduce its revenue by the underlying rate of return on the asset and the lessee of space would be able to credit only the excess of its rental payments over the underlying rate of return on the portion of the asset allocable to the space occupied.

There would be some concern that this treatment is not balanced because there would be no credits balancing the tax revenue from the organizations constructing the real estate. This is true, however, with any revenue from persons or entities outside the VAT system. Furthermore, all new financial assets would arise from taxed revenue so that this apparent imbalance would not constitute a real problem.

There would have to be some exceptions, however. For example, exceptions would be required for real estate developers in the housing area and for companies which build factories, office buildings or warehouses for their exclusive use. In these cases, the operational asset model would be more appropriate.

Although this has not been an exhaustive treatment of the subject, it is clear that leasing and real estate can be included in a VAT base using the models applicable to non-financial institutions (in the case of leasing) and financial intermediaries (in the case of real estate).

BORDER TAX ADJUSTMENTS

For border tax adjustment purposes, the sourcing of financial services is more difficult to pin down than the sourcing of products. This can have serious ramifications because "[w]ith open capital markets and international capital mobility, inappropriate tax treatment of financial services under a VAT may induce movements of capital out of the taxing country."[39]

The border tax adjustment will necessitate defining the locale of the consumption of services and will almost certainly involve fairly complex apportionment rules. Insurance is a case in point. One of the architects of the proposed Canadian VAT originally argued that the location of the purchaser of insurance should determine the location of consumption, not the location of the risk itself:

> Given that it is the purchaser of insurance who benefits from risk pooling, tax liability would logically seem to depend on where the benefits or risk pooling are consumed, i.e., the residency of the purchaser of any given policy. Thus, an individual who purchases insurance in his (or her) country of residence, even if it covers risks overseas (such as to property) would be viewed as consuming peace of mind in his (or her) country of residence.[40]

Yet, the actual Canadian proposal determined that the place of consumption for border tax adjustment purposes was the location of risk, not residency of the purchaser of the policy. The two views can have widely different implications for the insurance industry.

Policymakers will have to carefully define financial services in order to determine what constitutes the export and import of such services. Apportionment will be necessary, and it must be understood that decisions can have a great effect on the competitiveness of domestic institutions.

The Canadian proposal specifies separate rules for banks, insu-

---

[39]Gillis, p. 21.

[40]Barham, Poddar and Whalley, p. 20.

rance companies and brokerage houses with respect to the border tax adjustment. For brokerage firms the border tax adjustment is described as follows:

> To ensure that Canadian financial institutions are not placed at a competitive disadvantage, the payment to a non-resident investment firm that is not a taxpayer of a fee or commission for the purchase or sale of publicly listed financial instruments will be subject to tax. As will be the case for other imports or services ... the tax will be levied on the person importing the service on a self-assessment basis. Thus, if a pension fund purchases publicly listed securities from a non-resident broker and pays a fee or commission, the pension fund would be required to pay tax on the amount of the fee or commission. Where an explicit fee or commission is not charged, the tax will be calculated on the basis of a prescribed fee schedule to determine the appropriate amount as a tax base.[41]

For brokerage houses, in general, the location of the consumption of services is based on the country of residence of the buyer or seller from when the fee is received, on the one hand, and the location of the broker, on the other. The location of use of services for underwriting is based on the residency of the issuer of the security. Thus, a German company that has a new issue underwritten by a Canadian brokerage firm is viewed as an export.

For banks, an allocation formula is needed:

> [I]t will be necessary to employ a formula to determine what portion of the intermediation margin is from a foreign source and should not be subject to tax. The allocation of the intermediation margin between Canada and abroad will be based on the residence of the person paying the interest, dividend or similar type of income and fees or commissions for security transactions.[42]

The formula will be based on the ratio of total foreign source revenue to total revenue.

As discussed previously, the border tax adjustment for insurance will be determined by the location of risk:

> Accordingly, the allocation for a resident insurer will be the proportion of the insurer's worldwide margin from financial instruments other than insurance policies that its Canadian policy reserve liabilities bear to its total reserve liabilities.[43]

Reinsurance of foreign risks by Canadian companies is viewed as an export. If, however, a Canadian insurer reinsures Canadian risks with a foreign insurer, it will be viewed as an import.

---

[41]Wilson, p. 123.

[42]Ibid., p. 131.

[43]Ibid., p. 135.

The Canadian experience illustrates the difficulties in defining exports and imports for financial services. Should a VAT be considered in the United States, similar problems will arise. Considerable theoretical work remains to be done on the proper definitions for financial exports and imports. Beyond the theory, practical solutions must be derived which do not upset the competitive balance and guarantee cross border neutrality.

9

THE SECTORAL IMPACTS
OF A VALUE-ADDED TAX

by David G. Raboy
and Cliff Massa III

The published literature on value-added taxes does not give much attention to the differential effects of such a tax on various business sectors within the U.S. economy. There are no studies which seek to compute the relative amounts of value added among industries in order to determine where value-added tax (VAT) liabilities would be concentrated.

Similarly, while the effects of border tax adjustments on imports and exports are vitally important to the computation of a value-added base, data on the use of imported materials by specific industries are non-existent; information on exports is available for manufacturers but apparently does not exist for the service and financial industries.

There are no reported studies which compare anticipated VAT burdens with existing corporate income tax and payroll tax liabilities among industries to determine how tax burdens might be shifted if a VAT were a complete or partial substitute for such taxes. Similarly, until the last year or two, industry groups had not undertaken any serious internal work along these lines. What has occurred since then is still limited in scope. As a result, there is no ready-made body of data and statistics which can be used to reach even the most general conclusions about the likely sectoral impacts of a VAT in the U.S. economy.

CORPORATE INCOME TAX ANALYSIS

By contrast, the corporate income tax has been the subject of extensive sectoral analysis for many years. As a tax on profits (at least as "profit" is defined and computed by the various rules of the Internal Revenue Code), the corporate income tax has been dissected by economists, government statisticians, public interest groups, financial analysts, accountants and business executives who seek to determine the relative impact of the tax on particular sectors and even on particular companies. Congressional staff studies annually memorialize the "effective tax rates" paid by specific industries. For many years, "effective tax rates" for individual corporations have been computed and published by tax analysts. Some years ago, the financial accounting profession mandated the inclusion in annual financial reports of corporate tax rate reconciliations to illustrate why the reporting corporation was not paying a full 46 percent tax rate.

The cumulative result of 10 to 15 years of the various reports and studies -- and the controversy surrounding them -- may have been to simply confuse policymakers. But it now seems likely that much, if not all, of the corporate community took the results seriously.

No matter what study or computational method was used, it became apparent that the corporate income tax did not produce anything approaching uniform results among companies in different industries which had essentially similar levels of financial profits. The numerous "preferences" or special provisions in the law were creating widely disparate "effective tax rates" among industries and companies.

By the mid-1980s, the "high effective tax rate" industries were increasingly vocal in their support for tax rate reductions to reduce the disparities. Wide variations in effective tax rates were cited repeatedly by Treasury and congressional supporters of the tax reform initiatives which resulted in the Tax Reform Act of 1986.

Whether for good or ill, the perceived disparities in effective tax rates on corporate profits significantly influenced the substance of the 1986 Act. The expressed desire to tax all corporate profits at essentially the same tax rate was a motivating force within certain business sectors and among many federal policymakers. The studies and computations which were cited were controversial in many instances, but they were also authoritative because the data had been prepared and debated for years.

SECTORAL DATA ON VALUE ADDED

The absence of sectoral impact data and analyses regarding the effects of a VAT in the United States should not be surprising. The general acceptance of the traditional analysis of a VAT -- i.e., a tax which is paid for by consumers -- suggests that there is little reason to study the effects of such a tax on the industries which simply pass their intermediate VAT liabilities along to the next business and ultimately to the consumer. The traditional analysis would present a sectoral disparity only when a VAT includes a series of exemptions, zero rates or multiple rates which would affect consumer demand for products which bear differing rates of tax. In such a system, the industries which do *not* produce or sell the tax-preferred goods and services might be concerned about a drop in sales, but this does not relate directly to the tax burden on the industries themselves.

Effect of the Shared Incidence Analysis

The alternative economic analysis, which is discussed along with the traditional analysis in Chapters 3 and 4, leads to a different result. Suggesting that the ultimate economic incidence is shared among consumers, providers of labor services and providers of capital services in ways similar to existing income and payroll taxes, this analysis presents issues which could have a political impact similar to that of the effective tax rate issues which have dominated the corporate income tax debates in recent years. The initial reaction of industries with high VAT liabilities relative to sales or to profits (or any other traditional benchmark) is likely to be unfavorable. Yet, high concentrations of value added in one group of industries in contrast to lower concentrations in other industries necessarily results in relatively high VAT liabilities. If a VAT were implemented with a single rate applied to a very broad base, the disparate VAT liabilities should not attract much criticism on the grounds of discriminatory treatment. Value added which is taxed at a uniform rate naturally imposes a burden which falls most heavily on those with the highest concentrations of value added.

It is the comparison of VAT liabilities *to existing tax liabilities* which is likely to create the most heated controversy, not the comparison of relative VAT liabilities among industries. Whatever the real or perceived inequities in current income and payroll tax laws, there is some stability in the present situation. *Substituting* a VAT for some portion of current taxes would rearrange the burdens, and this is likely to be a very disconcerting prospect for

many industries.   The long-term economic merits of using a
comprehensive value-added base which taxes labor and capital in
proportional amounts would be forced to compete for political
attention with short-term changes in tax burdens.   It is in this
context of uncertainty that differential impacts upon industries
become as relevant for a VAT as they would be if major changes
were proposed in the corporate income tax.

ANALYZING INCIDENCE BASED ON WHO IS THE "INITIAL PAYOR"

The factors which determine who is the *initial payor* under
various forms of "consumption" taxes (including a retail sales tax, a
generic or subtraction method VAT, and an invoice and credit
VAT) were discussed in some detail in Chapters 2 and 4. For this
purpose, the initial payor is the one who first pays an amount which
is identified as a tax.   That payment could be either a company's
payment to the government when a VAT liability is first computed
under a generic VAT or an invoice and credit VAT (at least if levied
on a tax-inclusive base -- see Chapter 4), or a consumer's payment
to the retailer in the case of a retail sales tax.

Whether a VAT is shifted will depend first on conscious
decisions on the part of individual businesses, and ultimately on
market forces.   This much is certain; the business is the initial
remitter of a VAT, in contrast to a sales tax. The form of the VAT
may influence subsequent or coincident pricing decisions, and the
ultimate incidence may be uncertain, but it is business firms that
write the checks to the government.

Given the fact that businesses are the initial payors of a VAT and
that the ultimate incidence *may* be similar to other business taxes,
the study of sectoral impacts becomes an important policy issue.
This chapter will take a first step -- *but only a first step* -- toward
addressing the effects of a VAT on different industries.   A
thoroughly comprehensive analysis of sectoral impacts would
consider all of the following issues:

1. What is the relative size of the *initial* remittance of VAT by each
   industry to the government?

2. What varying market forces among suppliers and purchasers affect
   each industry?

3. What differences exist in internal company pricing mechanisms and
   corporate cultures in each industry?

4. How much of a new VAT would be passed forward in price in each industry (based on conclusions to question 3)?

5. To the extent that the VAT is passed forward in price, what will be the market response in each industry (based on conclusions to question 2)?

6. After all company and market forces have acted and reacted, what proportion of the tax will be borne by shareholders, lenders, and labor in each industry?

This chapter will consider only the first question, that of initial remittance. As is the case with corporate income tax analyses, the amount of tax payments is the quantitative factor which is important. Several approaches will be used to compare the initial remittance of a VAT to the remittance of other business taxes on an industry-by-industry and company-by-company basis.

CAVEATS AND LIMITATIONS

The chapter also will only consider the broadest measure of value added for comparison purposes. Preferential treatment for "necessities" and for certain sectors or groups (e.g., small businesses, financial services, charities, etc.) would reduce the base and rearrange the general conclusions. The reader is left to consider the implications of a VAT following the possible base-narrowing results of the political process. It will also be left to the reader to meditate on the extent to which a VAT may be shifted in each industry, and on the ultimate economic incidence in each industry. This chapter seeks only to provide a sense of the relative magnitude of tax payments (check-writing) which would occur in each industry, and even then caution must be observed. The data employed by this chapter are sufficiently sensitive that the numerical results *must not* be taken too literally.

The sectoral impacts discussion will involve two separate analytical pieces. The first section uses aggregate data compiled by the federal government to compare the proportion of a VAT which each industry might pay to the proportion of the corporate income tax and the employer's portion of the Social Security payroll tax that each industry currently pays. The second section of the chapter presents the results of a survey of individual companies on the initial remittance of a generic VAT. This micro data serves as a check on the aggregate data, but also shows the extent of variability across different companies.

Before beginning the review of the data and general conclusions which follow, it is essential to keep certain facts in mind.

- The data needed to prepare comprehensive summaries of value added by industries are not complete. Collection of some facts (such as the use of imported goods and services by each business sector) has not been undertaken.

- Corporate income tax and payroll tax data are not necessarily assigned to 2-digit SIC codes in the same manner as value-added statistics are compiled. Tax data for a corporation with multiple lines of business may be assigned to the SIC code of its largest business.

- The Tax Reform Act of 1986 has resulted in major changes in the corporate income tax. The income tax data in this chapter are for 1981 to 1984, because the latest year for which data have been released is 1984.

For these reasons, the tables and observations presented below must be read and used for what they are -- a first step in a longer term effort to develop better data and methods for assessing where value added arises within this economy and how VAT liabilities would compare to existing tax liabilities. The authors do not intend for other uses of, or inferences to be drawn from, the following discussion.

THE AGGREGATE DATA

The first step in the analysis is to describe the proportion of existing business taxes paid by each industry. Of interest are the two primary federal business taxes -- the corporate income tax and the employer's portion of the Social Security payroll tax. Once the industry-relative proportions of these two taxes (both individually and in combination) are determined, these proportions can be compared to the proportions of a VAT which each industry would pay.

For instance, it may be determined that Industry A pays 3 percent of the total corporate income tax, 2 percent of the total employers' portion of the payroll tax, 2.7 percent of the combination of these two taxes and 4 percent of a potential VAT. This is the same as saying that (i) for each $100 raised through the corporate income tax, $3 are paid by Industry A, (ii) for every $100 paid by employers into the Social Security Trust Fund, $2 has come from Industry A, and (iii) for each $100 of a potential VAT, $4 would be paid by Industry A.

Using this simple but illustrative process, any industry could compare the relative cost of one tax versus another, based on initial remittance. For instance, if the Congress were choosing between a corporate income tax increase or a VAT to raise a given amount of revenues for deficit reduction, Industry A would know that, in terms of initial check writing, it would be paying 4 percent of the total revenues from a new VAT, but only 2 percent of each new dollar of corporate income tax. Depending on Industry A's members' beliefs about final incidence, they may prefer to see a $20 billion economy-wide corporate income tax increase to a new $20 billion VAT.

Data was gathered based on the Standard Industrial Classification (SIC) at the 2-digit level for 39 separate industries. Data on the employer's portion of the Social Security payroll tax, by SIC 2-digit classification, was available from the Social Security Administration. Data on corporate income tax remittance by industry is reported in the Internal Revenue Service's *Statistics of Income* for each year. Since the latest available IRS data was for 1984, all tables are based on averages over the period 1981 through 1984. *Therefore, the tables clearly present a different picture than might occur today.* The significant changes in tax rates and the tax base enacted in the Tax Reform Act of 1986 may -- and probably have -- changed the proportions of the corporate income tax paid by each industry.

Since the taxable base for VAT purposes is defined as total payments to capital and labor, the closest one can come to determining a comparable tax under current law is the *combination* of the corporate income tax and the employer's portion of the payroll tax. Comparing the proportion of this existing "quasi-VAT" (which is labelled "total business tax" in the tables) paid by each industry to a potentially pure VAT is an exercise which should be of broad interest.

The first note of caution is that, in a sense, apples and oranges are being compared. The payroll tax applies to all businesses regardless of form, while the corporate income tax applies only to corporations. In industries such as agriculture and services, many entities are non-corporate. This is one reason that, whereas the service industries pay 23.9 percent of the employer's portion of the payroll tax, such companies pay only 5 percent of the corporate income tax. To truly represent "total business taxes," individual taxes by industry should be added for sole proprietorships and partnerships. However, no data by industry for individual income taxes exists. For most industries, this is not a problem because the majority of economic activity (whether measured by net worth, income, or value added) is performed by corporations. Nonetheless, this is one factor which requires that the tables and observations be read as indicating ballpark estimates rather than precise relationships among industries.

Table 9-1 presents the proportions of existing taxes paid by each industry. For example, out of every $100 of corporate income tax, the primary metals industry pays $1.08. It pays a greater proportion of the payroll tax than it does the corporate income tax -- $1.86 out of every $100. Of every $100 raised by the *combined* taxes, the industry pays $1.51. The chemical industry, however, pays a greater proportion of the corporate income tax (4.79 percent) than it does the payroll tax (2.12 percent). It can be determined, for each industry, whether the industry is more significantly affected by the payroll tax or the corporate income tax. These proportions can then be compared to a potential value-added tax.

VALUE ADDED BY INDUSTRY

In order to compare existing taxes to a potential VAT, a data series is needed for value added by industry. The Commerce Department publishes a series in the *Survey of Current Business* entitled "Gross Product by Industry." Each industry's contribution to GNP is defined to be its value added, which is measured by using the addition method. The components of value added include compensation of employees, proprietors' income, rental income, corporate profits, net interest, indirect tax liabilities, and some other minor bookkeeping measures.[1] The data series provides the results obtained by adding the components for each year.

There are several adjustments which must be made to the series in order to approximate a VAT base. Even after the adjustments, only a rough approximation of each industry's potential VAT base can be determined. Thus, extreme caution must be used when comparing potential VAT liability to the liabilities which exist under current business taxes.

The first adjustment which must be made concerns real estate. A substantial portion of the reported value added in this industry is an imputation of the consumption value of owner-occupied housing. This would not be part of any conceivable VAT base, and therefore, it has been subtracted from the industry total.

A more serious problem concerns exports and imports. Since

---

[1] For an explanation of the methodology, see Milo O. Peterson, "Gross Product by Industry, 1986," *Survey of Current Business* (Washington, D.C.: United States Department of Commerce/Bureau of Economic Analysis, April 1987), pp. 25-27.

Table 9-1

EXISTING TAXES ON BUSINESS
PERCENTAGE OF TOTAL[a]
PAID BY EACH INDUSTRY
(Averaged Over 1981-1984)

Industry	Payroll Tax[b] (Employer Share)	Corporate Income Tax	Total[c] Business Tax
Agriculture	1.38%	.67%	1.07%
Metal mining	.17	.06	.12
Coal mining	.40	.20	.31
Oil and gas extraction	1.10	1.57	1.31
Non-metallic minerals mining	.21	.19	.20
Construction	6.02	2.77	4.59
Food and kindred products	2.90	4.72	3.70
Tobacco products	.14	1.89	.91
Textile mill products	.90	.88	.89
Apparel	.96	1.33	1.12
Lumber and wood products	.78	.57	.69
Furniture and fixtures	.52	.74	.62
Paper and allied products	1.08	1.50	1.27
Printing and allied products	1.94	3.49	2.62
Chemicals and allied products	2.12	4.79	3.30
Petroleum refining	.68	7.39	3.64
Rubber and miscellaneous plastics	1.04	.95	1.00
Leather and leather products	.26	.40	.32
Stone, clay, glass, and concrete products	.88	.86	.87
Primary metals	.86	1.08	1.51
Fabricated metals	2.38	3.21	2.75
Industrial machinery and computer equipment	3.88	4.97	4.36
Electronic and other electrical equipment	3.13	4.08	3.55
Transportation equipment	4.62	3.13	3.96
Instruments	1.15	1.44	1.27

Table 9-1 (cont'd.)

Industry	Payroll Tax[b] (Employer Share)	Corporate Income Tax	Total[c] Business Tax
Miscellaneous manufacturing	.52	1.03	.75
Transportation	4.21	2.76	3.57
Communications	2.63	2.82	2.71
Electric, gas, and sanitary services	1.82	5.25	3.33
Wholesale trade	7.69	9.52	8.50
Retail trade	10.86	9.77	10.38
Depository institutions	2.04	2.68	2.32
Non-depository credit institutions	.81	.70	.76
Security and commodities brokers	.50	.93	.69
Insurance carriers	1.87	2.84	2.30
Insurance agents	.65	.38	.53
Real estate	1.29	2.24	1.71
Holder and other investment offices	.66	1.06	.84
Services	23.90	5.16	15.65

[a]Percentages may not equal 100 percent due to rounding.

[b]This includes the employer's share of payroll taxes from corporate and non-corporate entities. For industries such as services and agriculture, a considerable amount of payroll tax liability may come from non-corporate entities. It is assumed, however, that for most other industries, the majority of the liability comes from corporations.

[c]Total business taxes are the sum of corporate income taxes and the employer's share of Social Security payroll tax. The corporate income tax constitutes 44 percent of "total business taxes." Clearly, this category is only an approximation because individual income taxes for non-corporate entities and other industry specific business taxes are not included.

Source: Calculations by authors based on data from the Social Security Administration and Internal Revenue Service, *Statistics of Income*, 1981 through 1984.

value added for the data series is measured using the addition method, a portion of profits and compensation is associated with production of exported goods. Using the destination principle, which is assumed for any potential U.S. VAT, export sales must be subtracted from value added for each industry. This *should* be a simple exercise, but it turns out *not* to be. Data from the Census Bureau exist for the export of *products* on an SIC 2-digit industry basis, but only for 25 of the industries being considered. There are no data available from any government agency on exports for transportation, communications, financial services, or other service industries.

The reason for this data gap is that economists differ on the definition of an export in these service-oriented industries (see Chapter 8 for a description of definitional problems concerning the border tax adjustment for financial services) while the definition of an exported *product* is easy to grasp. Since an "export" or an "import" of a service is difficult to define, no data exist for a substantial group of industries.

Because an exact measure for value added net of exports is not possible for a large number of industries, the strategy of this chapter is to present results based on a *range of assumed values* for exports by industries for which data are not available.

Table 9-2 shows exports as a percentage of value added for industries where data are available plus construction. By definition, in the National Income and Product Accounts (NIPA), there are no construction exports. If a U.S. construction company builds a facility overseas, that value added is assigned to the "rest of the world" category, rather than to the construction industry. Thus, all reported value added in the construction industry is from domestic sources.

Table 9-3 shows several measures of the proportion of total value added by industry. The measure shown in the first column reports the proportion of total economy-wide value added by industry *without any adjustment for exports.* For export-intensive industries, this would be a worst-case illustration of relative concentration of value added.

The second column shows value added by industry with *gross export sales subtracted for only the industries where actual data is available.* This would be a best-case illustration for export-intensive industries.

The third column lists value added, with gross export sales subtracted for industries where the data are available, and *value added with an assumed 5 percent reduction for exports for certain other*

Table 9-2

EXPORT SALES AS A PERCENTAGE OF VALUE ADDED
FOR INDUSTRIES WHERE DATA IS AVAILABLE
(Averaged over 1981-1984)

Industry	Percentage of Value Added
Agriculture	32.00%
Metal mining	25.69
Coal mining	34.60
Oil and gas extraction	.61
Non-metallic minerals mining	23.33
Construction	0.00
Food and kindred products	18.40
Tobacco products	12.05
Textile mill products	11.08
Apparel	6.62
Lumber and wood products	15.05
Furniture and fixtures	5.28
Paper and allied products	15.61
Printing and allied products	3.30
Chemicals and allied products	36.32
Petroleum refining	19.59
Rubber and miscellaneous plastics	13.07
Leather and leather products	12.66
Stone, clay, glass and concrete products	9.59
Primary metals	16.22
Fabricated metals	14.50
Industrial machinery and computer equipment	46.59
Electronic and other electrical equipment	27.66
Transportation equipment	42.50
Instruments	35.36
Miscellaneous manufacturing	19.23

Source: Calculations by authors based on data provided by the Bureau of the Census.

industries.   These industries are transportation, communications, depository institutions, security and commodities brokers, insurance carriers, and services. Electric, gas and sanitary services; wholesale and retail trade; credit institutions; insurance agents; and holder and investment offices are assumed to have *no* exports.

Figures shown in the fourth column are based on the same assumptions as the third column except that *the assumed level of exports for the certain industries is 20 percent instead of 5 percent.* Under these various assumptions, the relative concentrations of value added can be compared, by industry, to the relative concentrations of existing business taxes.

There is one further caveat to the numbers presented in Table 9-3. This chapter is concerned *only* with the initial remittance of taxes. Under the destination principle, the importer of goods and services is statutorily liable for the border tax associated with imports. Accordingly, Table 9-3 should be based on numbers which add the gross value of imports used by each industry to that industry's value added. The actual VAT payment by each industry should equal the rate applied to value added minus export sales plus import purchases. Regardless of final incidence, the actual checks written by companies in an industry will be based on this formula.

Unfortunately, no government data exist to describe imports *used* by each industry, and there is no way to statistically allocate imports by industry. For instance, the level of oil imports in any year may be known, but the proportion of oil imports used by any 2-digit SIC industry is not known. Because there is no means to spread imports among industries, no attempt is made to add assumed levels of imports to value added by industry. The initial remittance results may be distorted as a result.

Results of the Aggregate Data Comparisons

The proportions paid by each industry of the corporate income tax, the employer's portion of the payroll tax, and the total business tax from Table 9-1 can be compared to the proportions of a VAT paid by each industry based on the various assumptions in Table 9-3. Subject to the major caveats previously mentioned, several types of comparisons can be made. The first comparison of interest is whether an industry would pay a relatively larger portion of total VAT liability than it does of the existing combination of business taxes. The second comparison would involve a possible policy choice for deficit reduction. If the choice were to reduce the deficit either by an equal-yield VAT or a corporate income tax increase,

Table 9-3

A VAT UNDER VARIOUS EXPORT SCENARIOS
PERCENTAGE OF TOTAL PAID BY EACH INDUSTRY
(Averaged Over 1981-1984)

Industry	Value Added Including Exports in the Base	Value Added Excluding Exports for * Industries	Value Added Excluding Exports for * Industries, 5% of Value Added Assumed to be Exports for ** Industries	Value Added Excluding Exports for * Industries, 20% of Value Added Assumed to be Exports for ** Industries
Agriculture*	3.22%	2.37%	2.41%	2.54%
Metal mining*	.10	.08	.08	.09
Coal mining*	.53	.38	.38	.40
Oil and gas extraction*	3.91	4.21	4.28	4.50
Non-metallic minerals mining*	.19	.16	.16	.17
Construction*	5.55	6.00	6.10	6.42
Food and kindred products*	2.31	2.08	2.04	2.19
Tobacco products*	.38	.36	.37	.39
Textile mill products*	.60	.58	.59	.62
Apparel*	.73	.73	.75	.78
Lumber and wood products*	.71	.65	.66	.69
Furniture and fixtures*	.39	.39	.40	.42
Paper and allied products*	1.03	.94	.96	1.01
Printing and allied products*	1.51	1.58	1.61	1.69
Chemicals and allied products*	2.13	1.46	1.49	1.57
Petroleum refining*	.98	.85	.87	.91
Rubber and miscellaneous plastics*	.78	.74	.75	.79
Leather and leather products*	.15	.14	.14	.15
Stone, clay, glass and concrete products*	.74	.73	.74	.78
Primary metals*	1.40	1.27	1.29	1.36

Table 9-3 (cont'd.)

Industry	Value Added Including Exports in the Base	Value Added Excluding Exports for * Industries	Value Added Excluding Exports for * Industries, 5% of Value Added Assumed to be Exports for ** Industries	Value Added Excluding Exports for * Industries, 20% of Value Added Assumed to be Exports for ** Industries
Fabricated metals*	1.83	1.70	1.72	1.81
Industrial machinery and computer equipment*	3.02	1.74	1.77	1.87
Electronic and other electrical equipment*	2.49	1.95	1.98	2.09
Transportation equipment*	2.74	1.70	1.73	1.82
Instruments*	.88	.62	.63	.66
Miscellaneous manufacturing*	.43	.38	.38	.40
Transportation**	4.41	4.77	4.61	4.08
Communications**	3.33	3.60	3.47	3.08
Electric, gas, and sanitary services	3.65	3.94	4.01	4.22
Wholesale trade	8.52	9.22	9.37	9.86
Retail trade	11.30	12.22	12.43	13.08
Depository institutions**	2.34	2.53	2.44	2.16
Non-depository credit institutions	.30	.32	.32	.35
Security and commodities brokers**	.60	.65	.63	.55
Insurance carriers**	1.26	1.36	1.31	1.16
Insurance agents	.65	.70	.71	.75
Real estate	6.30	6.82	6.93	7.30
Holder and other investment offices	.30	.32	.33	.35
Services**	18.30	19.80	19.12	16.95

Source: Calculations made by authors based on data from the *Survey of Current Business*, U.S. Department of Commerce, various issues.

under which choice would an industry's initial remittance be greater?[2]

Three general categories can be created from these comparisons -- industries which would pay a lesser proportion of total taxes under a VAT (the winners), those which would pay a greater proportion (the losers) and those with no significant change (the indifferent). A prime example of an industry which likely would bear a much greater proportion of VAT liability than of current taxes is the oil and gas extraction industry. Currently, the industry pays 1.1 percent of payroll taxes, 1.57 percent of corporate income taxes, and 1.31 percent of total business taxes. Depending on export assumptions, this industry would pay between 3.91 and 4.5 percent of a VAT. This is a high value-added industry with a low level of exports (.61 percent of value added).

This is in stark contrast to the other end of the petroleum industry -- refining. Although the petroleum refining industry pays only .68 percent of payroll taxes, it pays 7.39 percent of the corporate income tax and 3.64 percent of total business taxes. Its VAT proportion ranges from .85 percent to .98 percent. A fairly large proportion of this industry's value added would be subtracted from the VAT base due to exports (19.59 percent of value added would be eliminated). While imports may be an important factor for this industry, the VAT burden probably would be less than the total business tax burden, and petroleum refining would almost certainly bear a lesser proportion of total taxes under a new VAT than under an equal-yield corporate tax hike -- at least on an initial remittance basis.

Food and kindred products is another industry which would probably be better off under a VAT than under existing taxes. This industry pays 2.9 percent of the payroll tax, 4.72 percent of the corporate income tax, and 3.7 percent of total business taxes. Its VAT remittance would range from 2.04 percent to 2.31 percent, depending on the export assumptions for other industries. Export sales account for a significant portion of the industry's value added (18.4 percent).

Textile mill products might realize a lesser proportion of total tax under a VAT, but this is a much closer call. Given all the caveats on these comparisons, the relative burdens are sufficiently close that this is probably one of the indifferent sectors. This industry pays .9 percent of payroll taxes, .88 percent of the corporate income tax, .89

---

[2]The reader must keep in mind that the corporate income tax burdens are based on pre-1986 tax law.

percent of total business taxes, and would pay between .58 and .62 percent of a VAT. A similar story is told for the related apparel industry.

Another industry showing indeterminant or indifferent results is lumber and wood products. The industry pays .78 percent of the payroll tax, .57 percent of the corporate income tax, and .69 percent of total business taxes. Its VAT liability would range between .65 and .71 percent of the total, depending on the export assumptions for service-oriented industries. The results are indeterminant despite the fact that exports are not trivial (15.05 percent of value added).

An apparently major winner under a VAT would be the chemicals and allied products industry, although this result must be qualified. The industry pays 4.79 percent of the corporate income tax and 3.29 percent of total business taxes. Its VAT proportion is between 1.46 and 2.13 percent of the total amount for all industries, but because it is highly export intensive (exports sales account for 36.32 percent of value added), its VAT liability proportion would probably not be much higher than 1.57 percent. However, to the extent that imported oil is used as an input, this liability proportion may be understated.

The electronics industry, which finds itself in four industry classifications, probably would bear a lesser proportional burden under a VAT than under existing taxes. Part of the industry is contained in the industrial machinery and computer equipment category. Under any comparison, a lesser proportion will be paid under a VAT than under existing business taxes. This is also true for the electronic and other electrical equipment category and the instruments category. The one category which may end up worse off under a VAT is the communications industry.

An obvious loser under a VAT is the transportation industry. This industry pays 4.21 percent of payroll taxes but only 2.76 percent of corporate taxes. The transportation industry pays 3.57 percent of total business taxes. It would pay between 4.08 and 4.77 percent of a VAT, depending on assumptions concerning this industry's exports.

Another apparent loser is the retail trade industry. This industry pays 10.86 percent of payroll taxes, 9.77 percent of the corporate income tax and 10.38 percent of total business taxes. Retailers would pay between 11.3 and 13.08 percent of all VAT liabilities, depending on export assumptions for other industries. In fact, on an initial remittance basis, the VAT proportion is probably greatly understated due to the large amount of imports used by this industry.

The results for the financial services industries should be interpreted with caution. It is in this area that definitional problems with exports are the greatest. The results are different for the major sectors: banks, insurance companies, and brokerage houses. The results appear indeterminant for brokerage houses and banks. Insurance companies appear to be both better off under a VAT than under existing business taxes or a corporate income tax hike. These results must be qualified, however, because many financial services companies have large real estate portfolios and there appears to be substantial value added in real estate.

A rough, subjective criterion can be established to determine how many industries would be net losers, winners, or indifferent if a VAT were compared to the total of existing business taxes, or a corporate income tax increase. Substantial differences in remittance proportions are required to move an industry into either the winners or losers category. If the proportions are numerically close, the results are deemed indeterminant.

Based on this subjective comparison, 16 industries would be better off, on a strict remittance basis under a pure VAT, than under the existing business tax system. Eleven industries would be worse off, and the results would be indeterminant for the remaining 12 industries. Three of these remaining 12 industries are border-line cases which could conceivably be moved to the winners category. These results are summarized in Table 9-4, which compares a VAT with total business taxes.

Table 9-5 provides a policy choice comparison. What would happen if policymakers could choose between a VAT or an equal yield corporate income tax increase for deficit reduction? Based on initial remittance, 17 industries would be better off under the VAT, 11 industries would be worse off, and the results would be indeterminant for the remaining 11 industries. Of the 11 with indeterminant results, 3 are border-line cases which could be moved to the winners category, and 2 are border-line cases which could conceivably be moved to the losers category.

COMPANY SURVEY DATA

Manufacturing in General

To supplement the aggregate data, a survey was conducted among a limited number of companies to develop a handful of "real-

Table 9-4

WINNERS AND LOSERS UNDER A VAT AS COMPARED
TO TOTAL EXISTING BUSINESS TAXES

Winners	Losers	Indifferent
Food and kindred products	Agriculture	Metal mining
Tobacco products	Oil and gas	Coal mining
Furniture and fixtures	extraction	Non-metallic
Printing and allied products	Construction	minerals mining
Chemicals and allied products	Transportation	Textile mill
Petroleum refining	Electric, gas	products[a]
Leather and leather products	Wholesale trade	Apparel[a]
Fabricated metals	Retail trade	Lumber and wood
Industrial machinery and	Insurance agents	products
computer equipment	Real estate	Paper and allied
Electronic and other equipment	Services	products
Transportation equipment		Rubber[a]
Instruments		Stone, clay, and
Miscellaneous manufacturing		glass products
Non-depository credit		Primary metals
institutions		Depository
Insurance carriers		institutions
Holder and other		Security and
investment offices		commodities
		brokers

[a]These are border-line cases which could be in the winners category.

life" fact patterns for analysis. Survey participants represented the electronics, aerospace, motor vehicle, pharmaceutical, food production, and other industries. Data were compiled by line of business and by total company results. Several companies reported data for two or three years.

The survey form was designed to isolate the initial remittance for each company as if a generic, border-adjustable VAT had been in place for the years surveyed (1985 through 1987). Thus, the survey was applied to actual company data without any assumptions or

Table 9-5

WINNERS AND LOSERS UNDER A VAT
AS COMPARED TO AN EQUAL YIELD
CORPORATE INCOME TAX INCREASE

Winners	Losers	Indifferent
Food and kindred products	Agriculture[a]	Non-metallic mineral mining
Tobacco products	Metal mining	
Furniture and fixtures	Coal mining	Textile mill products[b]
Printing and allied products	Oil and gas extraction	Apparel[b]
Chemicals and allied products	Construction[a]	Lumber and wood products[c]
Petroleum refining	Transportation	
Leather and leather products	Electric, gas	Paper and allied products
Fabricated metals	Retail trade	Rubber[b]
Industrial machinery and computer equipment	Insurance agents[a]	Stone, clay, and glass
Electronic and other equipment	Real Estate	Primary metals
Transportation equipment		Communications[c]
Instruments		Wholesale trade
Miscellaneous manufacturing		Depository institutions
Non-depository credit institutions		
Insurance carriers		
Holder and other investment offices		

[a]These industries contain large numbers of non-corporate entities.
[b]These are border-line industries which could be moved to the winners category.
[c]These are border-line industries which could be moved to the losers category.

adjustments concerning tax-shifting. For the most part, data came directly from each company's corporate income tax returns.

The survey form itself was relatively simple. The first section of the form collected data regarding includible gross receipts from the sale of goods and services, domestic royalties, rental income and the sale of capital assets. Export values were separately stated and then subtracted from receipts. The second section of the form calculated deductible expenses. These included all purchases of tangible and intangible property (raw materials, components, plant and equipment, etc.), services and any imports (the import tax, although paid by the importer, is a deductible expense).

Net business receipts were calculated as the difference between gross receipts (net of exports) and total deductible expenses. The tax liability under the generic VAT was the rate (10 percent) times net business receipts plus the border tax (the rate times total imports).

Financial intermediation services provided by banks and insurance companies were taken into account by assuming that percentages of such costs are deductible.[3] Based on information from executives in the financial services industry, it was assumed that 15 percent of gross insurance premiums represented the previously taxed value added, and that 25 percent of interest expense represented the value of intermediation services by banks. These amounts were deductible expenses.

A word about the import tax is needed. The survey form used actual tax data for the years surveyed. Since the prices of both inputs and outputs were not adjusted to reflect any tax-shifting, one interpretation could be that there is an *implicit* assumption that firms bear the entire burden of the tax. But the import tax is added onto the existing price of imports, seeming to imply that the tax on imports is fully shifted. There is an apparent contradiction.

In fact, the experiment only attempts to measure *initial remittance* as if the numbers that existed in the years surveyed were what would have existed with a VAT in place. In reality, one would expect the prices of outputs and inputs, including imports, to adjust. On an initial remittance basis, however, it is appropriate to add the import tax as a separate item. The experiment attempts to measure only the initial check writing for each company. Since the importer presumably would be statutorily liable for paying the import tax, the treatment of the import tax is appropriate for purposes of the survey.

The data supplied were confidential, so absolute numbers and company names will not be used here. Because the number of companies surveyed was so small, the results provide only anecdotal evidence and a direct comparison with the aggregate results is not possible. Of interest is a comparison of VAT liabilities and the

---

[3]Chapter 8 provided a framework to tax value added for financial services companies. If such value is taxed at the level of the financial services company, then a deduction must be allowed for the business user, in order to avoid tax cascading.

components of VAT liabilities by company. Probably the most useful piece of information is the extent of the variability of these liabilities and the factors which affect the VAT base among companies.

Factors of primary interest are levels of exports, imports, capital purchases, and the purchase of outside services relative to receipts from sales of goods. To mask the data, VAT liability and the listed items are expressed in Table 9-6 as a percentage of gross receipts *before the subtraction of exports* by each company. Table 9-6 provides the ranking, from lowest to highest for each category, for VAT liability and various factors which affect the VAT base as a percentage of gross receipts. Each data point represents a total company or line of business in a given year (thus some companies may have more than one data value displayed). Besides showing the extreme values of items of interest, Table 9-6 gives a feel for the *dispersion* of the values of such items. The reader can get a feel for the variability among companies of VAT liabilities and the components that are affected.

There are considerable differences in the relative VAT liabilities for different companies or lines of business. VAT as a proportion of total gross receipts ranged from .63 percent to 5.94 percent. Within the manufacturing sector, there is considerable variability in the initial remittance liabilities of various companies.

This variability is even more dramatic for various factors which affect the VAT base. Exports ranged from 0 to 36.58 percent of gross receipts. Imports ranged from 0 to 25.34 percent of gross receipts. Capital purchases were less variable (although this may be illusory because many companies did not provide separate information on capital purchases). Capital expenditures ranged between 2.52 and 9 percent of gross receipts. There was also considerable variability in the purchase of deductible outside services. As a percentage of gross receipts, these purchases ranged from 2.94 percent to 40.76 percent.

Purchases of insurance and banking services were small. Deductible bank value added ranged from .1 to .7 percent of gross receipts, with most firms in the .5 percent range. Deductible insurance value-added ranged from .02 to .15 percent of gross receipts with most firms in the .06 range.

The micro data can also serve as a check on the aggregate data. Some of the data is interesting, although not enough was accumulated on individual company corporate and payroll tax liability to make any substantive statements. Ideally, enough companies would have been surveyed to allow a direct comparison to the aggregate

Table 9-6

RANKING OF SUMMARY DATA FOR MANUFACTURING
FIRMS FROM VAT SURVEY
(Data Expressed as a Percentage
of Gross Company Receipts)

VAT	Exports	Imports	Capital Purchases	Services
.63%	0.00% (15)	0.00% (2)	2.52%	2.94%
.94	.073	.72	2.91	3.17
1.14	.32	.75	2.97	3.18
1.47	.40	1.36	3.22(2)	3.27
1.53	.43	1.46	3.25	3.57
1.77	.65(2)	1.49(2)	3.27	3.36
1.78	.91	1.52	3.43	3.64(4)
2.03	.92	1.54	3.51	3.73
2.36	.95	1.60	3.61	3.74
2.37	1.37	1.61(2)	3.66	3.95
2.39	2.03	1.64	4.04	4.15
2.76	2.48	1.67(2)	4.07	4.17
2.78	3.41	1.69(2)	4.46	4.33
2.83	3.46	1.70	4.51	4.39
3.03(2)	4.34	1.72	4.67	5.59
3.11	4.99	1.85	4.75	6.24
3.23	5.34	1.92	5.43	6.63
3.33	5.40	1.93	6.76	6.65
3.34	5.59	2.01	8.79	6.83
3.37	7.73	2.04	9.00	6.86
3.38	8.03	2.11		6.95
3.39	11.81	2.68		7.30
3.52	12.57	2.72		7.70
3.53	12.58	3.06		9.35
3.54	12.61	3.50		11.31
3.64	13.19	4.38		11.88
3.65	13.25	4.61		12.27
3.75	14.31	4.96		12.99
3.80	15.23	5.16		13.48
3.81	15.31	5.50		14.02
3.83	16.24	5.99		14.24
3.84	19.39	6.19		14.46

Table 9-6 (cont'd.)

VAT	Exports	Imports	Capital Purchases	Services
3.85	30.82	7.96		14.46
3.99	36.58	8.16		16.15
4.23		9.19		16.85(2)
4.24		9.40		18.02
4.29		11.48		19.01
4.30		11.90		19.51
4.65		15.00		20.68
4.89		15.60		22.07
4.91		21.30		23.00
5.13		22.27		26.35
5.38		23.20		28.48
5.41		25.34		38.44
5.43				40.76
5.66				
5.91				
5.94				

Source: Survey conducted by the authors.

results. It is hoped that, in the future, the research can be extended to survey many companies from many different industries. In the interim period, the results from these few companies provides some anecdotal evidence.

One company -- call it Company A -- fell into an industry category which we would project to be a "winner" under a VAT as compared to both total existing business taxes and a corporate income tax increase. Company A would have paid 3.02 percent of its gross receipts in VAT while its total business tax liability (corporate income tax plus payroll tax) was 4.28 percent. In this experiment, the VAT rate was set at 10 percent. Such a tax would raise more than enough revenue to replace the corporate income tax and the employer's portion of the Social Security payroll tax. Thus, this company would be better off under a 10 percent VAT than under existing business taxes. This confirms the industry result.

A 3.5 percent VAT would raise approximately the same revenue as the corporate income tax. Such a VAT would have resulted in a liability equal to 1.06 percent of Company A's gross receipts. Company A currently pays corporate income taxes equal to 1.17 percent of gross receipts. This is sufficiently close that it is unclear which system Company A should prefer on an initial remittance basis.

Company B comes from an industry which was obviously better off under a VAT in both comparisons (existing business taxes or an equal yield corporate income tax increase). Yet, Company B's VAT liability (3.38 percent of gross receipts) exceeded its total business tax liability (3.15 percent). The VAT rate necessary to replace total business taxes would probably be slightly lower than 10 percent (maybe 8 or 9 percent). Under such rates, Company B would probably be indifferent between a VAT and existing business taxes.

On the other hand, Company B currently pays 2.22 percent of its gross receipts in corporate income tax. At the VAT rate necessary to replace the corporate income tax, it would pay only 1.18 percent of its gross receipts. Company B would be better off under a new VAT than an equal yield corporate income tax hike.

Company C was from a third industry which also would fair better under a VAT than under either total business taxes or a corporate tax increase in the aggregate experiment. As was the case with Company B, Company C would probably be indifferent, on a remittance basis, between replacing existing total business taxes with a VAT, but would greatly prefer a VAT to an equal yield corporate tax hike.

Company D would have been obviously hurt by the replacement of existing business taxes with a VAT. Even with a VAT rate as low as 8 percent, its VAT liability would be almost twice its total business tax liability. If a VAT were to replace the corporate income tax, its VAT liability would be almost 4 times as large as its current corporate income tax liability. Thus, under both comparisons, Company D would fair worse under a VAT. This is true despite the fact that the industry results showed company D's industry to be better off under a VAT for both comparisons.

That there is considerable variability among companies in an industry is shown by the results for Company E. Company E is in the same industry as Company D. Yet its corporate income tax liability is *three times greater than its liability would be under an equal yield VAT*. Company E, due to its large payroll tax liability, would be indifferent, on an initial remittance basis, between an equal yield

VAT, or the total of existing business taxes.

The data on general manufacturing shows great variability among manufacturing firms, and indicates that at least some companies would fare worse than industry results predict. To really get a feel for variability among firms, an intra-industry comparison is necessary. This was done for the electronics industry.

The Electronics Industry

Fourteen separate electronics industry companies participated in the VAT survey. These firms included computer firms, communications and telecommunication companies, producers of instruments, microprocessor firms and other producers of electronic equipment. Some of the companies provided data for more than one year. The only difference in the electronics industry survey, as compared to the general manufacturing survey, was that there was no provision for the deduction of value added associated with financial services.

In the section on aggregate results, it was stated that three out of the four industry categories which comprise the total electronics industry fared, on an initial remittance basis, better under a VAT than either the total of existing business taxes or an equal yield corporate income tax. These categories were industrial machinery and computer equipment, electronic and other electrical equipment, and instruments. The communications category was worse off under both comparisons.

The data for the electronics industry included current corporate income tax liabilities. VAT liability, corporate income tax liability, exports, imports, and investment were expressed as a percentage of gross receipts before the subtraction of exports.

The results show extreme variability within the industry. Table 9-7 ranks, from lowest to highest, VAT and corporate income tax liability as a percentage of gross receipts, as well as the important factors affecting the VAT base. Each data point reflects a company in a given year. There may be two or three data points for each company.

VAT liability ranges from .77 percent to 5.75 percent of gross receipts with values ranging continuously between the extremes. Corporate income tax was highly variable as well with companies paying anywhere from 0 to 15.25 percent of gross receipts in tax.

This industry is relatively export-intensive and yet companies differed dramatically here as well. Companies received from .74 percent to 47.39 percent of their gross receipts from export sales, although most companies' exports were in excess of 20 percent of

Table 9-7

RANKING OF SUMMARY DATA FROM VAT SURVEY
THE ELECTRONICS INDUSTRY

VAT as a % of Gross Receipts	Corporate Income Tax as a % of Gross Receipts	Exports as a % of Gross Receipts	Imports as a % of Gross Receipts	Investment as a % of Gross Receipts
.77%	0.00%(5)	.74%	0.00%(2)	1.70%
.88	.22	.97	.80	2.38
1.04	.23	1.08	.90	3.13
1.33	.31	11.07	1.26	3.15(2)
1.88	1.22	11.08	1.28	3.57
2.18	1.45	11.48	1.66	4.46
2.26	1.85	11.56	2.12	4.74
2.49	1.68	18.83	2.22	6.19
2.72	2.37	20.12	2.84	6.29
3.04	5.32	21.15	4.40	6.38
3.17	.67	3.45	4.80	8.31
3.79(2)	9.72	23.52	5.04	8.64
3.89	14.44	23.80	5.23	8.91
3.99	15.25	26.50	5.55	9.00
4.24		26.64	6.49	9.37
4.59		26.95	7.14	10.00
5.19		27.98	7.55	10.47
5.22		30.19	8.34	10.58
5.32		32.16	23.20	11.21
5.40		35.48	39.20	11.31
5.45		36.57	39.40	12.73
5.53		39.33	44.50	20.34
5.75		44.78		25.57
		47.39		

Source: Survey conducted by the authors.

gross receipts. In general, this industry appeared to use relatively low levels of imports although some companies were big users of imported components.   Imports as a percent of gross receipts ranged from 0 to 44.50 percent, but most companies spent less than 6 percent of their gross receipts on imported products.

Capital investment was more variable for the electronics industry than for manufacturing in general. Investment as a percent of gross receipts ranged from 1.7 percent to 25.57 percent.

With such variability for corporate income tax and VAT liability, as well as variability in the factors in the VAT base, it should come as no surprise that some companies would be better off and some worse off in a comparison between, say, a corporate income tax increase and an equal yield VAT. Since the corporate income tax is essentially a flat rate system, this experiment can be performed by assessing winners and losers, if a VAT replaced the existing corporate income tax. As previously discussed, a VAT levied at approximately 3.5 percent on a comprehensive base would achieve this result.

The data were manipulated to apply a 3.5 percent rate to the VAT base and compare the result, as a percent of gross receipts, with the current corporate income tax liabilities (generally for 1986 or 1987).   Two companies did not provide corporate income tax data. Of the twelve remaining companies, 3 companies would have been better off under the VAT, 5 companies would have been worse off under the VAT, and the results would have been indeterminant for the remaining 4.

The survey of the electronics industry was sufficiently limited in size that it provides no definitive results.   Nonetheless, the variability indicates that even if the aggregate results predict that an entire industry will be better off under a VAT than existing business taxes, within the industry there will be winners and losers.

CONCLUSION

This chapter has provided a first step in analyzing the sectoral impacts of a VAT. Much further research is needed. The aggregate data should be revised to reflect the 1986 tax law change and value-added data must be revised to better account for imports and exports.

To date, only one industry, the electronics industry, has been sufficiently surveyed to make a direct comparison to the aggregate results. Hopefully, data on other industries will become available in the future so that better comparisons can be made. It is crucial to have this micro data to check for variability within industries. Even the limited data presented here suggests that wide variability is to be expected and there may be many companies whose results differ from the aggregate predictions.

10

MACROECONOMIC EFFECTS OF A CONSUMPTION-BASED TAX

by Stephen C. Vogt

The Tax Reform Act of 1986 was hailed by its proponents as one of the most important pieces of revenue legislation in the history of the United States. The purpose of the law was to transform a tax system that was perceived to be increasingly complex, inequitable, and inefficient into a fairer, simpler, and more broad-based one.

Despite the passage of the 1986 Act, a time-honored debate on the proper base for taxation continues. Analysts began questioning whether a tax based on net income, or one based on consumption expenditures, held the greatest promise for U.S. economic health more than 40 years ago.[1] The debate was rejoined in earnest prior to deliberations on tax reform which culminated in the 1986 Act. Prior to tax reform, the Internal Revenue Code was best characterized as a hybrid system with elements of both consumption and income taxes.

In its original documentation, the Reagan administration made clear that its preference was to move the tax code closer to an income tax than a consumption-based tax. The end result, the 1986 Act, ratified this preference. Yet critics immediately surfaced, and the old debate on tax bases continues.

One objection by critics of the 1986 Act is that, in creating a more comprehensive income tax base, the new law does not help to

---

[1]Milton Friedman, "The Spending Tax as a Wartime Fiscal Measure," *American Economic Review, March 1943, pp. 50-62. Also see Nicholas Kaldor, An Expenditure Tax* (London: Allen and Unwin, 1957).

correct some of the distortions which existed under the previous Internal Revenue Code. For instance, the return on savings is still taxed twice under the new system. To some extent, savings now carries a larger burden, since the partial exclusion on dividend and capital gains income has been removed. The 1986 Act has also increased the tax burden on capital-intensive corporations, according to critics, and consequently has reduced incentives for business investment.

Indeed, critics contend that by using income as the underlying tax base, the revenue system in the United States will always be plagued with excess complication as policymakers try to devise more appropriate and precise measures of income. Proponents, however, argue that in fact the income tax is, in the long run, more efficient and that the 1986 Act will foster greater economic health.

The continuing debate on the appropriateness of income as a tax base, coupled with concerns for potential new revenue sources to reduce budget deficits, is reviving interest in a consumption-based tax. Thus, theoretical and empirical macroeconomic implications of one tax base versus another are a very current concern to policymakers.

The purpose of this chapter is to survey some of the macroeconomic evidence on different tax bases. Initially, some commentary is offered on some important questions of equity not covered elsewhere in this volume. Following the discussion of tax system "fairness," the ingredients and issues confronting an analyst faced with the task of quantifying the macroeconomic effects of income and consumption tax bases is discussed. Then, the empirical results of several studies are reported. These studies consider both the long and short run effects of one tax base versus another.

EQUITY CONSIDERATIONS

Chapters 2, 3 and 4 dealt at length with issues concerning the incidence of consumption taxes. Two views of incidence were provided. One, the traditional view, holds that consumption taxes are borne solely by consumers. The alternative view holds that the incidence is shared among consumers, workers, and the owners of capital.

As discussed in these earlier chapters, vertical equity or the concept of ability to pay relates to the incidence analysis. If a consumption tax is passed fully forward to consumers, then regressiveness -- the extent those least able to bear the burden of the tax -- is a critical issue. The alternative view, however, some-what diminishes the importance of vertical equity concerns. Remedies concerning the vertical equity question have also been covered in detail in Chapter 5. Therefore, this chapter will concern itself solely with the question of horizontal equity.

Horizontal Equity

Horizontal equity, or the requirement that "equals be taxed equally," also depends on which incidence analysis is correct. Both views do agree, however, that at least some, if not all, consumption tax liabilities are borne by individuals in their role as consumers. To simplify the discussion of horizontal equity, the following analysis assumes the traditional incidence perspective. It should be kept in mind, however, that, as is the case in vertical equity considerations, horizontal equity problems are diminished to the extent that the shared-incidence analysis is the appropriate one.

Under the current tax law, the requirement that "equals be taxed equally" is interpreted to mean that a fair tax is one under which individuals with the same current income pay the same amount of tax. Critics of the income tax argue that often times the standard of horizontal equity is not met since special provisions in the tax law serve to favor one form of income over another. Indeed, an impor-tant goal of the 1986 Act was to increase the degree of horizontal equity by eliminating favorable treatment of certain types of income (such as capital gains) and closing many tax "loopholes." However, critics of the income tax point out that current income is a poor index of equality since it disregards the ability of individuals to bor-row against future earnings to enhance their current lifestyles.

Horizontal equity is interpreted differently under the consump-tion tax. Proponents of the consumption tax argue that the appropriate measure of "equals" is not current income but rather lifetime income.[2] That rationale is based on the Life Cycle Hypothesis (LCH) pioneered by Modigliani and Brumberg.[3] The idea is that in a properly functioning capital market, individuals can save current income or borrow against future expected income in

---

2Thomas E. Vasquez, "Addressing Issues of the Regressivity of a Consumption Tax," in Charls Walker and Mark Bloomfield, eds., *The Consumption Tax: A Better Alternative?* (Cambridge, MA: Ballinger, 1987), p. 316.

[3]Franco Modigliani and Richard Brumberg, "Utility Analysis and the Consump-tion Function: An Interpretation of Cross-section Data," in Kenneth Kurihara, ed., *Post Keynesian Economics* (New Brunswick: Rutgers University Press, 1954), pp. 388-396.

order to attain the consumption path they desire. Therefore, individuals are likely to consume heavily early in their life-cycle, save in their prime income-generating years, and consume from savings during retirement. Under the LCH, two individuals with entirely different earnings streams can enjoy the same lifestyle as long as those streams have the same present value. Horizontal equity, consumption tax proponents argue, requires comparing individuals with the same lifetime income rather than merely identical current incomes.

The obvious question then becomes: How does tax policy insure that individuals with equal lifetime incomes are taxed equally? The answer comes from reconsidering the Life Cycle Hypothesis. Lifetime income can be spent in one of two ways. First, income can be consumed throughout the individual's lifetime. Secondly, any remaining income not consumed will be given either to heirs or to the state. Therefore, the appropriate means of taxing lifetime income is to tax consumption plus bequests.

The consumption tax insures that individuals with equal lifetime incomes will pay the same lifetime taxes (in present value terms). Individuals may postpone tax payments by consuming less, but the tax savings plus interest earned on the savings will be paid back at death when the individual's bequest is taxed.

Proponents of a consumption tax argue that, on horizontal equity grounds, taxation based on lifetime income is much fairer than the income tax. Under an income tax, two individuals with the same present value of lifetime income can pay drastically different amounts in taxes depending on how their income streams are arranged. Furthermore, since interest income is also included in the income tax base, individuals who choose to save early in life end up with a larger lifetime tax bill than those individuals with the same present value of lifetime income who choose to consume.

The argument for a consumption tax based on horizontal equity grounds is summed up by Bradford:

> The tax system should not bear more heavily on the individual who chooses to purchase better food than on the one who chooses to buy higher quality clothing. Nor should it bear more heavily on the individual who chooses to apply his endowment of labor abilities to purchase consumption late in life (by saving early in life) than it does on the one who consumes early in life.[4]

---

[4]David F. Bradford, *Blueprints for Basic Tax Reform* (Arlington, VA: Tax Analysts, 1984), p. 37.

Effects of Capital Market Imperfections

Critics of the consumption tax are quick to point out that lifetime perspective of horizontal equity is only valid under very restrictive assumptions.[5] Lifetime income is only a measure of a person's economic status at any particular point in time if he or she can freely borrow and lend to achieve his or her desired lifetime income-constrained consumption path. Conversely, if individuals are liquidity-constrained, their lifetime income is not an appropriate measure of economic status. Opponents argue that the individual with a larger yearly income is better off (i.e., has higher status) than an individual who must wait for his "ship to come in." The former, they argue, is less constrained in obtaining his desired consumption path than the latter, who cannot borrow against future income.

Imperfect capital markets further exacerbate the horizontal equity problem if the consumption tax is progressive. This results because imperfections make it difficult for individuals to smooth their consumption paths. Consequently, those with more volatile consumption paths would pay a higher lifetime tax.[6]

Another assumption implicit in taxing lifetime income by taxing consumption is that any changes in future tax rates must be completely anticipated. As long as individuals can accurately predict future tax rate changes, they can use this information when planning their consumption paths today. Alternatively, if individuals lack perfect foresight, future (unexpected) changes in tax rates will impose differential burdens on individuals at different stages of the life-cycle.

Unexpected changes in the consumption tax rate place a greater (or lesser) burden on those individuals already at the end of their life-cycles. These individuals made their optimal lifetime consumption path decision many years ago under the old cost of consumption. The new tax rate changes the cost of consumption at a time when these individuals are consuming out of past savings, thus forcing them to bear the entire cost (or enjoy all of the gains) over a short period of time. Younger generations do not face this problem since they can respond to the tax change by adjusting their lifetime consumption path to maintain their desired level of con-

---

[5]Joseph Pechman, "A Consumption Tax is Not Desirable for the United States," in Charls Walker and Mark Bloomfield, eds., *The Consumption Tax* (Cambridge, Mass.: Ballinger Publishing Company, 1987), p. 272.

[6]Don Fullerton, "The Consumption Tax Versus the Income Tax," in John Makin, ed., *Real Tax Reform: Replacing the Income Tax* (Washington, D.C.: American Enterprise Institute, 1985), pp. 8-9.

sumption after their income-producing years have past.

A final criticism raised deals with the treatment of bequests under the consumption tax. Policy proposals regarding the consumption tax often exempt gifts and bequests from the tax base. Such exemptions would violate the horizontal equity criterion since those individuals who prefer to save and make bequests would pay less taxes in present value terms.[7]

In addition, several problems might arise during the transition to a consumption tax. One serious drawback is that switching to a consumption base would cause an adverse redistribution of wealth among households of different ages. Older households that saved for years under an income tax (in order to consume more in retirement) would be hurt. Not only would these households have been taxed on previous income saved for retirement needs, but they also would be taxed on their retirement consumption. Some sort of transition rule might well be required to ease the excess burden on older households when switching to a consumption base if it is truly believed that consumption taxes are fully reflected in price.[8]

Another transition problem is the effect of a consumption tax on the value of existing assets. A switch to a consumption tax would effectively raise the tax on some assets (e.g., family homes) and reduce the tax on others (e.g., savings accounts). This switch would result in windfall gains and losses to owners of assets in a way that may be unrelated to any concept of fairness. For example, suppose an increase in a tax on the income or consumption stream of an asset will cause a decline in its price equal to the present value of the tax. Therefore, the owner of the asset effectively prepays any tax on the stream of income provided by the asset. But, under a consumption tax, the owner of such an asset will also have to pay a tax on his consumption stream from the asset. Therefore, the owner effectively would pay the tax twice. In switching to a consumption tax, those holding currently tax-favored assets would suffer windfall losses while those owning tax-disfavored assets would reap windfall gains.[9]

---

[7]Paul L. Menchik and David Martin, "The Incidence of a Lifetime Consumption Tax," *National Tax Journal* (June 1982), pp. 189-203.

[8]Fullerton, in Makin, ed., *Real Tax Reform*, p. 10.

[9]Ibid., p. 11.

MACROECONOMIC IMPLICATIONS OF A
CONSUMPTION/INCOME TAX SUBSTITUTION

The purpose of this section is to identify the factors influencing the change in economic welfare when substituting a consumption tax for the income tax. Simulating welfare changes is an extremely complicated endeavor, and many countervailing forces must be considered. The purpose of this type of simulation is to see if the economy would be better off under one type of tax regime than another. Ignoring, for the moment, equity questions, these macroeconomic simulations attempt to forecast whether the economy would be larger and grow faster under a revenue neutral consumption tax, than under an income tax.

Critics of the income tax cite two obvious types of distortions under current law -- altering returns for various types of assets and producing tax-induced preferences for current consumption. These two sources of non-neutrality are thought to artificially retard the economy's ability to grow.

Distortions Between Assets

First, the current, imperfect income tax creates differential effects across different types of assets and activities at any point in time, thus causing investors to make decisions they otherwise would not make, leading to an economic (deadweight) loss. These will be referred to as cross-sectional distortions. For example, individuals who own their own homes benefit from an income tax since they can deduct mortgage interest payments from their tax bills. Those who rent pay their housing bills with after-tax income. Also, corporate earnings are taxed at the corporate level and again at the individual level when dividends are taxed, while non-corporate earnings are taxed only once. Many types of payments for debt service are tax-deductible while dividends are not. Employees benefit from having a portion of their wages and salaries paid in the form of fringe benefits which are exempt from individual income taxes.[10]

Even though the 1986 Act set out to eliminate many such distortions, critics of the income tax argue that the ability to do so is inherently limited. Once income is selected as a base, these cross-sectional distortions are part of the package. Furthermore, they argue that those distortions which are correctable usually require fairly complex amendments to the tax law.

---

[10]Ibid., p. 7.

Intertemporal Distortions

A more common criticism of the income tax is that it creates intertemporal distortions (distortions involving choices on when to consume and save) in the economy. These tax-induced alterations of incentives result from the double taxation of savings and investment inherent in the income tax and were discussed in Chapter 4.

Double taxation occurs in two ways. As pointed out above, the return on savings is taxed twice, once when the income saved is received and again when the return on savings is realized. This implies that those choosing to consume today rather than save would actually reduce their intertemporal tax bill (again, the extent of this reduction depends on the actual incidence of the tax). The effect of the income tax is to drive a wedge between the price of consumption today and that price tomorrow -- encouraging present consumption and discouraging saving.

Secondly, returns to those investing in corporations are taxed at the corporate level and again when the individual receives the returns from that investment. This reduces the after-tax return to investment in corporate capital. Critics argue that such double taxation raises the cost of capital, thereby retarding the rate of capital development, slowing growth, and reducing social welfare.[11]

Finally, the income tax has an inflationary bias which further reduces the after-tax return to capital. Capital gains are defined as the difference between the realized value of the asset upon sale and the cost of purchase. Since these values are stated in nominal terms, inflation will affect the reported amount of capital gains. Thus, the owner of long-term assets will be taxed on both the real and inflationary gains upon sale of the asset.[12]

Prior to the 1986 Act, investment tax credits, accelerated depreciation, reduced tax rates for long-term capital gains, tax credits for research and development, and certain income shelters (i.e., IRAs, Keogh accounts, etc.) were used to enhance investment, thereby offsetting some of these distortions. Many of these special provisions were eliminated under the 1986 Act, thereby raising the tax burden on capital in the corporate sector by approximately six percent.[13]

---

[11]John H. Makin, "Income Tax Reform and the Consumption Tax," in Walker and Bloomfield, eds., *The Consumption Tax*, p. 90.

[12]David F. Bradford, "The Case for the Personal Consumption Tax," in Joseph Pechman, ed., *What Should be Taxed, Income or Expenditure?* (Washington, D.C.: Brookings Institution, 1980), p. 87.

[13]Makin, "Income Tax Reform and the Consumption Tax," in Walker and Bloomfield, eds., *The Consumption Tax*, p. 107.

There is a general consensus among researchers that the intertemporal distortions created under an income tax retards economic activity. Yet the extent of the loss and whether it can be corrected by a consumption tax is still open to debate. Quantitative differences in the estimates of this welfare loss result from differences in the methodology and assumptions used.

In fact, some argue that countervailing forces overcome any loss which may occur due to distortions in the saving/consumption choice. There are many forces at work in the economy which are affected by taxes. Some of these forces may react opposite to each other in the face of the same tax.

Simulation Studies

A certain evolution in simulation studies has occurred. Early studies analyzing the welfare costs of capital income taxation were done in the context of neo- classical growth models where the capital stock and factor prices were endogenously determined.[14] The problem with these models was that even though they *approximated* the effects of capital taxation on capital accumulation, they did not incorporate the individual responses of households concerning the saving/consuming choice. Later studies attempted to correct this by employing two-period models where the individual worked in one period, retired in the second and consumed in both.[15]

While this solved the problem of incorporating the individual's saving/consuming choice, a further problem was caused by assuming that individuals worked only in the first period. This is tantamount to assuming that taxes do not affect labor supply (labor supply is inelastic). The result of such a model would be to overstate the gains from moving to a consumption tax from an income tax. Later studies, some of which are reported later in this chapter, modeled both the household's saving/consuming choice and the labor/leisure choice.

In order for a researcher to truly simulate the effects of a tax substitution, each one of at least four potentially countervailing forces must be accounted for. The net result of this mix of indepen-

---

[14]See for instance Martin Feldstein, "Tax Incidence in a Growing Economy With Variable Factor Supply," *Quarterly Journal of Economics* (November 1974), pp. 551-573. Also Ann F. Friedlander and Adolf F. Vandendospe, "Capital Taxation in a Dynamic General Equilibrium Setting," *Journal of Public Economics* (August 1978), pp. 1-24.

[15]See, for instance, Martin Feldstein, "The Welfare Cost of Capital Income Taxation," *Journal of Political Economy* (April 1978), pp. 529-551.

dent reactions will determine whether the economy grows more, less, or remains the same, if a consumption based tax were substituted for the current income tax.

1. The Labor Response to Different Tax Rates. Any tax change is likely to affect the willingness of individuals to provide labor services. Clearly the more labor demanded and supplied, the greater the potential for economic growth. To the extent that consumption taxes end up being reflected in the prices of goods and services (see Chapters 2, 3, and 4), there will most likely be a difference in the rate of taxation under a consumption tax and income tax. This is because of the obvious relation determined from the National Income and Product Accounts (NIPA). It is clear, in a national accounting sense, that a tax base which excludes savings will require a higher tax rate to produce a given amount of revenue than one which includes savings.

Thus, if a consumption tax were substituted for an income tax, the tax rate may be higher. To the extent that this rate is applied to labor, less labor may be supplied under a higher-rated consumption tax than a lower-rated income tax. This may result in less output than otherwise would be the case and countervail the benefits of removing intertemporal and inter-asset distortions.

The extent of this countervailing force depends on labor's responsiveness to the after-tax wage rate or, in economic terms, it depends on the "elasticity of labor supply." This elasticity measures the percentage increase in labor supplied due to a one percent increase in the after-tax wage. If labor supply is very elastic, then higher tax rates may greatly reduce the amount of labor provided and the higher rates associated with a narrower base may be significant.

This elasticity is measurable and is an important component in any simulation purporting to measure the economic effects of a shift from an income tax to a consumption tax.

2. The Response of Savers. The fact that income taxes distort the individual's choice on how much to save and consume has already been discussed. The rate of saving effects economic growth through its effect on the rate of investment. To the extent that taxes negatively impact savings, economic growth may be retarded. How responsive savings behavior is to taxation, however, is an empirical matter. The important empirical measure is the elasticity of savings with respect to the after-tax rate of return. This measures the percent increase in the saving rate due to a one percent increase in the *after-tax* return to saving. If saving is very responsive (elastic), then the economic gains from moving to a consumption tax will be greater than if saving is inelastic. But there are countervailing forces which determine the saving response to tax changes.

McLure has pointed out that, even if a change to a consumption tax would increase welfare by reducing the distortion between current and future consumption, it does not follow that its adoption would result in more saving.[16] The tax policy impact on the saving rate depends on how the "income" and "substitution" effects of an interest rate change influence the level of savings.[17] While the substitution effect suggests a positive response of saving, the income effect is negative. Thus, the actual response of saving to a change in the after-tax interest rate is an empirical matter.

There is a long-standing debate over the influence of interest rates on the level of savings. As early as 1958, Denison noted the remarkable stability of the ratio of gross private savings to gross national product.[18] Howery and Hymans find empirical support for the proposition that the elasticity of saving is not significantly different from zero, implying that tax policy will not affect the level of savings.[19]

The opposing point of view, suggesting that the after-tax return does affect the level of savings, has been put forth by Boskin.[20] After running numerous econometric experiments on aggregate time series data over a variety of fundamental forms and estimation methods, Boskin has estimated the interest elasticity of saving to be approximately 0.4. This implies that a one percent increase in the after-tax rate of return produces a 0.4 percent increase in the savings rate.

The controversy on the response of the saving rate to after-tax rate of return has, in part, resulted from taking into consideration many theoretical and empirical factors involving bequests and other motives for saving. Since the early debates, the models have become more sophisticated. No longer are individuals' lives con-

---

[16]Charles McLure, "Taxes, Saving, and Welfare: Theory and Evidence," *National Tax Journal* (September 1980), pp. 311-320.

[17]The substitution effect occurs because the consumption tax reduces the cost of saving and therefore an individual may "substitute" saving for consumption. But because savings is taxed less in any rate, there is more income to both save and consume and there is, therefore, an income effect.

[18]Edward F. Denison, "A Note on Private Saving," *Review of Economics and Statistics*, Vol. 40 (August 1958), pp. 261-267.

[19]E. Phillip Howery and Saul Hymans, "The Measurement and Determination of Loanable Funds Savings," in Joseph Pechman, ed., *What Should Be Taxed?*, pp. 1-31.

[20]Michael J. Boskin, "Taxation, Saving, and the Rate of Interest," *Journal of Political Economy*, Vol. 86, no. 2, pt. 2 (1978), pp. S3-S27.

strained by models to occur in only two distinct periods -- a working period and a retirement period.

Summers has pointed out that when the model is extended to a more realistic, multi-period life cycle, the interest elasticity of saving becomes very large. In a multi-period model, labor income continues to be earned in subsequent periods. The higher after-tax rate of return on saving also discounts the individual's future earning stream by a larger amount. This lower present value of income (what Summers terms the human wealth effect) encourages even less consumption and more saving. The additional savings go toward further capital accumulation, creating greater economic growth. As a result of his multi-period model, Summers finds an elasticity of saving of 2.0.[21]

3. The Effects of Expectation Formulation. A third consideration affecting economic gains from removing the tax on capital is the degree of consumer foresight. Ballard has shown that the large welfare[22] gains from implementing a consumption tax that are predicted by some general equilibrium models may be slightly overstated. The reason for this is that most models assume that economic actors are myopic and that they base their future expectations on existing conditions. The consequence of these "static expectations" is that individuals do not foresee lower future capital prices (hence lower returns to investment) as a result of ongoing capital accumulation.[23] On the other hand, assuming perfect foresight allows agents in the models to foresee the lower price changes due to capital accumulation and adjust planned saving accordingly.

While perfect foresight does not change the final equilibrium growth rate of the economy, the path to that situation is altered. Ballard has estimated, however, that welfare gains under perfect foresight are only about 5 to 10 percent below the gains which occur under myopia.[24]

4. Open Economy Considerations. Probably the largest shortcoming of most general equilibrium models estimating the welfare gains from eliminating the tax on capital is that they assume a closed economy with no allowance for the international flow of capital.

---

[21]Lawrence Summers, "Capital Taxation and Accumulation in a Life Cycle Growth Model," *American Economic Review* (September 1981), p. 533.

[22]"Welfare" gain is economic parlance for the overall economic gain to society. It includes not only increased economic growth but also increased consumer satisfaction due to the fact that choices are less distorted by taxes.

[23]Charles Ballard, "Tax Policy and Consumer Foresight: A General Equilibrium Simulation Study," *Economic Inquiry*, Vol. 25 (April 1987), p. 280.

[24]Ibid.

Ballard *et al.* present a modified general equilibrium model that allows for an open economy. They run several specifications of the degree of openness and conclude:

> The consumption tax results certainly raise the possibility that a tax policy that appears to improve efficiency in a model of a closed economy may *reduce* efficiency in a model with an open world capital market.[25] (emphasis added)

The reason for this result is that, in an open economy, the removal of taxation on the return to saving need not encourage capital development in the domestic economy, since the increased saving can flow overseas and finance foreign capital development. In an integrated world capital market, individual national interest rates (and other risk factors) influence the flow of capital. Increased saving on the part of the United States would be put to use financing U.S. investment only if its return were greater than the return obtainable elsewhere. This serves to highlight the importance of reducing the double taxation of corporate income (which would increase the after-tax return on corporate investment). Removing the tax-induced bias against saving may not be enough in and of itself.

The degree of openness of the world capital markets has been subject to much debate. Harberger is associated with an open economy view of world capital markets. He studied the correlation between rates of return in different countries and their capital/labor ratios and found no relationship between the two. He suggests that this lack of correlation is the result of an efficiently operating world capital market.[26]

Feldstein and Horioka have taken a different approach. They suggested that there are many reasons why capital may not flow perfectly. They use data from major industrial countries to measure the extent to which a higher domestic saving rate is associated with a higher rate of domestic investment. The study discovers a positive relationship. Thus, they conclude that the degree of openness among major industrial countries is limited; therefore, tax policy encouraging saving may stimulate investment.[27]

Miskin also finds support for a less-than-perfectly-open world capital market. Using real interest rates in the Euro-deposit market

---

[25]Ballard et al., "Replacing the U.S. Income Tax," p. 228.

[26]Arnold Harberger, "Vignettes on the World Capital Market," *American Economic Review* (May 1980), pp. 331-337.

[27]Martin Feldstein and Charles Horioka, "Domestic Saving and International Capital Flows," *Economic Journal* (June 1980), pp. 314-329.

for the U.S., Canada, the U.K., France, West Germany, the Netherlands and Switzerland, he strongly rejects the hypothesis of equal interest rates across these countries.[28]

The debate appears to have reached a middle ground. Consensus supports the proposition that the economy is not entirely open and that there is room for tax policy designed to stimulate saving to ultimately stimulate investment as well. Even so, strong evidence exists that international capital flows are becoming increasingly important -- a factor that future tax policy must take into consideration.

Results of Long-Run Simulation Models. Various studies have incorporated some or all of the countervailing forces mentioned above. Some results are reported here (and summarized in Table 10.1). Auerbach *et al.* found that shifting to a proportional consumption tax leads to a welfare gain of approximately seven percent of lifetime resources.[29]   Ballard *et al.* considered replacing the income tax that was in place in 1985 with a consumption tax and found economic gains with present values between $841 billion and $2.3 trillion (in 1986 dollars) depending on the degree of progressivity and interest elasticity assumed.[30]

Boskin has estimated that the welfare loss from the double taxation of capital exceeded $50 billion a year with an overall present value of nearly $1 trillion.[31] Summers estimated that the long-run welfare gain from eliminating the double taxation on capital would be $150 billion annually.[32] Since he does not incorporate a labor response (which was pointed out to countervail the saving response), the effects may be overstated.

Table 10.1 provides a synopsis of various recent simulations of the effect of a substitution of a consumption tax for an income tax.

Short-Run Effects. Almost all studies addressing the macroeco

---

[28]Fredric Miskin, "Are Real Interest Rates Equal Across Countries? An Empirical Investigation of International Parity Conditions," *Journal of Finance*, Vol. 39, no. 5 (1984), pp. 1345-1357.

[29]Alan J. Auerbach, Laurence J. Kotlikoff and Jonathan Skinner, "The Efficiency Gains From Dynamic Tax Reform," *International Economic Review*, Vol. 24, no. 1 (February 1983), p. 97.

[30]Charles Ballard, Don Fullerton, John Shoven, and John Whalley, "Replacing the U.S. Income Tax With a Progressive Consumption Tax," in *A General Equilibrium Model for Tax Policy Analysis* (Chicago: University of Chicago Press, 1985) p. 183.

[31]Michael J. Boskin, "Taxation, Saving and the Rate of Interest," *Journal of Political Economy*, Vol. 86, no. 2, pt. 2 (1978), pp. S3-S27.

[32]Lawrence Summers, "Capital Taxation and Accumulation in a Life Cycle Growth Model," *American Economic Review* (September 1981), p. 533.

Table 10-1

SIMULATION STUDIES OF WELFARE GAINS
UNDER A SHIFT TO A CONSUMPTION TAX BASE

	Present Value Welfare Gain (in billions of 1986 dollars)	Percentage of Present Value Welfare
Auerbach *et al* (1983)	N.A.	5.0 - 7.1%[a]
Ballard (1987)	$1,097 - $1,501	0.9 - 1.3%
Ballard *et al* (1985)		
Closed economy	$841 - $2,300	0.7 - 2.0%
Open economy	$(1,399) - $1,281	(1.2) - 1.2%
Boskin (1978)	$45 - $56[b]	N.A.
Mankin (1987)	$1822 - $3115	1.5 - 2.5%
Summers (1981)	$100 - $200[b]	11.2 - 16.2%[a]

[a]Reported as a percentage of lifetime income
[b]Reported as annual gains

Source: See notes.

nomics of income/consumption tax substitution effects consider only the long-run welfare gains. Few studies reveal any information which may help answer questions regarding the macroeconomic effects of a consumption tax in the short run. Questions regarding the effects of the tax regime change on prices, economic activity, employment, and the trade and budget deficits have not been addressed.

A major concern with moving to a consumption tax, particularly to a VAT or national sales tax, is the short-term effect on prices. This concern is heavily dependent on the incidence discussed in Chapters 2, 3 and 4. Many observers believe that the introduction of a VAT will increase the price level by the VAT rate.[33] Even within the traditional analysis, where the VAT is deemed to be fully

---

[33]Joel Prakken, "The Macroeconomics of Tax Reform," in Walker and Bloomfield, eds., *The Consumption Tax*, pp. 117-166.

reflected in price, the effects of a VAT introduction on inflation rates is open to debate.

Using foreign experience as a guide, there appears to be little evidence that the introduction of a VAT exacerbates inflation. Tait (1981) has found that of the 31 countries adopting VATs between 1967 and 1980, only four showed evidence that a VAT had a major impact on prices. On the other hand, virtually no inflation effect occurred in 21 of those countries.[34] (This study is reviewed at the end of Chapter 4.)

In contrast to these findings, Prakken (1987) suggests that adopting a VAT will have at least a modest impact on prices. Using results from a macroeconomic model simulating the U.S. economy, he concludes that a one percent VAT, accommodated by a 1.35 percent increase in the nominal money supply (phased in over three years and beginning in 1989), would increase the GNP deflator 2.2 percent by 1991. By 1995, he forecasts the GNP to be down 1.4 percent, as higher prices slow economic activity.[35] (See Table 10.2.) He concludes that, even though a VAT will create short-term price rises, the likelihood of a prolonged bout of inflation is slight.

Of course, any econometric model is very sensitive to the original assumptions. If a VAT is modeled as a proportionate tax on factor incomes (as some models assume, see Chapter 3), rather than a tax on goods, the outcome can be radically different.

SUMMARY AND CONCLUSION

The flawless tax policy which performs its revenue-raising function without imposing costs on the economy does not exist. Even so, certain taxes perform better than others in several specific and crucial areas.

Measuring the macroeconomic effects of an income/consumption tax substitution is a very involved process. Many countervailing forces are at work and any econometric model is necessarily slave to a set of assumptions. Any simulation results should be viewed with extreme caution. Still the preliminary evidence seems to be that economic gains can be had by switching from a tax based on income to a tax based on consumption.

---

[34]Alan Tait, "Is the Introduction of a Value Added Tax Inflationary?" *Finance and Development* (June 1981), pp. 38-42.

[35]Prakken, in Walker and Bloomfield, eds., *The Consumption Tax*, pp. 133-134.

Table 10-2

ECONOMETRIC ESTIMATES FOR A 1 PERCENT VAT, MONETARILY ACCOMMODATED*

Category	1986	1987	1988	1989	1990	1991	1992	1993	1994	1995
Real gross national product	-0.00	-0.03	-0.09	-0.22	-0.43	-0.77	-1.10	-1.31	-1.40	-1.36
Personal consumption exp.	-0.00	-0.09	-0.16	-0.22	-0.25	-0.45	-0.74	-1.07	-1.43	-1.81
Business fixed investment	-0.00	-0.02	-0.01	-0.10	-0.41	-1.11	-1.96	-2.64	2.95	-2.83
As shares of gross national product										
Personal consumption exp.	-0.00	-0.06	-0.07	-0.00	0.18	0.32	0.36	0.24	-0.03	-0.46
Business fixed investment	-0.00	0.01	0.07	0.12	0.02	-0.34	-0.88	-1.34	-1.58	-1.49
Civilian unemployment rate (% pts)	0.00	0.02	0.04	0.11	0.21	0.43	0.68	0.93	1.13	1.27
Deflator, GNP	0.00	0.35	0.87	1.53	1.93	2.19	2.28	2.18	1.87	1.42
After-tax real bond yield (% pts)	-0.00	-0.02	-0.05	-0.07	-0.04	0.02	0.03	0.02	-0.01	-0.05
Real cost of business fixed capital	-0.02	-0.14	-0.30	-0.40	-0.15	0.28	0.50	0.47	0.24	-0.10
Real business fixed capital stocks	-0.00	-0.00	-0.00	-0.01	-0.04	-0.14	-0.32	-0.58	-0.87	-1.12
Personal savings rate (% pts)	0.00	-0.23	-0.51	-0.88	-1.04	-1.13	-1.16	-1.14	-1.07	-0.94
Federal deficit ($ billions)	-0.03	11.65	26.07	42.79	46.59	47.10	47.10	47.64	49.05	52.10

*Impacts are measured as percentage differences from baseline unless otherwise noted.

Source: Joel Prakken, "The Macroeconomics of Tax Reform," in The Consumption Tax, 1987, p. 135.

11

ADMINISTRATION AND COMPLIANCE

by Cliff Massa III

The introduction to Chapter 6 noted that the United States has not had much recent experience with implementing a new tax system which required consideration of transition issues. Although potentially important to some industries and companies, such matters do not attract universal interest. But the difficulties of developing from scratch the capacity to administer a whole new system would affect -- and probably aggravate -- *all* taxpayers.

Efficient implementation of a new tax would require trained administrators and tax collectors. There would need to be enough of them to assure that taxpayers would remit at the same high level of compliance which the United States is generally thought to enjoy, relative to many other industrialized countries. A body of clear and workable rules and regulations to enable both tax collectors and taxpayers to understand what is required would be equally important. The capacity to handle administrative and judicial appeals would also need to expand quickly once a new tax becomes effective.

Studying administrative issues clearly is less glamorous than debating economic incidence or international trade effects. Even the transitional issues and other company- or industry-specific problems would attract much more attention from the private sector than would administrative questions.

Yet, the perception that administrative and compliance problems would heavily burden day-to-day business operations *could* become a critical barrier to enactment of a value-added tax (VAT) in the United States. To provide some organization for the consideration of these matters, this chapter groups these administrative and compliance difficulties under three general headings.

The first part of the chapter discusses development of a framework for administration of a VAT. The principal questions are: "How much lead time should be allowed between enactment of a VAT and the date for implementing it? How long would it take to hire and train the necessary personnel? How quickly could basic regulations and procedures be developed and distributed to taxpayers? How much time would be required to educate taxpayers?"

The second section analyzes the numbers and types of people needed to create a knowledgeable core of government employees who could develop the regulatory structure and then implement and administer the tax. The Treasury Department's 1984 assessment of the costs of such activities is included.

The third section looks at a range of matters dealing with issues of simplicity, familiarity and precision. Many such issues could affect fundamental policy choices. For example, should administration and compliance burdens influence the fundamental decisions about the breadth of the VAT base and the use of a single or multiple rates? Should the widespread familiarity with the means for computing corporate and individual income taxes influence the choice of a structure for a VAT? Should the costs of auditing and collecting from millions of small businesses (relative to their tax payments) influence the decision about exempting such companies? Should simplicity take precedence over more complicated, but familiar, accounting rules?

The chapter concludes with a discussion of the administrative complexities of border adjustments. Issues such as what to use as the tax base and who must remit the tax are addressed.

No effort is made to identify exhaustively all of the administrative or tax accounting problems which a VAT would pose. Nor is a definitive set of potential solutions suggested. The list of tax accounting issues alone would be long, so only a brief mention is made of choices regarding accrual versus cash accounting, inventory capitalization and so on. It is hoped that the following discussion will encourage more business tax executives, accountants and attorneys, as well as federal policymakers, to give consideration to these and related subjects.

DEVELOPMENT OF A NEW SYSTEM

Enacting a new tax system of the magnitude of a VAT presents administrative challenges far beyond those required to accommodate recent major tax revisions. Substantial effort would be required to produce the body of regulations and procedures needed to administer the tax. The amount of time required to develop these materials, to hire and train the government employees and to educate taxpayers would be significant. The Treasury has estimated that a period of at least 18 months would be needed between the date of enactment and the date of implementation to prepare for administration of an invoice and credit VAT.[1]

If the United States were to enact the generic subtraction method VAT without the invoice and credit feature, the familiarity of taxpayers and tax collectors with the subtraction mechanics of the income tax might ease the educational problems. Efforts to construct a type of "short-form VAT attachment" to the regular income tax return (in lieu of a separate VAT return) suggest a desire to lessen the burdens on both taxpayers and tax collectors.

Perhaps the method for computing a VAT *could* lessen the magnitude of the compliance problems over the years. It seems plausible that familiarity with the basic mathematics would at least reduce major taxpayer mistakes. But it is not at all clear that the choice of the subtraction method over the invoice and credit method could materially lessen the amount of time needed to get ready for the new tax.

There are major substantive differences between net business income and a VAT base, and these must be addressed. Descriptions are easy in the abstract, but precise definitions of critical terms and concepts would take time to develop. In addition, the recordkeeping practices which are currently used to compute taxable income for a business might not lend themselves to simple adjustments for purposes of computing a VAT base.

The 1986 Act as an Example

Experience with the Tax Reform Act of 1986 (1986 Act) suggests that unforeseen practical difficulties can beset the best laid plans of tax reformers. The Treasury and the Internal Revenue Service (IRS) have responded to the massive task of implementing that legislation with a remarkable effort, including a series of "notices" and temporary regulations which have provided guidance that taxpayers

---

[1]U.S. Department of the Treasury, *Tax Reform for Fairness, Simplicity, and Economic Growth, Volume 3: Value-Added Taxes* (Washington, D.C.: U.S. Department of the Treasury, November 1984), p. 124.

can rely on when preparing their returns. This has helped to over-come the need to have final regulations before each major provision of the 1986 Act became effective.

However, more than two years have elapsed since enactment of the 1986 Act, and a series of major regulatory projects have not yet been completed. Furthermore, scores of noncontroversial technical corrections to the 1986 Act remained unenacted, as of October 1, 1988, thereby complicating the administration of the law in many areas in which that Act made substantive changes. Many of the reg-ulations which have been issued are not necessarily in final form and will require additional time to revise.

Furthermore, the difficulties encountered in implementing the 1986 Act have arisen in the context of a mature, well-developed tax system. That system is administered by well-trained and exper-ienced staffs at both the Treasury and the IRS. These professionals have been able to cope with the increasingly elaborate provisions of the Internal Revenue Code and accompanying regulations because substantial changes generally have developed in increments rather than in massive leaps, notwithstanding the magnitude of certain legislative revisions such as the enactments of the 1954 Code and the Tax Reform Act of 1986. Although the pace of legislation in the 1980s has greatly strained the system, the complexities and sub-tleties of income tax law have come into being at a pace which generally has allowed both tax collectors and taxpayers to absorb the changes.

Putting a New System into Effect

The process of implementing a new tax system, which by defini-tion does not have a substantial volume of rules and trained person-nel already in place, should be initiated long before the legislative process is completed. Ideally, a substantial amount of work could be undertaken before active congressional consideration even begins.

Such prior planning seems most likely if the executive branch proposes a VAT as a major policy initiative. Presumably, the Trea-sury would have a body of materials prepared before the proposal is unveiled. The results could either be released to the public or at least be discussed with congressional committees and staff as legisla-tion is drafted. The Treasury's work in preparing its 1984 commen-tary on a VAT is one example of this approach.[2] The detailed materials accompanying the proposals by the Canadian government

[2]Ibid., pp. 113-128.

is another.[3]

The prospects for such prior planning seem more remote if a VAT were to be essentially a creature of the Congress or, as is more likely, a type of political "joint venture" between the Congress and an administration after extensive political negotiations. In the latter scenario, the "prior planning" might take place as the legislative process was already underway.

Whatever the origin of a proposal, it would seem essential that there be a substantial period of time between enactment of a VAT and its implementation date. Arguably, this would provide opponents an opportunity to kill or maim the original legislation or for particular groups to add complicating preferential amendments. But it would also provide taxpayers and tax collectors an opportunity to get prepared. While all tax laws on the books are perpetually subject to efforts to reform or repeal them, a new tax system has only one opportunity to be efficiently and effectively implemented. Taking ample time to prepare for a newly enacted VAT would seem to pose a significantly lower risk than not doing so.

WHO SHOULD ADMINISTER THE VAT?

Although the IRS is the principal federal agency which administers and enforces federal revenue laws, the U.S. Customs Service is also a revenue agency. Indeed, there is precedent in the United Kingdom's experience for using the customs collection agency to administer a VAT system.[4] The choice of an agency (including the possibility of the creation of a new agency) to administer a VAT in the United States would be a decision which should be made early in the process to lessen the startup time, if for no other reason.

Presuming that the IRS is given the *primary* responsibility, a VAT with border tax adjustments would also require the Customs Service or another agency to administer the import tax.[5] The volume of imports into the United States through scores of major ports and thousands of miles of land borders would make this a sizable undertaking. A brief consideration of border adjustment issues is presented at the end of this chapter.

---

[3]Michael H. Wilson, *Tax Reform 1987, Sales Tax Reform* (Canada: Department of Finance, June 18, 1987).

[4]William J. Turnier, "Designing an Efficient Value Added Tax," *Tax Law Review* Vol. 39, (Summer 1984) pp. 455-457.

[5]Treasury, pp. 113, 116-117.

The IRS would seem to be the agency of choice for administering the VAT. The Treasury certainly contemplates this approach in its 1984 study,[6] and there appears to be no serious suggestion that a new or different agency be used. The IRS already has a well-developed structure for dealing with all aspects of tax administration, including drafting of regulations, responding to ruling requests, preparing forms and publications, answering informal taxpayer inquiries, processing returns and refunds, auditing returns, negotiating and settling audit controversies, collecting unpaid taxes and investigating criminal activities.

Beefing Up IRS Resources

At the end of FY 1987, the Internal Revenue Service employed approximately 108,000 people and had spent just over $4.4 billion for the year. The IRS collected approximately $886 billion in income, employment, gift, estate and excise taxes, resulting in administrative costs of approximately $.50 for each $100 of revenues collected.[7]

This expense-to-revenue ratio or "load factor" of 0.5 percent suggests a rather efficient system. However, it is important to keep in mind that the IRS has grown and evolved over a period of 125 years. The income tax was enacted 75 years ago. As the income tax began to grow in importance as a source of federal revenues relative to tariffs, the IRS was able to develop over time to its current level of efficiency.

In contrast to 75 years of developing the IRS as an income tax agency, the Treasury's 1984 VAT report estimates a four-year period (presumably in addition to the 18 months of lead time) for staff and budget expansion to implement a new VAT. Staffing is projected to rise from an initial year level of about 12,500 to approximately 20,700, and additional budget costs are projected to rise from $400 million to $700 million (in 1984 dollars).[8] An immediate need is anticipated for hiring over 7,900 personnel (reducing to about 7,400 over the four-year period) just to process the returns. In contrast, the initial force of 2,300 examination personnel would triple over four years to 7,000, as the number of trained agents could be expanded to provide a desired level of audit activity. Similarly, collection staffing would increase from 1,000 to about 2,900 over

---

[6]Ibid., pp. 113-128.

[7]*Internal Revenue Service Annual Report 1987* (1988), pp. 62, 65.

[8]Treasury, p. 128.

four years, and appeals staff would increase from 70 to 840.[9]

These estimates do not include any projections for the Customs Service's administration of the border tax adjustment. Nonetheless, the projections are probably as reasonable a set of target numbers as one could develop in advance of serious legislative consideration of a VAT.

Comparative Efficiencies

In the abstract, the creation of a 20,000-person bureaucracy at a cost of at least $700 million would appear to be a considerable undertaking. The potential political risks of proposing such an agency or such an increase in the existing resources of the IRS are clear.

Yet, these figures, when considered in the context of the revenue to be generated by a VAT, appear to present far less of a political risk. For example, if a VAT were to raise $100 billion in revenue, the 20,000 people and $700 million budget would impose a cost of $.70 per $100 of revenue, which would be a 0.70 percent load factor for the system. If a VAT were to raise $150 billion annually in new revenues (which is approximately the size of the annual federal deficit), the load factor would drop to about 0.47 percent, just about the average load factor for the past eight years.[10]

These Treasury projections of costs are somewhat more optimistic than load factors of up to two percent which have been incurred in Europe.[11] Thus, a U.S. load factor of even 0.70 percent or somewhat higher would still compare favorably to many European experiences.

However, the Treasury's cost estimates were four years old in November 1988. If a VAT were enacted for implementation by 1991 or 1992, it seems certain that such costs would increase by at least 25 to 30 percent to reflect increases in salaries and other costs since 1984, even if no additional personnel were needed. If so, the load factor for raising $100 billion of net new revenues would rise from 0.70 percent to around 0.90 percent. Furthermore, a significant amount of work would fall on the Customs Service or another

---

[9]Ibid., pp. 117-121.

[10]IRS, p. 62.

[11]William J. Turnier, "VAT: Minimizing Administration And Compliance Costs," *Tax Notes* (March 14, 1988), p. 1258; Alan Schenk, "Value Added Tax: Does This Consumption Tax Have A Place In The Federal Tax System?" *Virginia Tax Review*, Volume 7, Number 2 (Fall 1987), pp. 288-292.

agency which would administer the border adjustments on imports, and no estimates are available for these costs. Inflation and border tax administration combined could increase the load factor for any given amount of revenue by 35 to 40 percent.

The relative efficiency of the 0.50 and 0.70 load factors also assumes that the VAT is a net additional revenue source of $150 billion and $100 billion respectively. However, if a VAT were to produce more modest revenue gains (e.g., $50 billion) net of substantial income and/or payroll tax reductions, efficiency would erode. Assume a VAT were to raise $150 billion in gross revenues, with $100 billion of such revenue used to "pay for" income and payroll tax reductions. The load factor for those taxes would jump from around 0.49 to 0.56 (with a possible downward adjustment due to minor savings from reduced costs of administering those tax systems).

In summary, administrative load factors would be quite dependent on the amount of net revenue raised. Smaller added revenues imply either less VAT administrative efficiency or less-efficient collection of other taxes. On the other hand, a large net tax increase, with less administrative load factors, could hardly be considered good news for taxpayers.

SIMPLICITY, FAMILIARITY AND PRECISION: WHICH SHOULD GOVERN THE RULES?

Any new tax system is likely to be difficult to implement, no matter how much prior planning is done. It simply takes a certain amount of time for new concepts to be grasped. The massive revisions to the income tax in 1986 are a rough equivalent of the magnitude of the new concepts which a VAT would pose. Although several million taxpayers were either removed from the income tax rolls altogether or were shifted to short forms, administrative problems have actually increased significantly in many areas under that Act. The remaining individual taxpayers and corporate taxpayers are struggling to cope with the new rules which Treasury and IRS are striving to develop and publish.

If a VAT were to be enacted for the United States, there are several categories of issues which could affect the burdensomeness of administration. Some issues which should be given careful consideration are discussed below.

1. A system which applies a single tax rate to an extremely broad

*base would be easier to implement than a system with multiple rates,
zero-rating and exempt businesses.*

Most commentators assume that a VAT enacted in the United
States would follow the lead of European systems by imposing a
series of varying tax rates on sales of particular goods and services
and by exempting or zero-rating the sales of certain business sectors.
But these more complex systems require more regulations and more
complicated compliance procedures than would be the case if a single rate were applied to a very broad base.

Using the income tax as a rough gauge, audit and litigation
controversies could be expected to be significantly more time-
consuming under a VAT with various "preferences." For example,
two federal income tax "preferences" -- the classification of property
eligible for the investment credit and the characterization of income
as capital gain -- have routinely generated major audit and litigation
controversies. Similar disputes would blossom as taxpayers seek to
benefit from differential rates, zero-rates and exemptions under a
VAT.

For example, if medical care were zero-rated, imagine the controversies over what constitutes a sale of medical care goods or
services. When do sales of over-the-counter products and remedies
become sales for medical expenses? What about the sales of
equipment to doctors; are the suppliers' sales zero-rated or only the
doctors' services to patients? Could "health spas" to which doctors
send patients for various ailments avoid VAT liabilities?

Another leading candidate for the zero-rated category is the sale
of food for off-premises consumption. In general terms, that would
be intended to apply to food you buy at the grocery store to eat at
home. But what is treated as "food?" Are all sales of edible and
potable products to be zero-rated? How far "off premises" must the
consumption occur before the sale is zero rated; does the sale of
carryout or home delivery "fast food" qualify?

The case for multiple rates, zero-rates and exemptions under a
VAT rests primarily on the traditional analysis of incidence, which
finds that a VAT is passed forward in prices and therefore falls most
heavily on the lower income levels. Zero-rating or applying low
rates to necessities seeks to shift this burden away from low-income
households. But if a VAT were to be enacted with this analysis as
its economic foundation, would a simpler and more efficient system
be realized by addressing the regressivity effects through either the
income or employment taxes? Income taxes, after all, can target the
intended income-level beneficiaries without removing whole lines of

business from the VAT base. Treasury's estimates indicate that removing food from a comprehensive VAT base (which otherwise excludes only housing, educational and charitable items) would reduce the total base by about 13.5 percent, resulting in a 15 percent increase in the rate which must be applied to all other value-added to raise a given amount of revenue.[12] The greater the erosion of the base, the higher the rate(s) on the remaining base, which in turn increases the pressure for more preferences, which tends to push up rates, and so on. Each step along this path creates more law, more regulations, more litigation and more wasting of resources.

However, if the shared incidence analysis were to carry the debate or if a VAT were perceived to be solely a tax on business, it seems unlikely that substantial segments of the economy would be removed from the base. Absent the regressivity issue, zero-rating particular goods and services would appear to be concessions to special interests.

2. A subtraction method VAT could be more comfortable for business taxpayers in the United States. The mechanics of an invoice and credit VAT, which are widely used and understood by industrialized countries, could ease implementation and administration burdens.

A generic subtraction method VAT would operate in much the same manner as the federal income tax. During a taxable year (or whatever shorter accounting period is deemed preferable), the VAT taxpayer would compute receipts from sales of goods and services to determine the gross tax base. Then, all payments during that period to other businesses for their goods and services (which are includible in such businesses' VAT bases) would be deducted from the company's gross sales receipts. The balance would be the base to which the VAT rate is applied, producing either a tax liability or a refund (assuming that the system contemplates a refund mechanism). The deductible items would be different, but the computational process would be very similar to the income tax.

This computational process would contrast, at least in appearance, with the mechanics of the invoice and credit method which arguably requires a more sophisticated paper trail because the VAT stated on the invoice (at least on invoices prior to retail sales) becomes part of the computation and compliance processes. The extensive experience of European countries with the invoice and credit method might be drawn upon when preparing a U.S. VAT,

---

[12]Treasury, pp. 86-87.

thereby reducing the time and other resources required to initiate the system. The Canadian government also appears ready to propose a form of invoice and credit mechanism. By the time any U.S. proposals were actively considered in Congress, the Canadian experience could provide a nearby and contemporaneous case history for federal policymakers to consider.

3. While the revenues to be raised from small businesses may not justify the cost of administration, excluding small businesses could be highly destructive of public support for the system while creating other compliance problems.

From the perspective of efficiency, there is much to be said for removing small businesses from the reach of a VAT. Treasury's 1984 report asserted that an exemption for unincorporated businesses with less than $10,000 of gross receipts would, in 1979, have removed more than one-half of all sole proprietorships and about one-third of all partnerships from the tax rolls, at a loss of only 2.5 percent of gross receipts from the combined categories. A $50,000 gross receipts cutoff would have removed 90 percent of sole proprietorships and nearly 75 percent of partnerships, but only about 11 percent of gross receipts.[13] If IRS resources, which would otherwise be absorbed by five to eight million tax returns of small businesses, could be directed to the several hundred thousand larger companies, the effectiveness of the system might be improved at a relatively minor cost. There might also be some political appeal to excluding small firms from the system.

European experience is littered with small business exemptions although sales receipt levels are generally far lower than then $50,000 level.[14] And at least some European tax administrators are thought to favor even broader small business exemptions.[15]

But it is more difficult to conceive of such exemptions under a U.S. VAT, notwithstanding the efficiencies. The "recordkeeping burden" argument would not be too persuasive when considered in the context of income taxes, payroll taxes and, for most small businesses, state and local sales taxes. The *incremental* burden of a VAT could be noticeable on businesses of all sizes, but the unfamiliarity or inability of American small businesses to keep records and fill out tax returns would not seem to be a compelling or conclusive reason

---

[13]Ibid., pp. 58, 60.

[14]Ibid., pp. 59-60.

[15]Turnier, "VAT: Minimizing Administration and Compliance Costs," p. 1262.

for enacting an exclusion.

Furthermore, an exclusion for small businesses would present other issues. For example, several million exempt businesses scattered randomly throughout the economy would require considerable sophistication in recordkeeping by *other* businesses which purchase the goods and services from the exempt companies. Prohibiting the deduction of such non-taxed purchases under a subtraction method would be essential in order to capture the value-added attributable to such businesses. Properly segregating such purchases would require an extra step or two, including a notation by the seller that it was exempt and a system by the purchaser for separating such purchases. Even under an invoice and credit system, recordkeeping distinctions would be required to sort through the tens of thousands of invoiced purchases made by a large corporation during an accounting period.

A "brightline" exemption at, say, $50,000 of gross receipts would create some tax-motivated incentives for breaking up small businesses into even smaller units and for using creative bookkeeping to remain below that line. Responding to these initiatives would require complex "aggregation" rules and compliance procedures. The "all or nothing" nature of reaching just $49,999 could create resentment among owners of businesses which are just above that amount. To address such problems, a $50,000 "deduction" could be granted to all businesses. However, like zero-rating food, this benefits *everyone*. Or, the $50,000 exemption could be phased out as receipts increase, much like the benefits of the graduated income tax rate are recaptured from larger companies. Once aggregation and phaseout rules are decided on, two more complexities have been added.

Then, there is the "perception" problem faced by exempt small businesses which sell to other businesses. Being exempt because receipts are so low and being required to note this fact to the purchaser could be a circumstance which many small businesses would *not* want to face. Therefore, an exemption might need to be elective rather than mandatory, creating yet another administrative problem.

Other problems would also arise, depending on the observer's opinion about the incidence debate. If a VAT were fully passed forward in price, the exempt small business would pay the tax imbedded in its own purchases, but it would not receive a VAT credit because the company would not be filing a return. To recoup such costs, the exempt company would attempt to pass on the prior VAT in the form of higher prices to its customers. Although the exempt company's price might not rise quite as much as its taxable competitors' prices (because its own value-added would not be taxable), would a taxable *purchaser* willingly buy from the exempt company and be denied a deduction or credit for even the partial VAT which is included in the price? If the exempt company were making retail sales to non-business customers, this competitive problem *could* be a slight benefit, but only by assuming that the company's principal competitors were large enough to be taxable.

Alternatively, if a VAT were subject to shared incidence which is distributed among consumers, employees and shareholders as dictated by market forces, the price effects of an exemption could be more favorable for the small company. Its own purchase costs could have some VAT imbedded in them, but not as much as if a VAT were fully passed forward. However, the absence of VAT costs which a taxable company must absorb internally as reduced profits (or seek to shift to its employees as reduced wages) could provide a true competitive edge to the exempt seller in pricing its goods against taxable competitors.

4. Tax accounting concepts which are already familiar to taxpayers might be implemented quickly. Simplicity might be preferable for the longer term.

Erring on the side of simplified accounting and computational rules has not been a characteristic of federal income tax legislation or regulations in recent decades. Simplicity may be an initial objective of tax reform, but even the most vocal business opponents of complexity will accept -- and often affirmatively lobby for -- complex rules which work to the general benefit of taxpayers, or at least to the benefit of the taxpayer who is speaking. This human factor, coupled with the need to provide relief from excessively high individual and corporate tax rates several years ago, led to an extremely complex system for those taxpayers who engage in business or investment transactions.

While the Tax Reform Act of 1986 arguably simplified the system in many ways, it would be difficult to convince affected taxpayers that the uniform inventory capitalization rules, the passive loss rules or interest expense limitations in the Act have resulted in reduced administrative burdens.[16] These concepts and others are requiring

---

[16]It is interesting to note the evolution of "simplicity" as an objective of the recent tax reform process. The initial Treasury proposal in November 1984 (called "Treasury I") was entitled *Tax Reform For Fairness, Simplicity, And Economic Growth*. When Treasury II was unveiled in May 1985, simplicity had slipped a notch to third place in *The President's Tax Proposals to the Congress for Fairness, Growth, and Simplicity*.

substantial time and talent to put into practice. As a result, significant levels of resources are being expended by government and the
private sector to implement the new rules. The benefits to be
derived from such complexities *may* justify the resources devoted to
them, given the context of the complicated income tax into which
they have been placed. While the familiarity of complex income tax
accounting rules could make the initial implementation of a VAT
somewhat easier and less fearful for all concerned, would such rules
serve the system well over a period of years? In the absence of a
long history of rising rates and expanding preferences in a new VAT
system, would simplicity be the better approach?

Of course, simplicity creates its own set of problems. Business
transactions are often very complex. Financial arrangements and
the timing of payments are often structured to minimize or delay tax
burdens. Simple rules could produce one of two effects at opposite
ends of the spectrum: (1) taxpayers could be given maximum flexi-
bility in structuring their purchases and sales to defer tax liability, or
(2) the tax could be imposed in a manner which errs on the side of
collecting too much too soon rather than give any opportunity for
"gaming" the system.

It is worth taking a brief look at the relative merits of simplicity
versus precision in a VAT environment. Whereas the income tax as
applied to businesses (whether corporate or noncorporate) is essentially a tax on profits which are available to shareholders, a VAT is a
much more far-reaching tax. A VAT base would include profits in
the general sense which is applied by the income tax. It would also
include other profits paid to lenders and to lessors as well as the
substantial compensation paid as wages and salaries to, or benefits
on behalf of, all employees.

The extreme complexities of the income tax could be unnecessary
in a much more broadly based system. The precision with which
inventory capitalization rules, "economic performance" standards
and other accounting provisions seek to define taxable income (i.e.,
profits) do not seem necessary in a low-rate, broadbased, value-
added context. Exact matching may be an accountant's dream, but
for VAT purposes the objective is to place all value added into the
system once and only once. Hopefully, exacting measurements of
the "shareholder profits" component of value added would not lead
to a massive array of accounting rules.

When the ultimate legislation was enacted, neither the short title nor the brief description of the 1986 Act made any reference to simplicity; only "reform" was mentioned.

5. Specific VAT accounting questions could be quite numerous and just as nettlesome as income tax accounting issues.

A complete list of potential VAT accounting issues would be long. The following discusses only a few of the problems for illustrative purposes. No effort is made to provide ultimate answers.

Accounting Period. Two principal federal taxes on businesses -- the income tax and the payroll tax -- both use an annual accounting period and more frequent payment or deposit periods. For the payroll tax, the choice of an annual accounting period is principally a matter of convenience for both the employer and the employee. The tax is applied to a specified amount of wages and salaries during the calendar year, and deposits of withheld taxes and the employer's portion are made after those wage and salary amounts are paid. Annual accounting simply tells you when to go back to zero and start counting wages and salaries again.

The annual accounting period is more complex for income tax purposes. A business can earn profits in a very "lumpy" pattern over a long period of years. Measuring profit in the loose manner called "taxable income" requires some beginning and ending points. For better or worse, the federal income tax uses a 12-month period, augmented by carrybacks and carryforwards of losses and credits which otherwise would be unjustifiably lost due to the constraints of annual accounting. Estimates of annual profits are used to compute quarterly payments of income taxes by businesses, but this is principally a cash flow mechanism for the government. Until the taxable year is over, no one can be certain whether tax liability will exist or whether prior year profits have helped to cover a current loss. This contrasts with the payroll tax under which the company knows the total liability after each short pay period.

For VAT purposes, both an accounting period and a payment schedule would be required. The accounting period would be necessary principally for administrative reasons. Value added would be realized in lumpy patterns because sales and purchases often are made in uneven amounts over a period of months and certainly over a period of years. To be able to compute liability (and to audit taxpayer computations) in an efficient manner, there must be a beginning and an end which defines the time for taking sales and purchases into account. Although quarterly returns have been suggested, an annual filing would seem to provide enough paperwork and audit responsibilities to get the job done.

Estimated payments of VAT liability would be principally a cash flow device for the government, although the incidence controversy could filter down even into this question. If a VAT were fully passed forward and collected from each purchaser along the chain, it could be argued that frequent tax payments are both affordable and appropriate. After all, since the purchaser has "paid" the VAT to the business, the business has the funds to pay to the government (leaving aside questions of late paying customers on sales which have been taken into account, installment sales, accrual accounting, etc.). Quarterly payments would give large, unjustified cash flow and time value of money benefits to the business. But if a VAT were to become one more cost which is shared in unpredictable proportions by consumers, employees and shareholders, the business would not be in the same cash position as if it collects the VAT in full from customers. Then, weekly or bi-weekly payments would become a more severe cash burden.

Basic Accounting Method. The fundamental question of cash versus accrual accounting probably would require a brightline test based on business form (corporate versus noncorporate) or some other objective standard. Large corporations presumably would be on the accrual method. Sole proprietors or partners in a service firm likely would be on the cash method. The treatment of small corporations, large limited partnerships and other situations merit study. Avoiding two different accounting methods for income tax and VAT systems seems highly desirable.

One feature of a VAT -- the nondeductibility of interest (or of all but a small percentage of interest[17]) -- should dramatically reduce the attractiveness to a cash basis taxpayer of borrowing money to prepay deductible expenses or to carry customer receivables from one tax year to the next. Income tax reforms have sought to deal with both of these matters in recent years.

The Reporting Unit. Corporate income tax returns can be filed on a consolidated basis. For value- added purposes, consolidated returns would certainly lessen the number of returns filed (assuming taxpayers elected to consolidate the returns of all members of one group). Intra-group purchases and sales could be held in a deferred account until value added was realized in a sale outside the group. Consolidated returns also could offer some administrative benefits with respect to multinational companies which import from their own foreign subsidiaries or which ship components back and forth across the Canadian or Mexican borders during stages of production.

On the other hand, consolidation could offer benefits to corpo-

---

[17]See Chapter 8.

rate groups with substantial vertical integration of production and distribution functions. Cash flow could be favorably affected as subsidiaries sold raw materials and components amongst one another rather than to unrelated parties.

"Trafficking" In VAT Losses. The opportunity for "trafficking" in VAT deductions or refunds would need to be considered. Extensive and complex income tax rules have been developed to limit the "sale" of operating losses or the carryover of such losses when a company is acquired. As noted above with respect to precise measurements of value added, hopefully the objective would be to tax value added once but only once using a low-rate broadbased system. If this were the case, consolidation of excess VAT deductions with another companies' taxable VAT receipts would not seem important. If a refund mechanism were allowed to clean out the VAT system at the end of the accounting period, this whole subject would diminish in importance.

THE BORDER ADJUSTMENT FOR IMPORTS

The role of the Customs Service (or another agency) in collecting the border adjustment on imports under a VAT would be essential to the efficient functioning of a new system. With over $540 billion of goods and services imported into the United States in 1987, imports represented approximately 22 percent of the total value added which was realized in the United States in 1987 and would likely be included in the most comprehensive VAT base.[18]

The mechanics for imposing the import adjustment would seem to be clear, although particular situations could create some difficulties. The objective would be to collect from someone -- the foreign producer, the shipping company or the domestic importer -- the appropriate amount of tax on foreign value added. If no VAT is collected at the U.S. border with respect to the cost of imported items, then only *domestic* value added will be subjected to the U.S. tax (unless domestic taxpayers are prohibited from taking import deductions or credits into account when computing their VAT liabilities). This result is appropriate under the "origin principle" which seeks to tax value added where it arises, but it is not appro-

---

[18]The likely comprehensive base is assumed to have been approximately $2.4 trillion in 1987. This amount was determined by using the estimated $3.0 trillion of personal consumption expenditures for 1987 and deducting rental value of housing and educational, religious and foreign travel expenses. *Economic Report of the President* (February 1988), Tables B-14 and B-20, pp. 264, 270; Treasury, p. 86.

priate under the "destination principle" which taxes value added where it is ultimately consumed.   However, the origin principle would also deny the export tax adjustment, thereby taxing the value added of U.S. producers who sell their goods and services overseas. It is the destination-principle VAT which is in use among the major trading nations and which is presumed to be the form of VAT, if any, to be enacted in the United States.

Administration of the import adjustment presents two issues. First, what is the amount of foreign value added to which the tax is applied? Second, who will be required to remit the tax?

What is the Amount of Foreign Value added?

The amount of value added for an imported item is easy enough to define. It is the total amount which the domestic purchaser pays to acquire the item and to get it to the purchaser's facility. Converting the definition into a workable administrative rule may be somewhat more difficult.

For example, assume that the selling price in Tahiti of 10,000 locally-manufactured widgets is $100K. Company C, a U.S. business, pays this amount to the Tahitian manufacturer, Company T, in order to buy the widgets for import into the U.S. A commission of $1K plus packing costs of $3K are also paid to Tahitians by Company C. Transportation costs of $10K are then paid by Company C to a Tahitian shipping company, Company M, which delivers the widgets to a dock in the United States. Company C then takes the widgets, repackages them and sells them for $135K.

Company C will have incurred total costs of $114K to acquire the foreign-made widgets and have them delivered to the U.S. and will want to deduct such costs from its $135K receipts when computing its VAT liability. But unless all $114K has been subjected to the import adjustment, Company C will be deducting some amount of foreign value added which has not been taxed by the United States.

The Treasury recommends applying U.S. Customs Service techniques to the process of computing valuations for import adjustments.   Valuation questions involving commissions, royalties, licenses or uncertain pricing would be addressed in a manner similar to that applied currently for customs duties. Goods which are simply "passing through" the United States and are held in bonded warehouses for export could be ignored, since the export exclusion presumably would more than cover the import adjustment.[19]

---

[19]Treasury, pp. 116-17.

The transportation component of imported value added poses a potentially more difficult problem. The shipping company which transports goods from foreign countries to the United States (and vice versa) clearly increases the value added of those goods. In the example above, the $104K paid to Tahitians for the widgets (including commissions and packing) is of no value to Company C until the widgets are delivered to the United States. The $10K paid to shipping Company M clearly enhances the value of the widgets to Company C and to its customers.

The question is how to include the $10K receipts of the shipping company in the U.S. value-added base. There are at least three options.

First, such receipts could be included in the tax base of the shipping company. Thus, transportation costs would not need to be included in the valuation of imports, because the shipper's tax base would include such costs. This approach would work reasonably well if all shipping companies were susceptible to effective U.S. administrative and compliance procedures. While U.S.-based companies would be reachable, it seems doubtful that many foreign shipping companies would be in that category. The controlled shipping companies of U.S. multinationals (e.g., those which use such shippers to import their natural resources and components) would probably be the only general category of foreign entities to which effective compliance measures could be applied.

Second, transportation costs for imports could be ignored for border adjustment purposes. If the domestic purchaser could effectively be denied a deduction for such costs, the value added by transportation would be included in the purchaser's tax base and need not be separately taxed to the shipping company. This is the approach which was proposed by the Canadian government in its initial package.[20]

A third option is to include transportation costs in the import adjustment. This would assure that the transportation element of foreign value added is taxed in the United States, while avoiding the necessity of distinguishing between deductible and nondeductible transportation expenses when computing the purchaser's VAT liability.

Under the third option, there is one import transportation issue which would require special attention because of the extensive coastline of the U.S. and particularly because of the locations of two states -- Alaska and Hawaii. Goods traveling from state to state via

---

[20]Wilson, pp. 94-95.

a foreign shipping company (including by truck or rail through Canada or Mexico) would not be considered imports, but the shipper's value added would need to be taken into account somewhere.

Who Will Remit the Import Adjustment?

Remittance of a tax to the government is an administrative matter which may or may not have a significant impact on where the economic burden of the tax falls. Incidence issues have been discussed in detail in Chapters 2, 3 and 4, along with questions concerning the effects on incidence of the form and source of remittance.

With respect to the import adjustment, incidence should be influenced by the same factors which affect purely domestic VAT liabilities. Presumptions that a VAT is passed forward in price or is shared among consumers, employees and shareholders are just as applicable in the import context as they are in the domestic context. The following discussion will not revisit those presumptions. Instead, it presents options as to who would pay the VAT.

Domestic businesses would be responsible for their own net VAT liabilities, after subtracting the costs (or crediting the VAT liabilities) of their purchased inputs. But the United States would have no effective means for imposing its jurisdiction on the producers of foreign value added related to imported goods (except for controlled foreign affiliates of U.S. taxpayers or foreign parents of U.S. taxpayers). Seeking to reach into a foreign country to collect the import adjustment from the foreign producer, such as the Tahitian widget manufacturer in the example, would be inefficient at best and probably would result in the erosion of a substantial portion of the import adjustment base.

A domestic taxpayer would be a more reasonable remitter, principally because the United States could look to that taxpayer for collections. Furthermore, since the domestic taxpayer is the one which will seek to deduct or credit its costs for imports, requiring that person to remit the border tax could ease the audit burden somewhat.

When and where the tax is remitted also has administrative implications. Collecting VAT remittances *at the border* would avoid the need for segregating nondeductible imported purchases when auditing a company's return. Aside from smuggled merchandise, all imports would have been subjected to the VAT. With on-the-spot-collections at the border, it would not matter whether the domestic purchaser or foreign seller paid the tax. If domestic companies were taxable on imports through disallowing deductions or credits, the Customs Service would not have any noticeable VAT responsibilities. However, the domestic audit work could be expected to increase as agents seek to assure that the 20 percent of the value added consumed in this country which is represented by imports was not being excluded from the system.

The dollar values of goods brought into the U.S. by tourists returning home are relatively minor, and forgiving VAT on such transactions probably would be an acceptable and desirable simplification. But the potential for creativity by purchasers of big-ticket items (luxury cars, wines, high-fashion clothing, etc.) would tend to support the proposition that *all* imports be subject to the border adjustment.

Foreign Services

Import adjustments for many services provided by foreign entities present a range of administrative problems.

Transportation of goods presents a relatively easy case, because such services can be tied to goods which are identified and monitored by Customs agents at the border. The options in this area were discussed above.

Financial services might be relatively easy because they flow through entities which are regularly monitored and subject to audit. Banking, insurance and brokerage activities are likely to be tied to the United States in such a way as to allow administration and compliance to occur with some ease. The question of what the taxable value added of such activities is would present other problems which are addressed in Chapter 8.

Services provided by foreign professionals -- attorneys, accountants, architects and others -- are another matter entirely. These services are not tied to goods in a manner which allows for a reasonable point of collection. Instead, the value of the service may come completely from an intangible result such as advice or representation or conveying of ideas. While valuation is easy because a fee is charged, finding a means for including foreign services in a domestic tax base is not. One option is to ignore such professional services for import adjustment purposes and deny the domestic taxpayer a deduction for such costs. This would include the value of the services in the VAT base without the need to monitor foreign persons' activities. A second option is to seek to collect the tax from foreign professionals, particularly those who regularly provide services in the United States or have particularly large projects underway. This would allow domestic taxpayers to deduct the amounts paid, but the monitoring of such services in a country of this size would seem virtually impossible. A third option is the collection of the import adjustment from the domestic purchaser of the services. A type of "withholding" could be required of domestic taxpayers who pay for foreign professional services.

All three options present roblems because of the absence of a border checkpoint which can serve as the collection point and the possibility of directing payments through entities which would clog the audit trail. The Canadian government opted initially for denying the domestic taxpayer a deduction.   However, a special rule based on the third option would be imposed on the importation of services by an exempt entity, in order to avoid competitive disadvantages between domestic and foreign providers of services to such entities.[21]

Passenger transportation services are another problem area. A domestic passenger carrier with international routes would theoretically be "importing" a service when carrying passengers into the United States from a foreign country. As a practical matter, such import services could be overlooked because the value of such services would be included in the carrier's VAT base. Foreign-based carriers would not be as readily reachable, although the extensive regulation of the air carriers by U.S. agencies might provide the opportunity for collecting value-added taxes on the value of fares paid by U.S.-bound passengers, with deductions for expenses incurred in the United States (e.g., terminals, landing rights, fuel, etc.). The Canadians have opted for treating travel between the U.S. and Canada as being purely domestic (i.e., no export exemption or import tax), but all other international passenger traffic would be ignored.   Therefore, no deductions (or credits) for international travel would be allowed.[22]

A Concluding Observation

Those who deal with the nitty-gritty of administrative, compliance and accounting issues often find themselves engaged in a perpetual effort to count the trees in a forest where new seedlings begin to grow and older trees die every year. We lawyers and accountants in particular seem susceptible to the allure of figuring out the precisely correct result at one moment in time, with little thought for

---

[21]Ibid., pp. 91-92.

[22]Ibid., p. 93.

how useful that result is in the overall scheme of things. Whether by training or by personal inclination, we share a professional trait of devoting time to seemingly endless iterations of examples and corresponding rules to handle every conceivable possibility.

If the United States ever seriously considers a VAT, substantial resources will need to be devoted to creating the system of rules and procedures to implement it. Preventing abuses and assuring that all value added is taxed once *but only once* are essential results and will require attention to numerous details. But whether the VAT is enacted to raise massive amounts of new revenues or to offset substantial reductions in income and payroll taxes, a simplified system seems highly desirable. Hopefully, those who have a talent for and interest in accounting and administrative problems would devote substantial time to developing a system which can function efficiently and effectively with much less need for precision than the current income tax.

BIBLIOGRAPHY

Adams, Thomas S. "Fundamental Problems of Federal Income Taxation." *Quarterly Journal of Economics* (August 1921): 552.

American Bar Association. *Report of the Special Committee on the Value-Added Tax of the Tax Section of the American Bar Association*. Washington, D.C.: American Bar Association, 1977.

American Institute of Certified Public Accountants. *Alternatives to the Present Tax System for Increasing Saving and Investment*. Washington, D.C.: AICPA, October 1985.

Andersen, Arthur & Co. "The Business Transfer Tax -- A VAT by Any Other Name." *Tax Legislative Update*, February 3, 1986.

Auerbach, Alan J., Laurence J. Kotlikoff and Jonathan Skinner. "The Efficiency Gains From Dynamic Tax Reform." *International Economic Review* 24, no. 1 (February 1983): 97.

Ballard, Charles. "Tax Policy and Consumer Foresight: A General Equilibrium Simulation Study." *Economic Inquiry* 25 (April 1987): 280.

_____, Don Fullerton, John Shoven, and John Whalley. "Replacing the U.S. Income Tax With a Progressive Consumption Tax." In *A General Equilibrium Model for Tax Policy Analysis*. Chicago: University of Chicago Press, 1985.

Ballentine, J. Gregory. "The Administrability of a Value-Added Tax." In *New Directions in Federal Tax Policy for the 1980s*, edited by Charls E. Walker and Mark Bloomfield. Cambridge, Mass.: Ballinger Publishing Co., 1983.

Bannock, Graham. *VAT and Small Business: European Experience and Implications for North America*. Canada: Canadian Federation of Independent Business and National Federation of Independent Business Research and Education Foundation, 1986.

Barham, Vicky, S. N. Poddar, John Whalley. "The Tax Treatment of Insurance Under a Consumption Type Destination Basis VAT." September 1986. Mimeo.

Blundell, John. "Britain's Nightmare Value Added Tax." *Heritage Foundation International Briefing*. Washington, D.C.: Heritage Foundation, June 13, 1988.

Boskin, Michael J. "Taxation, Saving and the Rate of Interest." *Journal of Political Economy* 86, no. 2, pt. 2 (1978): S3-S27.

_____ and William G. Gale. "New Results on the Effects of Tax Policy on the International Location of Investment." National Bureau of Economic Research Working Paper No. 1862, March 1986.

Bradford, David F. "The Case for the Personal Consumption Tax." In *What Should be Taxed, Income or Expenditure?* edited by Joseph Pechman. Washington, D.C.: Brookings Institution, 1980.

_____. *Blueprints for Basic Tax Reform.* Arlington, VA: Tax Analysts, 1984.

Brannon, G. "VAT and Financial Institutions." April 12, 1985. Mimeo.

Branson, William H. *Macroeconomic Theory and Policy.* New York: Harper and Row, 1979.

_____. "The Dynamic Interaction of Exchange Rates and Trade Flows." National Bureau of Economic Research Working Paper No. 1780, December 1985.

Brown, Harry Gunnison. "The Incidence of a General Output or a General Sales Tax." *Journal of Political Economy* (April 1939): 254.

Browning, Edgar K. "Tax Incidence, Indirect Taxes, and Transfers." *National Tax Journal* (December 1985): 525.

Buyer, Mark. *An Analysis of the Case of a Broadly-Based Consumption Tax in Australia.* Sidney, Australia: Department of the Parliamentary Library, Legislative Research Service, March 1985.

Carlson, George N. "A Federal Consumption Tax." In *New Directions in Federal Tax Policy for the 1980s*, edited by Charls E. Walker and Mark Bloomfield. Cambridge, Mass.: Ballinger Publishing Co., 1983.

Congressional Record. September 25, 1967. Washington, D.C.

Coopers & Lybrand. *Focus on the Value-Added Tax.* Washington D.C.: Coopers & Lybrand, March 1986.

Denison, Edward F. "A Note on Private Saving." *Review of Economics and Statistics* 40 (August 1958): 261-267.

Dornbusch, Rudiger and Jeffrey Frankel. "The Flexible Exchange Rate System: Experience and Alternatives." National Bureau of Economic Research Working Paper No. 2464, December 1987.

John F. Due. *The Theory of Incidence of Sales Taxation.* New York: King Crown Press, 1942.

_____. "A General Sales Tax and the Level of Employment: A Reconsideration." *National Tax Journal* (June 1949): 123.

_____. "Towards a General Theory of Sales Tax Incidence." *Quarterly Journal of Economics* (May 1953): 256-257.

_____. "Sales Taxation and the Consumer." *American Economic Review* (December 1963): 1078.

Engel, Charles and Kenneth Kletzer. "Tariffs, Saving and the Current Account." National Bureau of Economic Research Working Paper No. 1869, March 1986.

Fagan, Elmer D. and Roy W. Jastram. "Tax Shifting in the Short-Run." *Quarterly Journal of Economics* (August 1939).

Feldstein, Martin. "Tax Incidence in a Growing Economy With Variable Factor Supply." *Quarterly Journal of Economics* (November 1974): 1-24.

_____. "The Welfare Cost of Capital Income Taxation." *Journal of Political Economy* (April 1978): 529-551.

_____ and Charles Horioka. "Domestic Saving and International Capital Flows." *Economic Journal* (June 1980): 314-329.

Ferguson, C. E. and J. D. Gould. *Microeconomic Theory*. Illinois: Richard D. Irwin, Inc., 1975.

Frankel, Jeffrey A. "International Capital Flows and Domestic Economic Policies." National Bureau of Economic Research Working Paper No 2210, April 1987.

_____ and Kenneth A. Froot, "Short-term and Long-term Expectations of the Yen/Dollar Exchange Rate: Evidence from Survey Data." National Bureau of Economic Research Working Paper No. 2216, April 1987.

_____ and Richard Meese, "Are Exchange Rates Excessively Variable?" National Bureau of Economic Research Working Paper No. 2249, April 1987.

Friedlander, Ann F. and Adolf F. Vandendospe. "Capital Taxation in a Dynamic General Equilibrium Setting." *Journal of Public Economics* (August 1978): 1-24.

Friedman, Milton. "The Spending Tax as a Wartime Fiscal Measure." *American Economic Review* (March 1943): 50-62.

Fullerton, Don. "The Consumption Tax Versus the Income Tax." In *Real Tax Reform: Replacing the Income Tax*, edited by John Makin. Washington, D.C.: American Enterprise Institute, 1985.

Gillis, Malcolm. "The VAT and Financial Services." The World Bank, February 1987. Mimeo.

Gravelle, Jane G. "Corporate Tax Reform and International Competitiveness." Congressional Research Service Report No. 86-42E. Washington, D.C.: Library of Congress, February 25, 1986.

Harberger, Arnold. "Vignettes on the World Capital Market." *American Economic Review* (May 1980): 331-337.

Heller, Peter S. "Testing the Impact of Value-Added and Global Income Tax Reforms on Korean Tax Incidence in 1976: An Input-Output and Sensitivity Analysis." International Monetary Fund Staff Paper, June 1981.

Henderson, James M. and Richard E. Quaundt. *Microeconomic Theory: A Mathematical Approach*. New York: McGraw-Hill, 1971.

Hoffman, Lorey Arthur, S. N. Poddar, John Whalley. "Conceptual Issues in the Tax Treatment of Banking Under a Consumption Type, Credit Method, Destination Basis VAT." September 1986. Mimeo.

_____. "Taxation of Banking Services under a Consumption Type, Destination Basis VAT." *National Tax Journal* (December 1987): 547.

Howery, E. Phillip and Saul Hymans. "The Measurement and Determination of Loanable Funds Savings." In *What Should Be Taxed, Income or Expenditure?*, edited by Joseph Pechman. Washington, D.C.: Brookings Institute, 1980.

Insley, Gordon. "The Value-Added Tax and Financial Institutions." *Tax Policy* (October-December 1978): 73.

Kaldor, Nicholas. *An Expenditure Tax*. London: Allen and Unwin, 1957.

Koutsoyiannis, A. *Modern Microeconomics*. New York: St. Martin's, 1979.

Lipsey, Robert E. "Changing Patterns of International Investment in and by the United States." National Bureau of Economic Research Working Paper No. 2240, May 1987.

Makin, John H. "Income Tax Reform and the Consumption Tax" In *New Directions in Federal Tax Policy for the 1980s*, edited by Charls E. Walker and Mark Bloomfield. Cambridge, Mass.: Ballinger Publishing Co., 1983.

Marston, Richard C. "Exchange Rate Policy Reconsidered." National Bureau of Economic Research Working Paper No. 2310, July 1987.

McLure, Jr., Charles E. "The Tax on Value Added: Pros and Cons." *Value Added Tax: Two Views* Washington, D.C.: American Enterprise Institute, 1972.

_____. "Taxes, Saving, and Welfare: Theory and Evidence." *National Tax Journal* (September 1980): 311-320.

_____. "Value Added Tax" in *New Directions in Federal Tax Policy for the 1980s*, edited by Charls E. Walker and Mark Bloomfield. Cambridge, Mass.: Ballinger Publishing Co., 1983.

_____. *The Value-Added Tax*. Washington, D.C.: American Enterprise Institute, 1987.

Menchik, Paul L. and David Martin. "The Incidence of a Lifetime Consumption Tax." *National Tax Journal* (June 1982): 189-203.

Miskin, Fredric. "Are Real Interest Rates Equal Across Countries? An Empirical Investigation of International Parity Conditions." *Journal of Finance* 39, no. 5 (1984): 1345-1347.

Modigliani, Franco and Richard Brumberg. "Utility Analysis and the Consumption Function: An Interpretation of Cross-section Data." In *Post Keynesian Economics*, edited by Kenneth Kurihara. New Brunswick: Rutgers University Press, 1954.

Musgrave, Richard A. "On Incidence." *Journal of Political Economy* (August 1953): 312.

_____. *The Theory of Public Finance*. New York: McGraw Hill, 1959.

Nicholson, Walter. *Microeconomic Theory*. Illinois: Dryden Press, 1978.

Pardon, Jean. "Banks and VAT -- Lessons from Belgium." *Banker*, August 1974.

Pechman, Joseph. "A Consumption Tax is Not Desirable for the United States." In *New Directions in Federal Tax Policy for the 1980s*, edited by Charls E. Walker and Mark Bloomfield. Cambridge, Mass.: Ballinger Publishing Co., 1983.

Peterson, Milo O. "Gross Product by Industry, 1986." *Survey of Current Business*. Washington, D.C.: United States Department of Commerce/Bureau of Economic Analysis, April 1987.

Prakken, Joel L. "The Macroeconomics of Tax Reform." In *New Directions in Federal Tax Policy for the 1980s*, edited by Charls E. Walker and Mark Bloomfield. Cambridge, Mass.: Ballinger Publishing Co., 1983.

Rolph, Earl R. "A Proposed Revision of Excise-Tax Theory." *Journal of Political Economy* (April 1952): 102.

Schenk, Alan. "Value Added Tax: Does This Consumption Tax Have A Place In The Federal Tax System?" *Virginia Tax Review* 7, no. 2 (Fall 1987): 288-292.

Seligman, Edwin R. A. *The Shifting and Incidence of Taxation*. New York: Columbia University Press, 1927.

Smith, Dan Throop and Bertrand Fox. *An Analysis of Value Added Taxation in the Context of the Tax Restructuring Act of 1980*. Washington, D.C.: The Financial Executives Research Foundation, 1981.

Studenski, Paul. "Toward a Theory of Business Taxation." *Journal of Political Economy* (October 1940): 653.

Sullivan, Clara K. *The Tax on Value Added*. New York and London: Columbia University Press, 1965.

Summers, Lawrence H. "Capital Taxation and Accumulation in a Life Cycle Growth Model." *American Economic Review* (September 1981): 533.

_____. "Tax Policy and International Competitiveness." National Bureau of Economic Research Working Paper No. 2007, August 1986.

Tait, Alan. "Is the Introduction of a Value Added Tax Inflationary?" *Finance and Development* (June 1981): 38-42.

"Tax Policy Options." *Capital Formation* (May 1988): 3.

Ture, Norman B. *The Value-Added Tax -- Facts and Fancies*. Washington, D.C.: IRET, 1979.

Turnier, William J. "Designing an Efficient Value Added Tax." *Tax Law Review* 39 (Summer 1984): 455-457.

_____. "VAT: Minimizing Administration And Compliance Costs." *Tax Notes* (March 14, 1988): 1258.

U.S. Department of the Treasury, *Internal Revenue Service Annual Report 1987*. Washington, D.C.: Internal Revenue Service, 1988.

U.S. Department of the Treasury. *Tax Reform for Fairness, Simplicity, and Growth, Volume 3: The Value-Added Tax*. Washington, D.C.: U.S. Department of the Treasury, November 1984.

Vasquez, Thomas E. "Addressing Issues of the Regressivity of a Consumption Tax." In *New Directions in Federal Tax Policy for the 1980s*, edited by Charls E. Walker and Mark Bloomfield. Cambridge, Mass.: Ballinger Publishing Co., 1983.

Williamson, K. M. "The Literature on the Sales Tax." *Quarterly Journal of Economics* (October 1921): 120.

Wilson, Michael H. *Tax Reform 1987, Sales Tax Reform*. Canada: Department of Finance, 1987.

ABOUT THE CONTRIBUTORS

ERNEST S. CHRISTIAN, JR. is a partner in the Washington law firm of Patton, Boggs & Blow. Mr. Christian served as Deputy Assistant Secretary for Tax Policy (Tax Legislation) of the U. S. Department of the Treasury from 1974 to 1975 and as Tax Legislative Counsel of the Treasury from 1973 to 1974.

HARRY D. GARBER is Vice Chairman of the Board of The Equitable Life Assurance Society of the United States. Mr. Garber, an actuary, has more than 35 years of experience in the financial services business. He participated actively in the development of the 1984 life insurance company tax law.

CLIFF MASSA III is a partner in the Washington law firm of Patton, Boggs & Blow. Mr. Massa was Vice President, Taxation and Fiscal Policy for the National Association of Manufacturers from 1979 to 1981 and Director of Tax Policy for the NAM from 1975 to 1978.

DAVID G. RABOY is Chief Economic Consultant to the Washington law firm of Patton, Boggs & Blow. Dr. Raboy served as legislative director to Senator William Roth (R-DE) from 1983 to 1986. Previously, he served as Executive Director of the Institute for Research on the Economics of Taxation from 1981 to 1983 and as Associate Director of Tax Analysis for the National Association of Manufacturers from 1979 to 1981.

STEPHEN C. VOGT is a Ph.D. candidate in Economics at Washington University in St. Louis. He is the recipient of the H. B. Earhart Dissertation Fellowship for 1988-89 and was the John M. Olin Research Fellow at the Center for the Study of American Business from 1986-1988.

MURRAY L. WEIDENBAUM is Director of the Center for the Study of American Business and Mallinckrodt Distinguished University Professor at Washington University in St. Louis. He was the first Chairman of the Council of Economic Advisers under President Reagan. Dr. Weidenbaum is the author of five books. His latest is *Rendezvous with Reality: The American Economy After Reagan*.

INDEX